Deep Inculturation

Deep Inculturation

*Global Voices on Christian Faith
and Indigenous Genius*

ANTONIO D. SISON, EDITOR

ORBIS BOOKS
Maryknoll, New York 10545

Founded in 1970, Orbis Books endeavors to publish works that enlighten the mind, nourish the spirit, and challenge the conscience. The publishing arm of the Maryknoll Fathers and Brothers, Orbis seeks to explore the global dimensions of the Christian faith and mission, to invite dialogue with diverse cultures and religious traditions, and to serve the cause of reconciliation and peace. The books published reflect the views of their authors and do not represent the official position of the Maryknoll Society. To learn more about Maryknoll and Orbis Books, please visit our website at www.orbisbooks.com

Copyright © 2024 by Antonio D. Sison

Published by Orbis Books, Box 302, Maryknoll, NY 10545-0302.

All rights reserved.

The permissions listed on page 237 represent an extension of this copyright page.

No part of this publication may be reproduced or transmitted in any form or by any means, electronic or mechanical, including photocopying, recording, or any information storage or retrieval system, without prior permission in writing from the publisher.

Queries regarding rights and permissions should be addressed to: Orbis Books, P.O. Box 302, Maryknoll, NY 10545-0302.

Manufactured in the United States of America

Library of Congress Cataloging-in-Publication Data

Names: Sison, Antonio D., editor.
Title: Deep inculturation : global voices on Christian faith and indigenous genius / Antonio D. Sison, editor.
Description: Maryknoll, NY : Orbis Books, [2024] | Includes bibliographical references and index. | Summary: "Original essays by leading global theologians with a focus on inculturation in Africa, Mexico, Japan, Australia, and Indonesia"— Provided by publisher.
Identifiers: LCCN 2023040741 (print) | LCCN 2023040742 (ebook) | ISBN 9781626985711 (trade paperback) | ISBN 9798888660270 (epub)
Subjects: LCSH: Christianity and culture. | Indigenous peoples—Religion. | Missions.
Classification: LCC BR115.C8 D345 2024 (print) | LCC BR115.C8 (ebook) | DDC 261—dc23/eng/20231026
LC record available at https://lccn.loc.gov/2023040741
LC ebook record available at https://lccn.loc.gov/2023040742

Contents

Foreword: Inculturation Revisited   vii
   Peter C. Phan

Introduction   xi
   Antonio D. Sison

Contributors   xxvii

Part I: Ritual and Performance

1   A Liturgy That Heals:
      An Interdisciplinary Approach to Mexican American Ritual   3
      Christopher D. Tirres

2   Dancing, Eating, Worshiping:
      Inculturated "Third Space" in Rarámuri Celebrations   25
      Ángel F. Méndez Montoya

3   Contemporary Inculturational Performing Arts
      in the Indonesian Christian Church   57
      Marzanna Poplawska

Part II: Method and the Lessons of History

4   Ceremonial Genius:
      Australia's First Peoples and Liturgical Inculturation   89
      Carmel Pilcher

5   Silent Inculturation:
      Japan's Hidden Christians and the Criterion of the Cross   127
      Antonio D. Sison

6 God, Canaan, Egypt, and the Stories of Migration
  in Intercultural Perspective   158
  Ferdinand Ikenna Okorie

7 Pedagogy of Hospitality:
  Transforming Missionary Onslaught into
  Mutual Transformation and Enrichment   187
  Agbonkhianmeghe E. Orobator

Acknowledgments   217

About the Cover Image   219

Index   221

Foreword

Inculturation Revisited

Peter C. Phan
Georgetown University

Antonio D. Sison does me a great honor by inviting me to write a foreword to this book on deep inculturation. I am deeply grateful to him for the opportunity to revisit one of the central themes of my theological work now trending toward a happy ending. This collection of the essays itself intends to offer a step forward in the understanding and practice of the ecclesial and theological process, which was brought to scholarly attention in 1984 by Arij Roest Crollius under the rubric of "inculturation" or, as I now prefer, "interculturation," and is still vigorously debated today.

The foreword that Sison has in mind for me to write does not consist of an overview of the book and a summary of the essays, which he himself offers in his brilliant introduction. Rather, what he asks me to do is to reflect autobiographically on what I have thought about inculturation, how I have gone about doing it, and what I think are its outstanding challenges and the ways to meet them. It is of course impossible to do all this in a few pages; what follows is a few random thoughts, for which the essays in this book provide rich elaborations.

To begin with, I fully endorse what Sison describes as the essential characteristics of a "deep re-rooting" of inculturation. To combine "global voices" and "indigenous genius" in presenting the Christian faith, he argues, inculturation today must be "contextual," "inductive," "creative," and "dialogical." These requirements are not unfamiliar to contemporary practitioners of the inculturation of the Christian faith. The issue is *how* to do it (methodology) and, more importantly, *doing* it (providing concrete examples beyond the throat-clearing methodological lucubration); happily, the essays in this volume offer instructive examples of both.

Whereas inculturation, both as conceptualized and practiced in the way mentioned above, is not a total novelty, especially in the Two-Thirds World, for people of my (old) generation who did theology in Rome, even a couple of years after the Second Vatican Council (1962–65), as in my case (1968–72), it was something literally unheard of. Even the word did not exist in the theological lexicon. However, I was fortunate enough to write on the Lutheran theologian Paul Tillich's Christology for my licentiate degree and on the theology of the icon in the work of Russian Orthodox theologian Paul Evdokimov for the doctorate. It was a rare incursion into non-Catholic theology that enabled me to see how theology was done differently from the neo-Thomistic theology then still dominant in Rome's pontifical universities. This theology and its categories were deemed globally normative and universally applicable, to be memorized and regurgitated during oral examinations, and exported to our countries and translated into our respective tongues. After my return to Vietnam in 1972, I was shocked to realize that the theology I had learned (and was given *summa cum laude* for) made no sense to the people I served, whom I completely bamboozled with an unintelligible discourse, liberally sprinkled with Greek, Latin, and German phraseologies to boost its bona fide orthodoxy!

Only after I left Vietnam for the United States as a refugee in 1975 at the end of the so-called Vietnam War and during my theological teaching career in Dallas, Texas, and later in Washington, DC, and under the beneficent pressure of the "publish or perish" axiom of academe, did I begin researching first theologies done in Latin America and Asia, and later in Africa, and Christian missions, especially the work of the seventeenth-century French Jesuit Alexandre de Rhodes.

For the first time, I encountered inculturation as a theological category and ecclesial process. I came to understand that inculturation is not a modern invention but is as old as Christianity. Without inserting the Christian faith into the "indigenous genius," its "global voices" would not have been heard; without it, Jesus' good news, and his very identity, would not have been properly understood in the Hellenistic and Roman worlds, the two cultures in which the gospel was first announced. This expression of the gospel in innumerable local cultures would continue down the centuries. Without inculturation, the church's evangelizing mission would have been impossible.

It became clear to me that the metaphor of "incarnation," which is much in favor with magisterial teaching on inculturation, is rather misleading, as it suggests that the gospel, like the divine culture-free Logos becoming flesh, is something culture-free, to be "incarnated" in other cultures. On the contrary, the gospel is never culture-independent. There is simply no culturally "pure" gospel. It always comes already enfleshed in a particular culture, first Jewish, then Greek, and subsequently various European cultures. Consequently, "inculturation" is by necessity "interculturation"—that is, an encounter between the culture(s) of the Gospel (not the "pure" Gospel), most often the missionaries' cultures, and other cultures and must abide by the laws of intercultural dialogue. (Recall the four requirements of inculturation listed above.)

Furthermore, this interculturation is not an irenic "*Horizontverschmelzung*," a harmonious and peaceful "blending" of cultural horizons. Because Christianity came to many parts of the globe in collusion with Western colonization and imperialism, its inculturation was, in many hidden and subtle ways, an exercise in dominating, subjugating, and at times erasing local cultures. Historically, interculturation has become a site for power struggles and contested relations in which more often than not the indigenous cultures come out as the vanquished. Consequently, I have consistently twinned inculturation with the work for liberation from systemic oppression and exploitation. Without the latter, inculturation, especially in liturgy and spirituality, runs the risk of becoming a pastime of the cultural elite.

Furthermore, since in most countries of the Two-Thirds World, religion—a system of beliefs, values, and practices—is a constitutive dimension of culture, inculturation necessarily requires interreligious dialogue. I have included this dialogue with not only the so-called Great Tradition that is embodied in the so-called world religions but also with the Little Tradition that is exemplified in indigenous and popular religions, often marginalized, such as the religious traditions of the Dalits, the Adivasis, and other minorities.

In light of the above, I have attempted to reconceptualize the main *loci theologici* in a triple dialogue—repeatedly advocated by the Federation of the Asian Bishops' Conferences—of liberation, inculturation, and interreligious dialogue. These include God as Holy Mystery in diverse cultures and religions; Jesus as the Ancestor, the Enlightened One (Buddha), and the Paradigmatic Migrant; the Holy Spirit as the Power of Migration; Mary and the Goddess of Compassion; sacramental celebrations; liturgy and popular devotions; and sundry other topics.

Despite these manifold attempts at interculturation, I am deeply aware that I have only scratched its surface. The challenge I see in the near future is not the lack of initiatives for interculturation at the grassroots level, as the essays in this volume amply demonstrate, but the Roman Curia's obsession with hierarchical control and fear of "heterodox" innovations. There is nothing more ludicrous than the requirement of obtaining the "approval" for, let's say, translations of the Roman Missal into various vernaculars or liturgical rituals by the officials of the Roman dicasteries who have little if any knowledge of these languages and cultures. Fortunately, Pope Francis has lent his voice and authority to this interculturation project, especially in his *Evangelii Gaudium* and *Querida Amazonia*. He constantly speaks of "social friendship" and "the culture of encounter," especially in his *Fratelli tutti*. In the meantime, confident in Pope Francis' encouragement and support, let's do what the ubiquitous sign says: "Keep Calm and Carry On Interculturating"!

Introduction

Antonio D. Sison

"What is so new about inculturation?"

Four decades ago, the question appeared on the cover of the series *Inculturation: Working Papers on Living Faith and Cultures* published by the Pontifical Gregorian University in Rome. The title of the issue's lead article by the Dutch Jesuit scholar Arij Roest Crollius, it engages certain queries as to whether inculturation was legitimately innovative in view of comparable concepts from the social sciences. Clarifying its usage in missiology, Crollius describes inculturation in a sequence of three interdependent moments.[1] In the initial stage, Christian missionaries and members of the local culture "assimilate elements of each other's cultures." Not much is offered in terms of the character and dynamics of this cultural assimilation, but the process is identified as "acculturation,"[2] a cognate term appropriated from cultural anthropology. Clearly, acculturation is understood here to be a first step to the deeper, more substantive assimilation that is presumed to characterize inculturation. This then leads to the next stage: as

---

[1] Ary Roest Crollius, SJ, "What Is So New about Inculturation?: A Concept and Its Implications," *Inculturation: Working Papers on Living Faith and Cultures*, vol. 5 (Rome: Centre "Cultures and Religion": Pontifical Gregorian University, 1984), 1–18.

[2] In view of the terminological confusion surrounding inculturation, acculturation, and related terms, identifying the often fine distinctions between them is illuminating. For this, see Aylward Shorter, *Toward a Theology of Inculturation* (Maryknoll, NY: Orbis Books, 1988), 3–13, and, in relation to liturgy, Anscar Chupungco, *Liturgical Inculturation: Sacramentals, Religiosity, and Catechesis* (Collegeville, MN: Liturgical Press, 1992), 13–54.

the numbers of those who join the church incrementally increase, a corresponding shift in agency occurs; the evangelized members of the local culture, now described as the "young Church," move from a stance of passive adaption to the wider home culture, to become the active, principal agents of transformation for that culture. The final stage, "the moment of active reorientation of the local culture," is the evident outcome of the triadic process.

By Crollius' own definition, "'Inculturation' is here meant as an expression of the process by which the Church becomes inserted in a given culture."[3] No doubt, this reflects a traditional missiological perspective where inculturation is understood as a strategy employed by missionaries—presumably, from the West—to evangelize local or non-Christian cultures. While reflecting the optimistic, dialogical stance toward local culture as evinced in conciliar documents—namely *Gaudium et Spes* and *Ad Gentes*, and further expressed in a continuum of papal documents thereafter such as *Evangelii nuntiandi* (1975), *Catechesi tradendae* (1979), and *Redemptoris missio* (1993)—it is instructive to point out how this is specifically configured in the second moment of Crollius' schema. The decentering of agency in favor of the local culture refers to a process-of-becoming on the part of its members— their eventual assumption of the role of lead agent in the missionary strategy of Church insertion. Said differently, the young Church itself eventually takes on the missionary task so that the evangelizing mission is, tactically, effectuated by the members of the selfsame culture; this is the locus and extent of the cultural assimilation.

The foregoing tactical approach to inculturation suggests that agency is not organically situated in the identity of the local culture, it is an acquired asset, earned when its members assimilate the evangelizing message that foreign missionaries had inserted into their culture. Consequently, their contribution to the presumed two-way assimilation is to become the local counterparts of the foreign missionaries, taking on their mandate, and delivering the gospel message to their own kind, in their own homeland. They are recognized then as agents, not necessarily of their own cultural identity and Indigenous genius, but

---

[3] Crollius, *Inculturation: Working Papers on Living Faith and Cultures*, 6.

of the missionary strategy. As Crollius concludes, the transformation predominantly takes place on one side of the equation, the side of the local culture; essentially, it loses control of its own cultural narrative.

It is noteworthy that a second essay in the *Inculturation* series, "Inculturation and the Specificity of Christian Faith" by the Rwandan Jesuit philosopher Théoneste Nkeramihigo, offers an alternative critical assessment of inculturation based on the historical contingencies that shape the local culture's encounter with the default Western expression of Christian culture. He interrogates two false, de-historicizing presumptions: (1) Cultures that have been marked by Western contact and influence have maintained their integrity, and (2) Christianity can be divorced from Western culture within which it had been, for centuries, contexted and marked.[4]

In a clear-eyed synthesis, Nkeramihigo asserts,

> What is really at stake in the phenomenon of inculturation is the identity search of a people, to whom it has become clear that this identity cannot be found either in the importation of a foreign culture (acculturation), or in the restoration of its past (tribalism, nationalism). Rather, it is to be sought in the acceptance of the present conflict resulting from two heterogeneous past situations whose meeting constitutes the beginning of a new phase of its history, seen in an attitude of reconciliation in hope of two traditions which are presently clashing.[5]

While expressing an appreciative awareness of the perspective of the local culture, he keeps in check, on one hand, the cultural "importation" of acculturation—essentially a critique of Crollius' unidirectional "insertion" model—and on the other hand, the romanticizing tendencies on the part of the local culture.

---

[4] Théoneste Nkeramihigo argues, "Whether we want it or not, if Christianity is the historical event of the incarnation of God in Jesus, by reason of the law of incarnation and its historical Destiny, it is bound to the West and it has been presented to us within this framework." See "Inculturation and the Specificity of Christian Faith," *Inculturation: Working Papers on Living Faith and Cultures*, 21.

[5] Ibid., 22.

In Nkeramihigo's thesis, the interaction between Western Christian culture and local culture is not so much a site of consensus as a site of contention. It is within the givenness of this conflict that both cultures move to a new reality, a new creation. He argues that it is Christianity—"the singular specificity of the man Jesus of Nazareth who has a universal destiny by reason of his power to break all other specificities"—that lays down a bridge toward reconciliation:

> I believe that the inculturation of Christianity in non-Western parts of the world depends on the capacity of this very Christianity to start and open up a history which calls peoples, in search of their identity, to get out of their situation of distressing and anxious ambivalence of uncontrolled conflict of cultures for future reconciliation of all peoples of God.[6]

As I understand Nkeramihigo's hermeneutics of reconciliation, it is the incarnation of Jesus—in the paradoxical both/and of being culture-specific and culture-transcending—that brings Western Christian culture and local culture from a state of conflict to a place of dialogue. In this creative dialectic, a more genuine inculturation becomes a promise and a possibility.

That said, Nkeramihigo's vision of the latent potential of conflict for a reconciled Christian cultural reality does not quite address the collective stigmata from the sentence of colonial history and its aftermath, which cannot be ignored if the local culture is to gain a renewed sense of identity and agency, and become a true dialogue partner in inculturation. It does serve as a kind of prolegomenon to an inclusive understanding of inculturation that is based on mutuality. At this relatively nascent stage in the development of the concept of inculturation, Nkeramihigo's perspective, as against Crollius', is the more viable response to the question "What is so new about inculturation?"

In 1999, fifteen years after *Inculturation*, another relevant collection of papers was published. Titled *Popular Catholicism in a World Church: Seven Case Studies in Inculturation*, it sets out to examine the *status quaestionis* in

---

[6] Ibid., 26.

the evolving concept of inculturation, clearly postulating a new starting point for theological inquiry that recognizes the epistemological privilege of local culture.

> Today, there is a growing awareness that the majority of the world's Roman Catholics are no longer located in the global North. Christianity's center of gravity has shifted dramatically during the second half of the twentieth century.... The Catholic thing, historically shaped and colored by popular cultures, is thriving in Latin America, in Asia, and in Africa. The "world church" that is emerging is stunningly diversified.[7]

Judiciously, the book draws attention to the experience of European colonization, a collective trauma that threads across the histories of a significant number of countries in the Global South—"Foreign domination, enslavement, and processes of cultural *uprooting* [emphasis mine] are part of their historical inheritance." The ghostlife of Eurocentrism continues to haunt local cultures in multiform ways, often compounded by geopolitical and sociopolitical issues that perpetuate various inequalities. On account of this cruel context, the book identifies popular Catholicism as the *locus theologicus* for understanding and doing inculturation. This represents a significant turn since it examines the phenomenon of inculturation as it takes place on the other side, the side traditionally seen as the context of the beneficiaries, not the principal agents, of inculturation. Covering Chile, Peru, St. Lucia, Ghana, Tanzania, South India, and Hong Kong, the case studies follow the mediations of the pastoral cycle, employing historical, anthropological, and sociological research tools as prior steps to theological reflection.

Ultimately, the anthology lives up to its main title *Popular Catholicism*; it presents thick descriptions of the rituals of popular piety in a variety of forms. Lamentably, however, its explanatory title, *Seven Case Studies in Inculturation*, proves to be an overpromise. In each of the case studies, the phenomenon of inculturation is pushed off to the

---

[7] Thomas Bamat and Jean-Paul Wiest, eds., *Popular Catholicism in a World Church: Seven Case Studies in Inculturation* (Maryknoll, NY: Orbis Books, 1999), 1.

far side of the stage, relegating it to a mere addendum to the research foci and conclusions. Moreover, it falls short of offering a renewed understanding of inculturation. As expressly stated, "'Inculturation' was more elusive. Despite having agreed to our working definition, we were drawn into employing some of the other meanings it has acquired in ecclesial parlance since it was coined in the 1970s."[8] Notwithstanding its earnest intentions, an awareness of the need to shift the center of gravity from the domain of the professional standard-bearers of mission to the local cultures of the World Church, the project remains hamstrung to inculturation in the top-down sense inherited from an older missiology. One step forward, two steps back.

A comprehensive review of published research works in the area is beyond the purview of this essay but from this brief but purposeful re-visiting of inculturation as an evolving concept,[9] we ourselves can ask anew the question, "What is so new about inculturation?"

A Deep Re-Rooting

Deep Inculturation: Global Voices on Christian Faith and Indigenous Genius represents a renewed polyphony for speaking about inculturation based on the immersive research work of seven scholars of diverse cultural backgrounds, each paying regardful consideration to contextual, inductive, creative, and dialogical approaches.

- **Contextual.** A contextual approach cannot be principally dependent on abstract, ivory-tower categories and traditional epistemologies disconnected from the organic, shifting realities of culture, social location, historical contingencies, and collective human experience. It is necessarily rooted in lived faith where local cultures are essential *loci theologici*, sites of religious-theological discovery and insight.

---

[8] Ibid., 7.

[9] For an earlier essay dealing with related questions on differing perspectives on inculturation, see Andrew Byrne, "Some Ins and Outs of Inculturation," *Annales theologici* 4 (1990): 109–49.

- **Inductive.** Necessarily affiliated with contextual theologies, inculturation is "a path, a *poeisis*, and a performance";[10] as such, it is a critical reflection *in via*. Interdisciplinary engagement allows for a range of perspectives to be brought together in a creative dialectic, which contributes to the inductive, forward movement of the hermeneutical flow.
- **Creative.** Beyond *logos*-based sources, local, grassroots, and Indigenous art, dance, music, ritual, oral narratives, and other nontextual cultural expressions are constitutive of the fusion of horizons that inform the scholarly quest for meaning. It is expedient to expand the view of what may be considered as acceptable references for theological wisdom, paying close attention to how local faith expressions are often a pilgrimage of touch, sight, sound, taste, scent, and movement.[11]
- **Dialogical.** The question of mutuality in inculturation —"How does the dynamic confluence between Christian faith and local culture evince mutual enrichment, critique, assimilation, and transformation?"—is an important heuristic touchstone for assessing whether a pathway to inculturation, in some shape or form, has been actualized. If the gospel message is presumed to kindle a transformative "incarnation" in the culture (as proposed by Arrupe, John Paul II, Shorter, Chupungco, among others), what, dialogically, are the essential features of the contribution of the local culture to

---

[10] Contextual theology as described by Robert J. Schreiter. He adds, "It is a path upon which a community embarks as a kind of journey or pilgrimage, evoking the image of the pilgrim people of God presented in the Dogmatic Constitution of the Church, *Lumen Gentium*." See Foreword to *Doing Theology as if People Mattered: Encounters in Contextual Theology*, ed. Deborah Ross and Eduardo Fernández (New York: Herder & Herder, 2019), x.

[11] Local, grassroots faith expressions lie "in the intersection of the artistic, the cultural, and the theological," thus often subverting textual, doctrinal expectations. This is expressed, for instance, in the Filipino popular devotion to the Black Nazarene, a material-tactile pilgrimage innervated by a laity-based communitas. Antonio D. Sison, *The Art of Indigenous Inculturation: Grace on the Edge of Genius* (Maryknoll, NY: Orbis Books, 2021), 9–10, 163–71.

the enrichment and transformation of Christian faith? While there are no simple answers, relevant ecclesial and theological insights have served as a forelight for the ongoing discussion.

In the 1985 encyclical *Slavorum Apostoli* ("The Apostles to the Slavs"), St. Pope John Paul II defines inculturation as "the incarnation of the Gospel in native cultures and also the introduction of these cultures into the life of the Church."[12] While a mutual interchange is proposed here, it's noteworthy that the contribution of each dialogue partner differs qualitatively. "Incarnation," a theological term that bears profound salvific-transformative import, is applied to the sharing of the gospel message, while "introduction," a neutral, unnuanced term, is designated for the bestowal of the local culture. The definition is unequivocal about cultural interaction, but the descriptive reference to a mutual transformation is limited to a bare allusion.

Ten years later, in his 1995 post-synodal apostolic exhortation *Ecclesia in Africa*, John Paul II expresses what is evidently a deepening ecclesial confidence in the mutual engagement between gospel culture and local culture. In profoundly meaningful phraseology, he proposes a compelling vision of inculturation that affirms a preferential option for African cultures:

> By respecting, preserving and fostering the particular values and riches of your people's cultural heritage, you will be in a position to lead them to a better understanding of the mystery of Christ, which is also to be lived in the noble, concrete and daily experiences of African life. There is no question of adulterating the word of God, or of emptying the Cross of its power (cf. *1 Cor* 1:17), but rather of bringing Christ into the very centre of African life and of lifting up all African life

---

[12] Thus, in speaking about the legacy of Saints Cyril and Methodius who preached the gospel to the Slavs, St. Pope John Paul II adds, "By *incarnating* [emphasis mine] the Gospel in the native culture of the peoples which they were evangelizing, Saints Cyril and Methodius were especially meritorious for the formation and development of that same culture, or rather of many cultures." *Slavorum Apostoli*, encyclical (1985), section 6.21. www.vatican.va.

to Christ. Thus not only is Christianity relevant to Africa, but Christ, in the members of his Body, is himself African.[13]

Expressing what is at stake in an inculturation that is truly mutual, John Paul II effectively sends an inclusive, culture-affirming message of signal impact: the introduction of the local culture to Christian life may also be, by God's grace, an "incarnation." For African life to be placed on a lampstand as incarnational throws a liberative, salvific light on African identity, which, having been subjected to unrelenting colonial domination, oppression, and erasure—in Cameroonian liberation theologian Engelbert Mveng's diagnosis, Africa suffers from "anthropological poverty,"[14] the collective trauma having reached an ontological level—holds additional claim to be celebrated as a coequal bearer of *imago Dei*. Upholding "anthropological dignity," Africa takes its rightful seat at the table of genuine inculturation.

The esteemed African theologian Laurenti Magesa echoes the cultural and theological inclusiveness that *Ecclesia in Africa* so eloquently expresses. In *Anatomy of Inculturation: Transforming the Church in Africa*, he describes "the shape of the encounter" between missionary Christianity and African culture in terms that reiterate mutuality as the cornerstone of an authentic process of inculturation:

> The revelation of God in the Christian scriptures meets the God who is already present in the values of the culture and in the history of a people. The two bond together, transforming and fulfilling each other in the process. And in the same process, people's perceptions and self-understanding on one hand, and of God in their midst on the other, are changed.[15]

---

[13] St. Pope John Paul II, *Ecclesia in Africa*, post-synodal apostolic exhortation (1995), section 127, www.vatican.va.

[14] For fuller treatment, see Engelbert Mveng, "Impoverishment and Liberation: A Theological Approach for Africa and the Third World," *Paths of African Theology*, ed. Rosino Gibellini (Maryknoll, NY: Orbis Books, 1994). In relation to inculturation, I examine "anthropological poverty" and Mveng's theological-aesthetic contribution in chapter 1 of Sison, *The Art of Indigenous Inculturation*, 21–75.

[15] Laurenti Magesa, *Anatomy of Inculturation: Transforming the Church in Africa* (Maryknoll, NY: Orbis Books, 2004), 143.

The description offers an assured, incarnational understanding of local culture, affirming that it is a *topos* where God's grace also finds a home. Thus, in the process of inculturation, a transformative experience takes place on both sides of the equation: the side of the local culture and the side of Christian culture. From a fuller consideration of the subject as it is problematized in *Anatomy of Inculturation* and Magesa's wider scholarship, this does not suggest a cultural romanticism that sidesteps critical analyses of local culture; rather, it emphasizes the urgency of a hermeneutics of appreciation,[16] precisely because local cultures have been historically othered and diminished.

The theologically reasonable, optimistic approach to culture seen in both Magesa and John Paul II dovetails with what Stephen B. Bevans describes as the "anthropological model" of contextual theology, which is grounded on the notion that culture is a locus for divine revelation.[17] At variance with an understanding of revelation as an external additive, a "supracultural" reality, the anthropological model proposes that revelation is deeply and organically rooted in the very complexity of culture. From within, local culture is good, very good.

In view of the cultural "uprooting" that ensued from a Eurocentric missionary history, a renewed, relevant pathway for inculturation is a "re-rooting"[18] to the fertile humus of the local culture, whose members are the rightful principal agents of deep inculturation. Thus, "what is so new about inculturation," quite ironically, is not so much a breaking of new ground; it is a cultural *ressourcement*. This is the premise and vision of this anthology.

---

[16] Filipino theologian José M. de Mesa, when discussing inculturation in the Philippine postcolonial context, proposes a comparable trajectory: "What is sorely needed is a hermeneutics of appreciation which methodologically highlights the positive in the culture." See de Mesa, *Why Theology Is Never Far from Home* (Manila: De La Salle University Press, 2003), 120.

[17] Stephen B. Bevans, *Models of Contextual Theology*, rev. ed. (Maryknoll, NY: Orbis Books, 2006), 56–59.

[18] To my knowledge, José M. de Mesa was the first to use the descriptive term "re-rooting" in the theological sense, specifically as applied to the development of an inculturated Filipino theology. See de Mesa, *In Solidarity with Culture: Studies in Theological Re-rooting* (Quezon City: Maryhill School of Theology, 1987).

A Rotating Prism:
Global Facets of Inculturation

The prism, an illustrative symbol that I have used on not a few occasions,[19] applies yet again here to indicate that the seven chapters of *Deep Inculturation* represent variegated hues of a common, unifying rubric. Each of the seven contributing authors, engaging the interdiscipline pertinent to their respective scholarly areas, rotates the hermeneutical prism so that diverse facets in the phenomenon of inculturation are refracted, revealed, and brought into sharper relief.

In the opening chapter "A Liturgy That Heals: An Interdisciplinary Approach to Mexican American Ritual," Christopher Tirres explores a Catholic Good Friday ritual called the *Pésame*, as it is performed at the San Fernando Cathedral in his hometown of San Antonio, Texas. At the heart of the *Pésame* is a liturgical dance dramatizing the bereavement of Mary of Nazareth. This opens up into a moving participative experience when a family in the pews, crossing the border that separates the sphere of performance from real life, is invited to console Jesus' grieving mother. Drawing from liberationist, pragmatist, aesthetic, and theological frames of reference, Tirres examines an unexplored discursive layer in the ritual, an ethical dimension that gives rise to an "aesthetics of the moral imagination," which bears profound resonances in the lives of its participants. In this deftly executed interdisciplinary drill-down, Tirres argues for a critical balance between a theoretical-hermeneutical examination and "the actual qualities and force of a given ritual" as described from experience—the consideration of which, as evinced by his study, breaks open an abundance of meaning. Ultimately, the essay sheds light on the phenomenon of inculturation as it occurs in a particular social context, a Mexican American community "dancing" in the interstices of culture, religion, and history.

The succeeding chapter "Dancing, Eating, Worshiping: Inculturated 'Third Space' in Rarámuri Celebrations" by Mexican scholar Ángel F. Méndez Montoya, traipses a similar pathway, this time widening the aperture to an examination of Holy Week liturgy as it is mutually

---

[19] For example, as used in Sison, *The Art of Indigenous Inculturation*, 18–19.

implicated with Indigenous devotional practices, dance, and foodways. Méndez invites us to be his virtual co-sojourners as he travels to the Mexican village of Samachique, southwest of Chihuahua, to immerse in the *Semana Santa* festivities and rituals of the Indigenous Rarámuri peoples, who, within the rich and vibrant matrix of their cultural heritage, are at home in the both/and of an embodied human existence and a cosmic, eco-spiritual imaginary. A central focus of Méndez' project is what he identifies as the inculturation of a "Third Space" that births from the theopoetics of the Rarámuris' own creative genius. Here, life-giving currents converge into a hybridized incarnation of the very paschal mystery, affirming both the integrity of the Rarámuris' cultural identity and the prophetic-liberating Christian gospel, while disarming the colonial specters that bedevil their sociopolitical milieu.

In "Contemporary Inculturational Performing Arts in the Indonesian Christian Church," Marzanna Poplawska brings to bear her deep, long-standing engagement with Catholic and Protestant communities in the Indonesian islands of Java, North Sumatra, and Flores to examine the dynamic interchange between Indigenous and European cultural elements inflected in local sacred music and their related expressions in dance. "Inculturational" is the descriptive term she proposes, an appellation that meaningfully connotes the kinetic, ongoing character of inculturation as a profoundly communitarian phenomenon. With astonishing clarity and a meticulous attention to nuances of ethnomusicology and cultural aesthetics, Poplawska authenticates how such an inculturational harmonizing represents the flourishing of Indigenous cultural identity, agency, and genius.

Carmel Pilcher's contribution, "Ceremonial Genius: Australia's First Peoples and Liturgical Inculturation," takes seriously the relativizing view of history to map the ongoing processes and modalities of inculturation in her native Australia. Her historical survey, based on primary sources rarely explored outside an Australian context, exemplifies a diligent and detailed accumulation of information, from the pioneering efforts of an earlier generation of Catholic missionaries, moving to the participation of Aboriginals and Islanders in the refracted light of the Second Vatican Council, and the incremental inclusion of

Introduction   xxiii

"ethnic genius" to liturgical ceremony and ritual. While drawing from the established methodological synthesis of liturgical inculturation proposed by noted Filipino liturgist Anscar Chupungco, Pilcher does not stop at a mere application of method; she issues a critique of the same for presupposing the primacy of the Roman Rite over Indigenous ritual expressions, which, she argues, limits the potential for true cultural dialogue. Constructively, she proposes the alternative notion of "interculturation"[20]—proffered by Ojibwe Canadian Eva Solomon, CSJ, whose lifework is dedicated to First Nations spirituality and liturgy—as the relevant, historically urgent form of mutual engagement for Australia's Catholic Aboriginal people.

Is inculturation—as against "acculturation"—realizable in the unfreedom of terror? "Silent Inculturation: Japan's Hidden Christians and the Criterion of the Cross," my own contribution to this anthology, re-traces the long-drawn via dolorosa of Japan's *Kakure Kirishitan* or "Hidden Christians," who heroically defied and outlived the great persecution of the Tokugawa shogunate (1630–1867) as they found astonishing ways of preserving their Christian faith under the shadow of public humiliation, torture, and martyrdom. In the crucible of suppression and suffering, *Kakure* faith birthed religious iconography,

---

[20] The term "interculturation," as Aylward Shorter notes, was coined by Bishop Joseph Blomjous in 1980 for the purpose of safeguarding the mutual character of Christian mission, which had been traditionally based on an "insertion" model. See Shorter, *Toward a Theology of Inculturation*, 13–14. While Solomon proposes "interculturation" as an alternative to inculturation, noted Vietnamese American theologian Peter Phan does not construe these concepts as mutually exclusive: "The gospel, though not to be identified with any culture, is never independent of culture. It always comes already enfleshed in a particular culture. Consequently, inculturation is necessarily *interculturation* [emphasis mine] and must abide by the laws and dynamics of intercultural dialogue." Phan underscores that the concept of inculturation also encompasses the theology behind the phenomenon, e.g., as governed by the paschal mystery; interculturation refers more to the process of cultural dialogue. See Phan, *In Our Own Tongues: Perspectives from Asia on Mission and Inculturation* (Maryknoll, NY: Orbis Books, 2003), 6–9. Representing distinct yet related "language-games," the option for inculturation and/or interculturation, as exemplified by Phan's work, is a matter of emphasis.

prayers, liturgies, even a sacred text, from fragmentary recollections of missionary catechism and biblical narratives interwoven with influences from their Japanese Buddhist-Shinto heritage. What is the appropriate lens and criterion for ascertaining the phenomenon of inculturation among the *Kakure Kirishitan*, who, in their very bodies and memories, bear the stigmata of the crucified Nazarene? Through an inductive journey, the emergent response—"the criterion of the cross"—challenges misplaced, rigid notions of doctrinal and liturgical conformity, and argues for the critical importance of "context" in comprehending the irreducible synthesis of inculturation and lived faith experience.

Ferdinand Ikenna Okorie's essay, "God, Canaan, Egypt, and the Stories of Migration in Intercultural Perspective," also takes the historical assignment seriously but from the decidedly longer view of biblical history. Adhering to the methodological rigor of biblical exegesis, he examines the phenomenon of migration in ancient Egypt, with a special focus on the experience of the Israelite forebears in Genesis, and that of the remnant of Judah during the exilic period as chronicled in Jeremiah. A "hermeneutic of contextual expressions of religious value" illumines Okorie's exegetical project, opening for him a window to the abiding presence of the deity in the very existential realities of border crossing. As evidenced in the phenomenon of migration, then and now—to wit, the Jewish migrant experience in ancient Elephantine, to the plight of present-day Latino/a migrants at the Mexico-US border—religious meaning finds inculturated expressions, the creative crossings of cultures embodied in material objects and symbols, and the rituals that surround them.

In the final chapter, "Pedagogy of Hospitality: Transforming Missionary Onslaught into Mutual Transformation and Enrichment," Agbonkhianmeghe E. Orobator critically examines Christian missionary history in his home continent of Africa, with an incisive analysis of the process by which the "evangelical hubris" of the European missionaries, in the service of colonial hegemony, translated into relentless abuse and subjugation of African culture and identity. A fallout of such a brazen assertion of Eurocentric superiority is the false-naming of African Indigenous religions as deficient, detestable, demonic. Proving resilient in the face of the missionary onslaught, however, African religions were not supplanted by missionary Christianity; on the contrary, they formed a "cultural substratum" that engendered multiple identity–belonging, thus becoming a locus for re-rooting inculturation. Judiciously interweaving a variety of cultural and theological sources, Orobator affirms Africa's Indigenous genius in the "humanizing values" of hospitality, *Ubuntu*, and palaver, generatively advancing the development of a deep inculturation that may be described as—to borrow from Orobator's creatively original book on inculturation—a "Theology Brewed in an African Pot."[21]

Perhaps it is reasonable for me to extend Orobator's vibrant metaphor to say that, bar none, each of our contributing authors endeavors, modestly but meaningfully, to reverse the hermeneutical flow as we explore inculturation as it is "brewed in the pot of Indigenous genius":

- In the poetic, healing movements of liturgical dance performed by a Mexican American community in Texas, or the sacred rhythms of faith-footwork-foodways of the Indigenous Rarámuri communities in Mexico's remote, mountainous regions.
- In the symphonic blending of Indigenous and Christian "inculturational" music in Catholic and Protestant churches in Indonesia, or the continuing pilgrimage of Australia's First Peoples to interweave their story and symbols in Catholic liturgy.
- In the heroic faith of Japan's Hidden Christians who birthed astonishing, culture-affirming devotional expressions under the shadow of death and untold suffering; in the experience of the migrants of biblical history in Egypt and their contemporary analogues, who, en route and in flux, found the deity in the fluidity of intercultural exchange; or in the

---

[21] Agbonkhianmeghe E. Orobator, *Theology Brewed in an African Pot* (Maryknoll, NY: Orbis Books, 2008).

transformative contributions of African cultures to Christian faith practice, re-rooted in cultural values that run counterflow to the exclusion and condescension of a calcified missionary Christianity.

To say it again, the hope of this collection is for us to represent a renewed polyphony for speaking about inculturation based on a reasoned, appreciative valuation of local culture. Local culture is also a gift of God, a pearl of great value.

Pope Francis, in his 2013 apostolic exhortation *Evangelii Gaudium* ("The Joy of the Gospel"), advocates for such a valuation when he reaffirms the creative agency of the members of local culture. Standing on the truth of their authentic identity as "people of God," they are the lead artisans in the creative and self-creating process of inculturation:

> The different peoples among whom the Gospel has been inculturated are active collective subjects or agents of evangelization. This is because each people is the creator of their own culture and the protagonist of their own history.... Each portion of the people of God, by translating the gift of God into its own life and *in accordance with its own genius*, bears witness to the faith it has received and enriches it with new and eloquent expressions.[22]

Deep inculturation. In the spirit of synodality, this is our path, *poeisis*, and praxis.

---

[22] Pope Francis, *Evangelii Gaudium*, apostolic exhortation (2013), section 122, www.vatican.va (emphasis mine).

Contributors

Ángel F. Méndez Montoya, OPL, PhD, author, *The Theology of Food: Eating and the Eucharist* (Oxford: Wiley-Blackwell, 2012). Professor, Department of Religious Sciences, Universidad Iberoamericana, Mexico City, Mexico.

Ferdinand Ikenna Okorie, CMF, PhD, author, *Favor and Gratitude: Reading Galatians in Its Greco-Roman Context* (Lanham, MD: Fortress Academic, 2020). Vice President and Academic Dean, Catholic Theological Union, Chicago.

Agbonkhianmeghe E. Orobator, SJ, PhD, author, *Religion and Faith in Africa* (Maryknoll, NY: Orbis Books, 2018); *Theology Brewed in an African Pot* (Maryknoll, NY: Orbis Books, 2008). Former President, Jesuit Conference of Africa and Madagascar (JCAM), Nairobi, Kenya. Dean of the Jesuit School of Theology of Santa Clara University.

Carmel Pilcher, RSJ, PhD, editor and contributing author, *Vatican II Reforming Liturgy* (Adelaide: AFT, 2013). Liturgy and Sacraments consultant/educator, New South Wales, Australia; Former President, Australian Academy of Liturgy.

Marzanna Poplawska, PhD, author, *Performing Faith: Christian Music, Identity and Inculturation in Indonesia* (New York: Routledge, 2020). Assistant Professor, Institute of Ethnology and Cultural Anthropology, University of Warsaw, Poland.

Antonio D. Sison, CPPS, PhD, author, *The Art of Indigenous Inculturation: Grace on the Edge of Genius* (Maryknoll, NY: Orbis Books, 2021). Vatican Council II Chair of Theology, Professor of Systematic Theology, Catholic Theological Union, Chicago.

Christopher D. Tirres, PhD, author, *The Aesthetics and Ethics of Faith: A Dialogue between Liberationist and Pragmatic Thought* (New York: Oxford University Press, 2014). Vincent de Paul Professor of Religious Studies, Inaugural Endowed Professor of Diplomacy and Interreligious Engagement, DePaul University, Chicago.

Part I

Ritual and Performance

1

A Liturgy That Heals

An Interdisciplinary Approach to Mexican American Ritual

Christopher D. Tirres

For many years, I have been crisscrossing the disciplines of religious studies and theology. As an undergraduate in a department of religious studies, I was exposed to the approaches and methods of *Religionswissenchaft*, or "the scientific study of religion," yet I also fell in love with liberation theology, which I discovered through two courses in political science. I was drawn to liberation theology's critique of structural sin and its attention to the fullness of life in the here-and-now. Under the mentorship of a philosopher (Cornel West) and a historian of religion (Davíd Carrasco), I wrote a largely theological undergraduate senior thesis on the realized eschatology of Archbishop Oscar Romero. All of this goes to say that my early engagement with liberation theology was colored by the insights of a variety of scholarly disciplines (including religious studies, philosophy, and politics) that are not, properly speaking, theology.

Nevertheless, my interest in the ever-expanding tradition of liberation theology has remained steadfast and has deepened over the years, though I have made some valuable side journeys along the way. Upon entering a doctoral program in religious studies, I had intended to write a dissertation on some aspect of liberation methodology. But while on this journey, I discovered two methodological approaches that productively foregrounded questions of culture. These two discourses were US-Latino/a theology, a close cousin of Latin American liberation theology, and US pragmatism. To make a long story short, I ended up writing a dissertation on John Dewey's philosophy of religion and its connection to his aesthetic theory and theory of education. But my interest in liberation theology never waned. Indeed, this sustained interest is evident in my first book, which crafts a dialogue between US pragmatism and liberation theology, as it is articulated both in Latin America and in the United States.[1]

Some of my ongoing questions are these: How can liberation theology and pragmatism, when put in critical conversation, shed light on not only the aesthetic and cultural dimensions of ritual, which are often so readily apparent, but also the ethical dimensions of ritual, which tend to be more implicit? How does ritual intensify not only "an aesthetics of sense," but also "an aesthetics of the moral imagination"? Furthermore, how can inculturated rituals simultaneously point adherents in two seemingly opposite directions: on the one hand, toward a cultural memory of suffering and yet, on the other, toward the promise of new life, as expressed through culturally affirming rituals?

In what follows, I look at these questions in light of a liturgy that takes place on Good Friday at the San Fernando Cathedral in San Antonio, Texas.

San Fernando Cathedral is a flagship church for a number of reasons. It is one of the oldest churches in the country and one of the most dynamic. Over the years, its leaders have included visionaries who see great value in the lived faith expressions of the people.[2] For these pastoral leaders, the lived faith of the people helps to preserve cultural dignity, and it may serve as a springboard for individual and

---

[1] Christopher D. Tirres, *The Aesthetics and Ethics of Faith: A Dialogue between Liberationist and Pragmatic Thought* (New York: Oxford University Press, 2014).

[2] At the time of my initial research, these visionaries included Virgilio Elizondo, James Empereur, SJ, David García, and Sally T. Gomez-Jung. For a closer look at their exemplary pastoral work, see ibid., 14–41, 160–73.

communal transformation. San Fernando Cathedral is well known for its Good Friday processions, particularly its dramatic *Via Crucis*, or reenactment of Christ's trial and crucifixion, which draws upwards of fifteen to twenty thousand people to downtown San Antonio every year. For several hours, people literally walk alongside the portrayal of Jesus through the streets of San Antonio, accompanying him in his final hours of life.

San Antonio Cathedral during Holy Week.
Copyright © 2023 Marcela Szinnyey

As gripping as the *Via Crucis* is, I would like to focus on a lesser-known liturgy that happens at the end of the day on Good Friday, a traditional Mexican service called the *Pésame*. According to Miguel Arias, the *Pésame* has its origins in the region that today we know as Guatemala. It was introduced by Pedro José de Betancourt (1626–67), who was canonized a saint in 2002. Arias takes special note of the Indigenous elements of the *Pésame*. He writes,

Around 1670 Betancourt began processions with the *Nazareno* (an image of the suffering Christ) through the streets of old Guatemala City. Christ's body was extremely scourged, with no place for even one more wound. The people were impressed with this image because according to their story of the creation of the world, Quetzalcoatl, the feathered serpent, had to pierce himself to water the earth. As a result of this watering, human beings were born. This wounded Jesus, the new God introduced to them, really knew their pain and suffering.[3]

Over three hundred years later, Mexican American Catholics in San Antonio continue to know Jesus' pain and suffering through their own culturally appropriate crucifix and their own version of the *Pésame*.

However, rather than focus the liturgy around the singular figure of an "extremely scourged" Jesus, congregants instead confront Jesus' suffering in a more relational and interactive way by paying their respects to Jesus' grieving mother, Mary.

In a powerful part of the *Pésame* service that I witnessed in 2004, Mary performs a moving liturgical dance that invites participation from onlookers. In what follows, I focus my comments on the ways that Mary's dance ignites not only a visceral aesthetics of sense but also a more encompassing aesthetics of the moral imagination. Furthermore, the *Pésame* itself may be said to "dance" creatively between Latinx religious customs, which serve as bulwarks to cultural assimilation, and the Paschal message, thereby shedding light on what inculturation can look like in a particular time and place.[4] In offering this interpretation,

---

[3] Miguel Arias, "Stay with Me," *U.S. Catholic* 72 (2007): 48, https://uscatholic.org.

[4] As Robert Schreiter writes, "A close reading of the shape of popular religion gives us a unique perspective on the nature of religious activity and experience in concrete social contexts. It tells us something also of the role of religion in social change and in the continuing process of shaping identity in a particular cultural setting." Seen in this light, this chapter is an attempt to show that one of the particular "somethings" that the *Pésame* reveals is that cultural and religious identity can be significantly shaped both by sensorial experience

I draw on insights from religious studies and theology, showing how both may address similar concerns.

A crucifix evincing Christian-Indigenous inculturation.
Viernes Santo at the San Fernando Cathedral.
Image courtesy Christopher D. Tirres

The Aesthetics of *Viernes Santo*

Across the country, Good Friday is an important day among Latinx communities of faith. Although Easter is, theologically speaking, the high point of the liturgical year, in many parishes it is not uncommon for more Latino/as to attend services on Good Friday than on Easter Sunday. How does one account for this phenomenon?

One reason is that many Good Friday liturgies are performed in open, public spaces. Accordingly, these liturgies can accommodate hundreds, if not thousands, more people than a traditional church service. In Chicago's largely Mexican American Pilsen area, for example, over ten thousand ritual participants process down

---

and imaginative moral reasoning. Robert Schreiter, *Constructing Local Theologies* (Maryknoll, NY: Orbis Books, 1985), 123.

Eighteenth Street, Pilsen's main thoroughfare.[5] Similarly, thousands of Hispanics publicly commemorate the *Via Crucis* in New York City's Lower East Side.[6] Given the steady influx of immigrants from Latin America, one can find similar events in countless urban and rural areas throughout the country and the world.[7]

For many Hispanics, the *Via Crucis* also proves meaningful because it is a liturgy guided by lay parishioners themselves. Although official church leaders like priests and deacons participate in it, everyday parishioners are often the ones who assume the lion's share of responsibility for the reenactment. Months in advance of Good Friday, parishioners organize tryouts, lead practices, and in some cases organize religious retreats for all those involved in the liturgies. Perhaps most significantly, Latino/as are drawn to Good Friday because of the aesthetic charge that it holds. This aesthetic charge alludes not only to ritual's physical and sensorial qualities—or what we could refer to as an "aesthetics of sense"—but also to its epistemic and imaginative qualities—its "aesthetics of the moral imagination."[8] The aesthetics of sense is experienced through the embodied, tactile, and sensorial encounters one has on Good Friday. Participants walk with Jesus for

---

[5] In 2009, it snowed in Chicago on Good Friday, yet thousands of people still participated.

[6] Wayne Ashley, "Stations of the Cross: Christ, Politics, and Processions on New York City's Lower East Side," in *Gods of the City: Religion and the American Urban Landscape*, ed. Robert A. Orsi (Bloomington: Indiana University Press, 1999), 341–64; Alyshia Gálvez, *Guadalupe in New York: Devotion and the Struggle for Citizenship Rights among Mexican Immigrants* (New York: New York University Press, 2010), 107–39.

[7] For a look at the most ambitious annual passion play in the world, which takes place in Mexico, see Richard C. Trexler, *Reliving Golgotha: The Passion Play of Iztapalapa* (Cambridge, MA: Harvard University Press, 2003).

[8] I am drawing here, in part, on Alexander Baumgarten's broad understanding of aesthetics as the "science of (all) sensory knowledge." Unfortunately, Baumgarten's wide-reaching definition, which he offered in 1735, was soon limited to a more circumscribed discussion of exceptional pieces of fine art, as seen in the shift from Immanuel Kant's wide-ranging discussion of the transcendental aesthetic in the *Critique of Pure Reason* (1781) to G. W. F. Hegel's more limited ruminations on the fine arts in his *Introductory Lectures on Aesthetics* (1835).

hours. Over the course of the day, they also see and hear the agony that Christ endures, they smell incense, they taste the Eucharist, and they touch and kiss the statue of Jesus on the cross. Through these kinds of bodily encounters, participants "sense" ritual in a real and direct way.

At the same time, these liturgies also prove aesthetic insofar as they engage participants at the level of the moral imagination. Through their ritual actions, participants forge new epistemic connections between realities that may seem, at first glance, to be disconnected. As I elaborate further momentarily, ritual allows participants to engage multiple identities simultaneously, to merge past and present, to straddle universal and inculturated meanings of the *Via Crucis*. Ritual action creates a subjunctive, ludic, and liminal space that allows participants to imaginatively conjoin what may, at first, appear to be discrete and independent aspects of experience.

As a participant-observer, I found that it was fairly easy to see an aesthetics of sense manifested in the many ritual practices of the day. Clearly, the San Fernando Good Friday liturgies heightened and intensified experience in myriad ways. What was less apparent, though, and therefore worthy of further study, was how these liturgies also prove ethically significant. In what ways do the aesthetics of sense give rise to an aesthetics of the moral imagination, and how far does the latter extend? How is the aesthetic charge of Good Friday tied to God's kingdom here and now? How is the feeling of ritual experience connected to the action of living out one's life beyond Good Friday? While such questions may be clearly tethered to psycho-social analyses, it is worth noting that they also extend out to religious-theological considerations, especially given the theological context of the *Pésame* itself.

Such questions, I soon came to realize, are best answered in light of particular cases. In what follows, I share my experience of the *Pésame* service.

The *Pésame* and the Power of Liturgical Dance

On Good Friday, there are four liturgies at San Fernando: an ecumenical prayer service that begins the day, the *Via Crucis*, the *Siete Palabras* service (which commemorates the seven last phrases of Jesus), and the *Pésame*.[9]

Pésame at the San Antonio Cathedral.
Copyright © 2023 Marcela Szinnyey

Of all the services on Good Friday, the *Pésame* perhaps best engages what I am calling here the "aesthetics of the moral imagination." This simple twilight service begins at 7:00 p.m. The entire church is dark, except for the main altar area located in the center of the church. Congregants hold lit candles in the pews. Three male parishioners, who are dressed as disciples, come forward to take down the life-size statue of Jesus from the cross. The men gently disengage the Christ figure from the cross and fold his movable arms

---

[9] The descriptions I offer reflect my experience of the *Pésame* in 2004. Though the liturgy took place in the past, I write about it here in the historical present to give the reader a sense of what is was like to experience it firsthand.

down to the sides of his torso. This detail, which is a trait common to the processional art of Golden Age Spain, adds a certain realism to the ritual.[10]

Pésame at the San Antonio Cathedral.
Copyright © 2023 Marcela Szinnyey

The repositioning of the body from the cross to the funeral bed is a touching moment, as Jesus, who has suffered high upon the cross, is now brought down to be with the people. The men carefully secure Jesus' body to the funeral bed with rope. They exit the cathedral. With candles in hand, parishioners follow. It is now dark. Everyone processes slowly across the street and around the city plaza directly in front of the church. People sing as cars pass by. The warm, yellow

---

[10] Susan Verdi Webster, *Art and Ritual in Golden-Age Spain: Sevillian Confraternities and the Processional Sculpture of Holy Week* (Princeton, NJ: Princeton University Press, 1998).

lights from the candles overlap with the more industrial white lights emanating from the plaza's streetlamps and car headlights. After slowly processing around the plaza, the parishioners solemnly return to the church and fill the pews once again.

When everyone has returned and the body of Jesus has once again been lain at the altar platform, three older women approach the body and tenderly rub the statue with burial oil.

Pésame at the San Antonio Cathedral.
Image courtesy Christopher D. Tirres

As they do so, a solo baritone from the choir begins singing the heart-wrenching refrains of the American folk hymn "What Wondrous Love Is This?" and twelve female liturgical dancers in black dresses and shawls circle the altar area. Their movements and facial gestures signal pain and loss. The three older women finish generously slathering the body with oils. They cover Jesus' body and limbs with a white cloth, leaving his face exposed, and they place some rose petals on the cloth. They leave the platform. About this time, another dancer enters the sanctuary. Her black shawl is distinctively marked by a thin piece of white cloth at the brow, distinguishing her from the others.

A Liturgy That Heals

She assumes a central role within the dance, and it quickly becomes apparent that she is playing the role of Jesus' mother, Mary.

Mary runs across the area in front of the altar, stops, folds her hands together, pauses, and faces upward with a pained and sorrowful look. She bows her head. She runs in desperation to the other side of the church and does the same. Alone she stands, in agony.

Then, in an unexpected turn of events, a family of four who are seated near the front of the church rises from the pews. The father, mother, and two adolescent girls move toward Mary. At this point, it is not clear what is happening. Are they part of the liturgy? The family members approach Mary and embrace her, one by one. This is repeated twice more. Their movements are expressive and intentional. Perhaps more than any other gesture of the day, this embrace embodies and inculturates how the audience is one with the actors, how they are connected to the passion in a real way. It reminds parishioners that they have come to this church service with an express purpose: to console a grieving mother at her son's funeral.

The family sits down, and Mary then goes up to each of the twelve dancers who are standing in a wide semicircle around the altar area. Mary consoles the dancers and is consoled by them. The reciprocity seems to suggest that there are many Marys in need of consolation. Another group of parishioners rises from the pews. This time, it is a family of three older women. They approach Mary and take turns embracing her multiple times. The effect is again powerful. Through ritual, the congregation is, in a very real way, sharing Mary's suffering.[11]

Finally, after these ritual gestures of consolation, the dancers exit. In silence, ushers guide parishioners out of their pews and direct them toward the altar, giving each parishioner a single-stemmed flower. In

---

[11] This is just one inculturated example of Marian devotion. For a detailed discussion of Marian devotions in San Antonio, see Timothy Matovina, *Guadalupe and Her Faithful: Latino Catholics in San Antonio, from Colonial Origins to the Present* (Baltimore: Johns Hopkins University Press, 2005). Matovina builds on this work in his excellent *Theologies of Guadalupe: From the Era of Conquest to Pope Francis* (New York: Oxford University Press, 2019), which offers a broader historical overview of the many ways in which Our Lady of Guadalupe has been interpreted theologically throughout the hemisphere.

two lines, congregants slowly walk up to the altar platform and place their flower atop Jesus' body. Almost everyone makes some kind of physical contact with the body. They kiss and touch Jesus. Soon, the pile of flowers is so substantial that several fall to the floor. After having paid their tribute to Jesus, the parishioners solemnly exit the church in silence. The *Pésame* and Good Friday have come to an end.

Ritual Theory, Practical Theology, and Actual Experience

At San Fernando, ritual clearly engages participants in an embodied and visceral way. On Good Friday, participants hear, smell, touch, taste, and see; they move their bodies through a variety of spaces, often becoming part of the ritual itself. But in addition to involving participants at the level of an aesthetics of sense, ritual at San Fernando also engrosses participants at the level of the aesthetics of the moral imagination, wherein ritual practices structure and shape a larger outlook on life. In so many words, the felt quality of ritual experience gives rise to a larger *Weltanschauung*, or cosmovision, with all of the ethical implications that this implies.

What do I mean here by the "moral imagination"? To begin with, I understand morality not in terms of an eternal "moral law" or even a "system" of rules for living, but rather as a continuous, reflective response to a life that is inevitably unstable, precarious, and tragic. Morality, in this sense, begins with an actual, real life situation of instability; it involves some form of deliberation to deal with this situation of instability; and it leads to some form of judgment, which itself is always unstable and contingent.[12]

Ritual, I believe, can be a powerful mode for engaging moral dilemmas. This is especially true if we take to heart John Dewey's

---

[12] I am following here John Dewey's situationalist and pragmatic understanding of morality. For a compelling example of how a pragmatic hermeneutic may be applied to a truly precarious and tragic situation, see Eddie S. Glaude Jr.'s "Tragedy and Moral Experience: John Dewey and Toni Morrison's *Beloved*," in *In a Shade of Blue: Pragmatism and the Politics of Black America* (Chicago: University of Chicago Press, 2007), 17–46.

insight that moral deliberation can take the form of "dramatic rehearsal" wherein, through processes like ritual performance, ritual participants can imaginatively engage precarious situations and consider our possible courses of action, without the threat of direct harm. Victor Turner, the noted cultural anthropologist and ritual theorist, understands this point well, underscoring how stage dramas serve as mirrors to larger social dramas, and vice versa.[13] As Turner makes clear, stage drama is not simply a powerful form of entertainment. In a more profound sense, it is a means to deal with various forms of social instability, ruptures, friction, and pain. It is for this reason, writes Turner, that "society has always had to make efforts, through both social dramas and aesthetic dramas, to restabilize and actually *produce* cosmos."[14]

In producing cosmos, ritual performance proves moral in the sense I have described it. Through structured gestures and actions, ritual confronts social instability and reestablishes a sense of order. Almost by definition, then, we could say that ritual serves an important ethical function. But how else may ritual performance—and, in particular, the *Pésame* service at San Fernando—prove ethical? Ritual theory offers us a range of helpful concepts for understanding how the moral imagination can be enlarged through ritual. Most crucially, perhaps, the *Pésame*'s liturgical dance functions to create a liminal experience where concepts of time and identity collapse. In the liturgical dance, we see figures of the past—the grieving Mary—come into direct physical contact with figures from the present—the grieving families of San Fernando—through the intentional embraces that they exchange. In an embodied and symbolic way, the past meets the present, giving way

---

[13] Victor Turner, "Are There Universals of Performance in Myth, Ritual, and Drama?," in *By Means of Performance: Intercultural Studies of Theatre and Ritual*, ed. Richard Schechner and Willa Appel (Cambridge: Cambridge University Press, 1997), 8–18. It is instructive to note that Turner turns to Dewey's philosophy at several junctures in his essay to elaborate several key themes, including the meaning of experience (8, 13), the instability of social life (as captured by the "doings and sufferings" of the present community) (9), and the connection of aesthetic drama to sociocultural life (12).

[14] Turner, "Are There Universals of Performance in Myth, Ritual, and Drama?," 18, emphasis in original.

to a wider sense of what Turner refers to as *communitas*, or liminality experienced socially.

This liminal experience is further reinforced by the fact that the liturgical dance blurs the line between actors and audience. This happens when select families leave the pews to console the grieving Mary. When I witnessed this part of the liturgy, my initial reaction was confusion. *Why are these people getting up from the pews and embracing the dancers?* I asked myself. *What is going on?* I felt as if a social norm were being broken. Soon, however, I realized that this was indeed part of the liturgy. I was moved deeply. The moment dissolved the boundaries between actors and onlookers, between "us" and "them." The ritual gestures reminded participants that the drama did not only take place in Jerusalem two thousand years ago but continues in a real way in our own time and within our own communities. Even more significantly, as I discovered later, both sets of parishioners who console Mary were selected for a very particular reason: they, too, had lost loved ones in their own families during the year. Many in the congregation would have no doubt been aware of this fact, adding significantly to the meaning of their gestures.

All told, the *Pésame* creates liminal, intercultural experiences that are both sensual and epistemic. As we have seen, the liturgical dance creates new configurations of space, time, and identities, and, in doing so, it expands the moral and cultural imagination of participants. Congregants come away from this liturgy with a wider sense of community and a heightened sense of their own capacity to accompany those who suffer, whether this be the grieving Mary of two thousand years ago or grieving fellow congregants who have lost loved ones in their own immediate families. By entering into the ritual experience of the *Pésame*, congregants affirm life, even in the face of tremendous difficulty and loss. As Virgilio Elizondo, one of San Fernando's most influential pastoral leaders, puts it, the *Pésame* is "in a way, already resurrection" because it assumes "the most incredible suffering of that day." Through ritual, parishioners can identify with Jesus and say, "'I have gone through [the suffering], but it has not destroyed me. I have gone through it, but it has not diminished my hope and my enthusiasm. I have not run away from it, I have not denied it. I have faced it.'" This is "Good Friday in the Latino world," continues Elizondo. It is "the radical acceptance of life as it is, but you don't let it destroy you."[15]

As I have argued, interpreting the *Pésame* through the categories of liminality and communitas helps to shed light on the ethical dimensions of the ritual. The *Pésame*'s liturgical dance opens up a liminal space where many usual distinctions—such as past and present, us and them, and official presider and everyday layperson—merge together. When this happens, one's sense of community significantly broadens. At the same time, a qualitatively new experience emerges through the performance itself, through gestures, movement, embrace, reappropriation of space, and role reversals. For this reason, a performance-based approach to ritual, as exemplified in the work of Turner, may be especially illuminating for better understanding a fluid, inculturated liturgy like the *Pésame*.[16]

I would now like to consider how a similar set of insights might emerge from within particular strains of theology itself. Part of the irony here, as I fully recognize, is that I have been using interpretive categories often associated with religious studies to shed light on a ritual that emerges from a context that is clearly theological. I am, after all, talking about a liturgy centered on Mary, the mother of Jesus, which takes place on Good Friday within a Catholic church.

As someone who has been trained in religious studies yet who engages contextual and liberation theologies, I have found it helpful to bring resources from ritual theory to bear on theological symbols and rituals. Indeed, I think that theology has much to learn from religious studies. But I also have become increasingly aware that religious studies has much to learn from theology, especially from theologies that emerge from the underside of history, or what noted historian

---

[15] *Soul of the City: Alma del Pueblo*, videocassette, directed by Gerardo Rueda (Houston: JM Communications, 1996).

[16] As Walter Capps notes, for Turner, the very occurrence of performative action "effects changes in the environment within which it occurs, and it effects changes in the identities (both collective and individual) of those who participate in such action." For this reason, Turner urged his colleagues in anthropology to take theatre studies seriously. Walter H. Capps, *Religious Studies: The Making of a Discipline* (Minneapolis: Fortress Press, 1995), 197.

of religion Charles Long refers to as "theologies of the opaque."[17] Such theologies not only ground their reflection in concrete forms of human suffering, but they also indict theology at large for assuming certain normativity in its claims to knowledge. San Fernando allows for the flourishing of this kind of theology.

I have grown to appreciate how the theology espoused at San Fernando is not only contextual and liberationist but also highly intercultural. In his recent, elegant study, *The Art of Indigenous Inculturation: Grace on the Edge of Genius*, Antonio Sison offers a comparative look at the liberating dimensions of Indigenous inculturation as it emerges in three representative sites in the Global South: Kenya, Mexico, and the Philippines. Sison crafts a theological method that interprets processes of inculturation using three overlapping lenses: a *hermeneutics of suspicion*, which interrogates a protracted experience of cultural and religious colonization; a *hermeneutics of appreciation*, which foregrounds the "astonishing creativity, resilience, and tensile strength" of communities that have resisted cultural assimilation; and a *hermeneutics of serendipity*, which brings to light "how unanticipated historical turns kindled ironic emancipatory currents that allowed for the flourishing" of the local culture's creative

---

[17] Charles H. Long, *Significations: Signs, Symbols, and Images in the Interpretation of Religion* (Philadelphia: Fortress Press, 1986), 185–99. Along these lines, I resonate with Michael Hogue's pragmatic understanding of theology as "not limited to critical reflection on the symbol 'God.'" Instead, the objects of theology can be conceived of as "those diverse constellations of symbols and practices and institutions that orient us ultimately by formatting (i.e., giving shape to, stylizing, embedding) the religious meanings, purposes, and desires through which we negotiate the hazards and graces of vulnerable life in an ambiguous world." As Hogue notes, this conception of theology is made possible by drawing on a particular philosophy of religion, one that takes quite seriously Charles Long's conception of "orientation in the ultimate sense," Paul Tillich's understanding of "ultimate concern," and Charles Sanders Peirce's understanding "that religion is a life, and can be identified with a belief only provided that belief be a living belief—a thing to be lived rather than said or thought." See Michael S. Hogue, "Toward a Pragmatic Political Theology," *American Journal of Theology and Philosophy* 34, no. 3 (2013): 274–75.

genius.[18] As Sison shows, inculturation and liberation are, in fact, often coextensive. This is especially the case in postcolonial contexts such as found at San Fernando, where cultural and aesthetic performances serve as valued modes for expressing communal agency.

Sison's threefold method applies well to a faith community like San Fernando, which consists primarily of Mexican Americans, born in San Antonio, who, in the words of Virgilio Elizondo, have been "twice conquered, twice colonized, and twice mestized" first by the Spanish conquest of Mexico beginning in 1519, and again with the Anglo-American invasion of the Mexican northwest beginning in the 1830s. Elizondo elaborates:

> The ancestors of today's Mexican-Americans have been living in the present-day United States since the early 1700s. Our group did not cross the border to come to the United States; rather the United States expanded its borders and we found ourselves to be a part of the United States. Since the early beginnings, many generations have crossed the Rio Grande to come over to the other side of family lands. Yet we have always been treated as foreigners in our own countryside—exiles who never felt at home.... This is our socio-cultural reality![19]

For liberation to take root in an existential, social, and cultural situation like this, a hermeneutics of suspicion becomes an indispensable tool for unmasking and critiquing inherited narratives.

At the same time, what Sison identifies as a hermeneutics of appreciation and a hermeneutics of serendipity should also be utilized, as these help to account for the cultural treasures and creative forms of resistance that communities like San Fernando draw upon to overcome structural forms of marginalization and dehumanization. Sison's

---

[18] Antonio D. Sison, *The Art of Indigenous Inculturation: Grace on the Edge of Genius* (Maryknoll, NY: Orbis Books, 2021), 14–18.

[19] Virgil P. Elizondo, "Mestizaje as a Locus of Theological Reflection," in *Frontiers of Hispanic Theology in the United States*, ed. Allan Figueroa Deck, SJ (Maryknoll, NY: Orbis Books, 1992), 106.

theological method may be described as an assets-based approach to inculturation insofar as it highlights the inherent gifts and ingenious techniques that postcolonial peoples put to use in creating meaning and agency. Indeed, San Fernando's *Pésame* service may be seen as one shining example of this, as it succeeds, as Anscar Chupungco puts it, in "evok[ing] something from the people's history, traditions, cultural patterns, and artistic genius."[20] Furthermore, the San Fernando *Pésame* may also be seen as an especially good conduit of what Sison identifies as serendipity and surprise, given how ephemeral and improvisational the art form of dance is and how fluid and open-ended its meanings are for onlookers.

Though it doesn't speak of "interculturality" per se, another book that moves in this general direction is Ruth Illman and W. Alan Smith's *Theology and the Arts: Engaging Faith* (2013), which I found pleasantly surprising. Usually, when one sees a title with the words "theology," "arts," and "faith," one can expect a book that presupposes a certain Christian normativity in terms of its approach and basic commitments. While the language of this book does at times fall back on Christian categories, its overall aim is to subvert some of the more traditional ways that theology has tried to make sense of the arts. It attempts to articulate a practical theology of the arts that is not limited to "the conceptual and systematic claims of theology."[21] Rather, it takes ritual experience as both its methodological starting and ending point.

Like Sison's work, one of the striking features of this book is the attention it gives to the centrality of praxis. In the book's core chapter, "Outlining a Practical Approach to Theology and the Arts," Illman and Smith underscore the importance of praxis to their methodological

---

[20] Anscar Chupungco, "Methods of Liturgical Inculturation," in *Worship and Culture: Foreign Country or Homeland?*, ed. Gláucia Vasconcelos Wilkey (Grand Rapids: Eerdmans, 2014), 263. As Chupungco goes on to explain, "The immediate aim of inculturation is to create a form of worship that is culturally suited to the local people—so that they can claim it as their own. Its ultimate aim, on the other hand, is active, intelligent, and devout participation that springs from the people's conviction of faith."

[21] Ruth Illman and W. Alan Smith, *Theology and the Arts: Engaging Faith* (New York: Routledge, 2013), 10.

approach. Following the work of Robert Schreiter, Rebecca Chopp, Thomas Groome, and others, the authors present praxis as a process "in which agent subjects reflect critically on their social/historical situation and present action therein."[22] Praxis, they explain, is the "ensemble of social relationships that include and determine the structure of social consciousness."[23] This "ensemble of social relationships" may be understood in terms of three dimensions: an active dimension that includes and engages intentional historical activities, a reflective dimension that uses critical and social reasoning to reflect critically on individual and social action, and a creative dimension that leads to concrete forms of individual and social transformation.[24]

Just as Gustavo Gutiérrez, the father of liberation theology, has underscored the central role that orthopraxy, or "right action" (and not just orthodoxy, or "right belief") must play in one's expression of faith,[25] so too do Illman and Smith maintain that a practical theology "does not consist in propositional claims or positivistic statements of doctrine as much as it does in critical reflection on living as persons of faith."[26] For

---

[22] Ibid.,, 54, quoting Thomas Groome, "A Religious Educator's Response," in *The Education of the Practical Theologian*, ed. Don Browning, David Polk, and Ian Evison (Atlanta: Scholars Press, 1989), 88. In addition to the three authors mentioned above, Illman and Smith also draw generously from the work of Paul Ballard and John Pritchard, especially their *Practical Theology in Action: Christian Thinking in the Service of Church and Society* (London: SPCK, 2006).

[23] Illman and Smith, 51, quoting Schreiter, *Constructing Local Theologies*, 91.

[24] Illman and Smith, 51. See Rebecca Chopp, "When the Center Cannot Contain the Margin," in Browning et al., eds., *The Education of the Practical Theologian*, 85.

[25] Gutiérrez explains that in underscoring the importance of orthopraxis, his "intention, however, is not to deny the meaning of *orthodoxy*, understood as a proclamation of and reflection on statements considered to be true. Rather, the goal is to balance and even to reject the primacy and almost exclusiveness which doctrine has enjoyed in Christian life and above all to modify the emphasis, often obsessive, upon the attainment of an orthodoxy which is often nothing more than fidelity to an obsolete tradition or a debatable interpretation." Gustavo Gutiérrez, *A Theology of Liberation: History, Politics, and Salvation* (Maryknoll, NY: Orbis Books, 1973), 10.

[26] Illman and Smith, *Theology and the Arts*, 51.

all of these authors, faith, at its best, demands critical reflection and actually "doing the truth."[27]

Though *Theology and the Arts* can certainly be read as a contribution to contemporary debates in Christian practical theology, it can also be understood as pointing toward a much larger intercultural horizon. The book seeks to move not only "beyond the bias of modern systematic and constructive theology," but also, and perhaps even more significantly, beyond narrow understandings of "theology" at large. Toward this end, the book, like Sison's, focuses on a set of projects around the world that serve as concrete sites of transformation and healing, many of which do not seem to have a formal connection to theology at all. These case studies, all of which embody praxis, include the Philadelphia Mural Arts Program, a set of Peruvian women's cooperatives that create fabric arts, a collection of short stories, improvisation theatre, a documentary film about a heart transplant that bridges the separation between Palestinians and Israelis, an interreligious and intercultural music project, and a dance company that incorporates dancers with and without disabilities. As the range of these cases makes clear, the form of practical theology espoused in this book moves well beyond discussions of church-based or even faith-based activities. Rather, the book seems to reverse the "hermeneutical flow" between the arts and theology.[28] Or, in the words of Sison, such an inductive and contextual approach emancipates the art form from "being a mere handmaid of a given theological proposition and agenda." Instead, the art form is "offered prior leave to speak on its own terms as a condition for a respectful and honest dialogue with theology."[29]

Methodologically speaking, Illman and Smith's book draws eclectically upon a number of discourses—including feminist, postmodern, liberationist, and dialogical/dialectical discourses—with the aim of decentering a narrow and modern emphasis on reason and the scientific method, which traditional forms of theology often

---

[27] Gutiérrez, *A Theology of Liberation*, 10.
[28] This phrase comes from Craig Detweiler, as cited in Antonio D. Sison, *World Cinema, Theology, and the Human: Humanity in Deep Focus* (New York: Routledge, 2012), 5.
[29] Sison, *World Cinema, Theology, and the Human*, 5.

uncritically accept. Drawing on the antifoundationalist discourses just mentioned, the authors outline seven guiding characteristics of their approach, each one of which might well describe the ritual experience of the *Pésame*. First, a practical theology of the arts is embodied and not just reflected upon. Second, it has a "face" in the Levinasian sense of the term. Its truth emerges through the encounter of real-life, flesh-and-blood persons. Third, it gives pride of place to the voices of these who have been silenced. Fourth, a practical theology of the arts is accomplished through dialogue that need not be restricted to the spoken word, but instead, may emerge through various forms of intense and intentional listening. Fifth, it proceeds from and is characterized by the actual practices of the arts. Sixth, it clears a space for the emergence of the voices and concerns of the community. And seventh, it is committed to transformative praxis and social change.

Pésame at the San Antonio Cathedral.
Image courtesy Christopher D. Tirres.

Given my description of the San Fernando *Pésame* liturgy, one may note several connections here. The *Pésame* is an embodied ritual that honors the faces of those who grieve. It also gives center stage to voices—and bodies—that are not at the center of most churches, namely, the voices of women and everyday parishioners.

Furthermore, its gestures and symbols serve as an implicit, yet powerful form of dialogue, and the dance itself reconfigures a somewhat conventional church space (the altar) into a new kind of sacred space that allows the voices and sufferings of the community to take center stage. When one puts all of this together, it is not difficult to see how the *Pésame* may broaden the moral imagination, resulting in significant forms of healing and transformation.

In closing, I believe that a rapprochement between religious studies and theology is, indeed, a worthwhile endeavor, especially for those of us who cross these disciplines regularly.[30] But the real challenge, I think, is the extent to which these discourses stay true to the ritual experience itself. There is still often an unfortunate tendency in both scholarly fields to give more attention to the interpretive categories we use to understand ritual than to the actual qualities and force of a given ritual itself. To be clear, I am not suggesting that we need less theory and more descriptions of the practice of ritual. This would be too simple. What I am saying, rather, is that when we utilize theory, we need theory that sticks closely to the experience of ritual that people actually undergo. Whether we choose to approach a ritual like the *Pésame* through the lens of religious studies or theology, the real test is how well our theoretical interpretations adhere to both the actual and ideal qualities of ritual. It seems to me that a layered, intercultural approach, which borrows critically from a variety of disciplinary approaches, is at least a step in the right direction.

An earlier version of this essay appeared in *New Theology Review* 28, no. 2 (March 2016): 27–37.

---

[30] This is a recurring conversation for many in the American Academy of Religion. For a good overview of this ongoing debate, see Michelle A. Gonzalez, *A Critical Introduction to Religion in the Americas: Bridging the Liberation Theology and Religious Studies Divide* (New York: New York University Press, 2014).

2

Dancing, Eating, Worshiping

Inculturated "Third Space" in Rarámuri Celebrations

Ángel F. Méndez Montoya

A vast majority of religious celebrations of an extremely wide diversity of Catholic cultures throughout Mexico co-implicate food practices and traditions with different genres of dance. People dance and eat in religious celebrations such as baptisms, weddings, sweet fifteen presentations to society (*fiesta de quinceañera*), and locally important popular celebrations of saints and liturgical seasons. Secular and religious symbolisms are interwoven in the intersection of dance, food, and religion, producing choreographies in which these symbolisms overlap, crossing boundaries, as well as opening fissures in the separation between the body and the spirit, the I and the other, and humanity and divinity. Intercultural and transcultural contexts in Mexico, in which dancing and eating are mutually implicated, awaken images of a liminal and hybrid "Third Space."[1]

---

[1] For a succinct articulation of what is meant by "Third Space," see the discussion in the conclusion to this chapter. As a preliminary notion, the Third Space represents the liminal or the in-between space created by the encounter between two different social and cultural worldviews, and the negotiations, translations, and hybridization that take place after such overlapping and interaction of cultures. It is a sociocultural term that distinguishes home (First Space) from

This opens interstices for an encounter between the spiritual and material realms, between culture and religion. Given the ceaseless nature of researching the intersection between dance, food, and religion, as well as the constraints of this paper, we focus on some of the Rarámuri traditions emerging after the European colonization in which this intersection can be observed, using the analysis offered by Velasco Rivero's research into religion and resistance to domination in the Rarámuri culture.[2] Based on a critical reading of Velasco Rivero's work, this paper aims to answer the following questions: (1) Could the dance-food-religion intersection be replicating the Catholic religious syncretism[3] that reiterates hegemonic colonial systems of exploitation and subjugation of both the body and the

---

work (Second Space). While there is a sense of displacement on both sides, the Third Space brings about a new intercultural and hybridized common identity. We argue that the encounter between the Rarámuri and the Catholic cultural, social, and religious traditions creates a Third Space in their cultural-religious identity. As presented in this article, Rarámuri Catholicity manifests an interstitial religion that enriches both Christian and Indigenous experiences of God and creation. The postcolonial theorist Homi Bhabha is one of the main expositors of this term, and is an inspiration to better appreciate the creativity and genius created by the mutual enrichment of Rarámui and Catholic imaginations.

[2] Pedro J. de Velasco Rivero, *Danzar o morir. Religión y resistencia a la dominación en la cultura tarahumara* (Guadalajara: ITESO-IBERO, 2006).

[3] I follow Robert Schreiter's definition of syncretism as having "to do with the mixing of elements of two religious' systems to the point where at least one, if not both, of the systems loses basic structure and identity." While there are different varieties of syncretism, Schreiter mentions three forms: "(1) where Christianity and another tradition come together to form a new reality, with the other tradition providing the basic framework; (2) where Christianity provides the framework for the syncretistic system, but is reinterpreted and reshaped substantially, independent of any dialogue with established Christianity; (3) where selected elements of Christianity are incorporated into another system." As there could be negative as well as positive outcomes of syncretistic religions, we will see that the Catholicism of Rarámuri culture and religion can be appreciated as being positive, insofar as the encounter between both religions enhances both the local culture and Christianity. However, as will be further suggested, the Catholicism of the Rarámuri communities, although displaying elements of syncretism, is an instance of inculturation. Robert J. Schreiter, *Constructing Local Theologies* (Maryknoll, NY: Orbis Books, 1985), 147–48.

earth? Or perhaps (2) could these hybrid and polyvalent transcultural expressions help us to envision the inculturation[4] of a Third Space that elicits somatic and kinetic grammars of resistance, using an "aesthetics of liberation"[5] in which "bodily theopoetics"[6] are re-created, incarnating God's liberating call to dance, eat, and worship, beyond Eurocentric and hegemonic Christianity?

The Rarámuri and Collective Resistance: Struggling to Survive

Samachique is a village located in the municipality of Guachochi, southwest of the state of Chihuahua in northern Mexico. An eight-hour drive from the state capital Chihuahua City, Samachique is a

---

[4] I agree with Anscar Chupungco, who follows Aylward Shorter's definition of inculturation as "'the creative and dynamic relationship between the Christian message and a culture or cultures.'" There is a process of mutual enrichment within this form of cultural engagement. As Chupungco adds, "Inculturation does not imperil the nature and values of Christianity as a revealed religion, nor does it jeopardize human culture as expression of society's life and aspirations. Christian worship should not end up being a mere ingredient of the local culture, nor should culture be reduced to an ancillary role. The process of interaction and mutual assimilation brings progress to both; it does not cause mutual extinction." See *Liturgical Inculturation: Sacraments, Religiosity, and Catechesis* (Collegeville, MN: Liturgical Press, 1992), 28–29; also Shorter, *Toward a Theology of Inculturation* (Maryknoll, NY: Orbis Books, 1988), 11. With Laurenti Magesa, I also consider the individual and communal deep experience enhanced by inculturation as part of the encounter between the Catholic and Rarámuri's religions: "True inculturation is a deep experience in the life of the individual and the community that occurs when there is a constant search for identification between gospel and culture, and when there is mutual correction and adjustment between them." Laurenti Magesa, *Anatomy of Inculturation: Transforming the Church in Africa* (Maryknoll, NY: Orbis Books, 2004), 144–45. Herein, I use the term "mutual inculturation" to emphasize the sense of mutuality in inculturation, particularly as expressed in the Catholic-Rarámuri encounter.

[5] Antonio D. Sison, *The Art of Indigenous Inculturation: Grace on the Edge of Genius* (Maryknoll, NY: Orbis Books, 2021), 6–9.

[6] Ángel F. Méndez Montoya, *The Theology of Food: Eating and the Eucharist* (Oxford: Wiley-Blackwell, 2009).

Rarámuri village almost twenty-two hundred meters above sea level; it is the deepest and most remote area of the Tarahumara Mountains, which form part of a mountain range known as the Sierra Madre Occidental.[7]

In 2020, 1,388 inhabitants were recorded. Although the population is 50 percent men and the other 50 percent women, the women have higher levels of illiteracy and precarious education compared to the male population. In terms of their religious affiliation, approximately 60 percent are estimated to be Catholic, 15 percent Christians of a diversity of denominations, and 15 percent do not practice an official religion. Almost 90 percent are Indigenous people, and 70 percent of the population speak Rarámuri, an Indigenous language. Although the majority are bilingual, just 5 percent of the total population of the state of Chihuahua speak only Rarámuri.

The Rarámuri language, of ancient Uto-Aztecan roots, was spoken over a wide area ranging from what is now the northern United States down to Central America. Despite its multiple variants, a certain standardized form had been preserved. Rarámuri is derived from the root words *rara* (foot) and *muri* (running); etymologically, it means "running feet." The Rarámuri are known for their athletic prowess, having great physical endurance to run untold kilometers along mountainous trails at a high altitude.[8] The Rarámuri culture is primarily oral and somatic; for them, the body and the corporeal senses form part of a language that is not only human but, according to

---

[7] In *Danzar o morir* ("Dance or Die"), Velasco Rivero explains, "The Tarahumara Mountain Range is formed by high mountains that reach from 2,000 to 3,000 meters above sea level. It has been divided geographically into the High and the Low Tarahumara Mountains. This group lives dispersed in *rancherías* and villages in the municipalities of Guadalupe y Calvo, Morelos, Balleza, Guachochi, Batopilas, Urique, Guazaparez, Moris, Uruachi, Chínipas, Maguarichi, Bocoyna, Nonoava, Carichí, Ocampo, Guerrero and Temósachi." Velasco Rivero, *Danzar o morir*, 33. See also Instituto Nacional de los Pueblos Indígenas, "Etnografía del pueblo tarahumara (rarámuri)," *Gobierno de México*, April 19, 2017, https://www.gob.mx/inpi/articulos/etnografia-del-pueblo-tarahumara-raramuri.

[8] For example, see Juan Carlos Rulfo's 2019 video documentary *Lorena, la de pies ligeros* ("Lorena, Light-Footed Woman"). Watch the trailer at https://www.youtube.com/watch?v=E04zNn9dFZo.

their intrinsic religious imaginary and sensibilities, also bears cosmic, ecological, and spiritual meaning.

Although rich in natural resources, the Tarahumara mountainous territory is marked by climate extremes and a rocky, mountainous terrain, posing a real challenge to the daily lives of its inhabitants. Fruit is scarce, but the few produce items include corn, beans, and squash. Aside from farming, most of the Rarámuri are engaged in shepherding and handicrafts. Given the scarcity of resources, the harsh weather, and the rugged landscape, their economy is precarious. Mining is an important economic activity and a significant source of employment. Since the arrival of the Spanish colonizers in the sixteenth century, the Tarahumara communities have been exploited by large-scale mining. Their mineral-rich lands bore the consequences of the early colonizers' predatory extractivism, a practice perpetuated by the neocolonial stakeholders who continue to exploit, abuse, and violently control the territories today.

Prior to the mid-sixteenth-century colonization, the origins of the Rarámuri, albeit unknown, seem to have been rooted in a culture with a deeply relational and intrinsically religious sensibility. In view of the harsh living conditions, communal life had always been an imperative; the Rarámuri are hospitable, generous, honest, and averse to warfare. Their communitarian orientation is characterized by reciprocal social relationships based on a kinship system. Their myths and everyday life are suffused with a predominantly religious and festive proclivity that considers the body, particularly dancing bodies, as a place in which an encounter with Father-Mother God can take place. A dancing body can even be understood as a place of deification. It should be noted that these original peoples are rooted in a festive tradition; celebrations provide meaning to their attitude of resistance and resilience. It can be said that the Rarámuri live to celebrate and celebrate to live.

For all these reasons, the evangelization process found fertile ground that enabled the emergence of a dynamic of transculturation and inculturation of pre-Hispanic and Christian traditions, practices, and symbols, some of which still survive to this day. However, the cruel mechanisms of the colonial enterprise and its aftermath—"the sword and the cross"—brought exploitation, destruction, and violence, giving rise to periodic bursts of rebellion and resistance among the Rarámuri.

Around 1607, the Jesuits established the first missions in the Valley of Santiago. In 1639, the Rarámuri territories of the Tarahumara Mountain Range were set up as an independent mission. Father Juan de Font, SJ, assumed the role of mediator in an intertribal conflict and facilitated a peaceful intervention. The Jesuits learned the Rarámuri languages and defended the Rarámuri against colonial exploitation. In turn, the Rarámuri adopted baptism and evangelization in an apparently peaceful manner.

Although the slave-based *encomienda* system was not allowed in this area, the Spaniards soon occupied these lands in order to gain profit from mining activities; this resulted in labor exploitation and ecological destruction:

> In 1631, the exploitation of the San José del Parral mine began. For the Rarámuri, Parral became an important market for their products and labor. Cattle raisers and farmers soon began to seize the best lands, forcing the Tarahumara to move deeper and deeper into the mountains. The Tarahumara, reduced to mission villages, were forced to work in the mines when this activity boomed in the mid-seventeenth century.
>
> The Jesuits who were established in missions traveled to regions pertaining to the "gentiles" in order to convert them and bring them together in villages, from which the indigenous people would escape. The Jesuits replaced the *caciques* with new authorities, such as governors, captains, generals, soldiers, prosecutors, elders, and *temastianes* [nonordained church assistants]. Village dwellers who did not comply with Catholic functions were subjected to punishments ranging from whipping to life imprisonment. Each mission cultivated land and raised cattle to supply mining centers and missionary populations.[9]

---

[9] Instituto Nacional de los Pueblos Indígenas, "Etnografía del pueblo tarahumara (rarámuri)."

Economic, political, and religious repression sparked the first armed uprisings that lasted from the early to mid-eighteenth century. However, in general, the Jesuits became defenders of the Indigenous people and sided with them during these uprisings. For this reason, Charles III, the king ruling Spain at the time, decreed the expulsion of the Jesuits in 1767, and it was not until 1900 that they were allowed to return. The twenty-eight missions that the Jesuits had abandoned fell into the hands of the diocesan clergy and some Franciscan communities. Despite these changes, the Rarámuri rebellion movements did not cease:

> In 1876, the Rarámuri from Nonoava rebelled because they had been dispossessed from their land by people of mixed heritage protected under the land expropriation laws issued in 1856. Although the conflict was resolved with the return of the lands, new uprisings were recorded in Agua Amarilla in 1895 and in Chinatú in 1898 caused by the abuses inflicted by mixed-heritage individuals.[10]

After the independence of Mexico in 1810, the mining activity intensified in the nineteenth century, lasting until the early twentieth century, when mining collapsed "with the worldwide drop in the price of silver and the boom in logging, which drew foreigners to Rarámuri territory and led to the construction of the Kansas City railroad."[11] The twentieth century witnessed a resurgence of the Jesuit missions; the Jesuits advocated for the defense and protection of the Rarámuri communities. After 1920, schools, hospitals, roads, and other vital infrastructure were built. However, unbridled capitalism also came with neocolonial guidelines that were marked by intimidation and violence, not to mention clandestine criminal groups engaged in illegal logging and land grabbing. The conflict over land and property rights also produced serious problems of abuse and violence among the Rarámuri and the *mestizo* / mixed-heritage communities. Organized crime and a drug-lord system took over

---
[10] Ibid.
[11] Ibid.

several Tarahumara territories, compounding the Rarámuri people's suffering and oppression.

When Velasco Rivero published the first edition of *Danzar o morir* in 1983, the narco-government and its accompanying drug trafficking activities were not as severe as they are today. The extreme level of violence inflicted by organized crime, as well as the domination and wars of the drug lords in the northern part of the country, invaded and increasingly devastated the Tarahumara Mountain Range. On June 20, 2022, two Jesuit priests, Father Javier Campos Morales and Father Joaquín César Mora Salazar, were murdered in the Rarámuri mission of Cerocahui, Chihuahua. Alleged members of the Sinaloa cartel hit-squad entered the Jesuit church and shot a local tour guide who was seeking refuge in the church. When the priests intervened, they too were shot dead. The three bodies were not found until two days later. The Jesuit Province in Mexico issued a strong denunciation, expressing concern about the escalating violence and unrest that affect both the religious and the laity serving in the Jesuit missions.[12] Currently, the Jesuits have three main missions in the Tarahumara Mountain Range:

> The first mission is in Creel, a village in the heights of the Sierra Madre Occidental, in the municipality of Bocoyna. There, the Santa Teresita clinic provides healthcare and nutritional services. In this same village, the Jesuits facilitate a project to drill for water and a program to address drought in the region through exchanging products such as corn and beans for community work. Another of their projects is in the Samachike parish, where they teach groups of children to recover the rites of the Rarámuri culture, as well as their history, cosmovision, and traditions. In Cerocahui, where the priests were murdered, the Jesuits carry out the pastoral work characterizing the mission accompanied by Rarámuri families and individuals who lead the celebrations in the area.[13]

---

[12] "Jesuitas exigen justicia a un mes del asesinato de dos sacerdotes en Chihuahua," *Expansión Política*, July 20, 2022, https://politica.expansion.mx/mexico/2022/07/20/compania-jesus-justicia-sacerdotes-asesinados-chihuahua.

[13] Scarlett Lindero, "¿Quiénes son los jesuitas asesinados en la Tarahu-

The community's resistance and resilience in the midst of such devastating realities—sociopolitical hegemony, exploitation, control, and power over their bodies and territories—is admirable, to say the least. Notwithstanding these extreme conditions, the Rarámuri continue to sustain a deep sense of rituality, celebration, and dance, which gives life and shape to their cultural and religious experience. I invite the reader to delve more deeply into this experience of religiosity in which sacred pre-Hispanic and Christian traditions are mutually interwoven, complementing each other in "aesthetic expressions of freedom"[14] made manifest precisely because of the Rarámuri's extraordinary ability to survive as a community in a hostile world.

Mutual Inculturation of the Experience of God: Feasting, Dancing, Living

The Rarámuri peoples carry an intrinsically sapiential religious and communal tradition. Since there is no separation between the sacred and the profane, there is no need for private prayers or to go to the temple in order to obtain salvation. Strictly speaking, there is no infinite moral guilt; although there is a sense of guilt for serious sins such as murder, theft, lying, and adultery, God does not compel infinite punishment, but rather infinite dancing. The only real sin, therefore, is not to dance.

Rarámuri altars are minimalist and do not express a traditional devotion to the saints. They only include images of Jesus Christ or the Virgin Mary. Rather than expressing "guilt," their religious sentiments are displayed through "celebration," especially through "feasting." Velasco Rivero notes that

> the *Rarámuri-Pagótuame* lack private religious expressions: they do not pray, they never go to the temple alone, they do not have images in their homes or make pilgrimages to shrines, they do not use sacramentals—so popular among other

mara?," *Gatopardo*, June 22, 2022, https://gatopardo.com/noticias-actuales/jesuitas-asesinados-sierra-tarahumara-cerocahui/.

[14] Sison, *The Art of Indigenous Inculturation*.

indigenous people in Mexico—nor do they use candles or votive offerings. There are no spoken prayers of their own, no creed, and, even less, theological reflection. Even myths are scarce and poor. The Tarahumares express themselves through feasting.[15]

Although some Jesuits attempted to persuade the Rarámuri to eliminate this inclination to feasting, either through sermons or physical punishment, they did not succeed. The missionaries did not particularly agree with their feasts, which often led to drunken revelry; they denounced the constant quarrels and orgies that accompany these celebrations. Feasting nonetheless persisted, and the Jesuits eventually recognized the enormous religious value and cultural importance of communal rituals and feasts. The missionaries also incorporated the Tarahumare preference to celebrate at night, not with preestablished or recited prayers, but with intensely corporeal expressions such as dancing, eating, and drinking, night and day, in the presence of God who feasts and dances with them.

This sense of God's presence within the celebratory community resonates with the Catholic belief in the sacramental presence of God, particularly in the Eucharistic theology that expresses this feast of divine and human desire conjoined in one, selfsame *corpus Christi*:

> Ultimately, what takes place in the Eucharist is a dynamic of desire: both God's desire to share divinity with humanity and humanity's desire for God. In theological terms, desire is as much a human reality as it is a divine one. Echoing Augustine, Graham Ward suggests that there is a fundamental appetitus, a radical hunger at the heart of humanity. Humanity perpetually hungers for another—this other being a piece of bread or another person. Appetitus is hunger that is desire, and in Augustinian terms it is an ultimate desire for God. Desire also exists within a relational God: as the mutual craving of the Father for the Son and the Son for the Father, as well as the eternal craving maintained by and united through the

---

[15] Velasco Rivero, *Danzar o morir*, 65.

Holy Spirit. In this Trinitarian community desire is ultimately enacted not from a reality of fundamental lack, but rather from one of plenitude. Because God loves God, God desires God, and God's desire does not go unfulfilled. God feeds God with God's excessive love.... The Eucharist is communion: with God and with one another. This act of participation in the Eucharist transforms the partakers into eucharistic people: Christ's body, an erotic/agapeic community that is called to feed both physical and spiritual hungers.[16]

A Rarámuri-Christian inculturation is thus observed, giving rise to a "Third Space" with a deeply incarnated religious sensibility; this mutually characterizes the Rarámuri communities and the missionaries, who, since the sixteenth century, introduced a Spanish-Western form of Christianity rooted in popular "Old World" devotional practices.

It is important to highlight the praise for the body that is expressive of the Rarámuri religious imaginary. The individual body is always relational since Rarámuri cultures and societies take into account not only interhuman relationality but also the relationship with the planet, the cosmos, and the supernatural realm. The natural and the supernatural are mutually implicated through the union of body and spirit; for this reason, the Rarámuri healing system is comprehensive or holistic, since body and spirit are in an inseparable, mutually constituted relationship. Healing methods involve shamanic elements and the use of nature-based concoctions. Some common disorders are treated at home with various herbal ointments and restorative body remedies, but for serious cases, they resort to medical specialists, who are very important figures in the community.[17]

A diversity of life passages are celebrated: birth, the arrival of adolescence (when *tesgüino*, an alcoholic beverage of fermented corn, is ingested for the first time at the age of fourteen), marriage, and death. There are warrior and agrarian feasts; the latter, revolving around the agricultural cycle from sowing to harvesting,

---

[16] Méndez Montoya, *The Theology of Food*, 67–68, 74.
[17] Instituto Nacional de los Pueblos Indígenas, "Etnografía del pueblo tarahumara (rarámuri)."

have endured. There are nighttime and daytime feasts, both in churches, and in outdoor settings without altars. In general, the feasts correspond to important liturgical seasons such as Advent and Christmas, and also importantly include the celebration of the Virgin of Guadalupe. Holy Week or the "Feast of the Pharisees" is the most important Catholic feast for the Rarámuri-Pagótuame because it celebrates the victory of Christian good over the evil of the Pharisees. All the Rarámuri houses have a patio from which to feast and dance, transforming the domestic space into a sacred place. Food is prepared by a few families appointed to host a specific feast or by any family offering their hospitality.

The Tarahumara culture is based on the principle of *kórima*, the virtue of sharing and redistributing of wealth in the spirit of co-responsibility and interdependence. This enables life to be preserved. Feasting and *kórima* are thus associated with each other:

> Both are polarized by the *conservation of life:* failing to dance or to give *kórima* would imply the *death* of the community and of each individual, either symbolically or in the realm of everyday reality. Both tend to distribute wealth and eliminate individual surplus. In this case, there is not only a correspondence but an integration of both institutions, so that both the feast and the obligation to give *kórima* rely mainly on the individuals themselves, thus favoring a real distribution of wealth.[18]

Feasting has a sense of constructing the world in the struggle against evil or in the struggle of good over evil. Far from being selfish or individualistic, feasts are communal, sharing just like God shares himself.

Living to Dance and Dancing to Live

I noted earlier that for Rarámuri religiosity, the only true sin is "not to dance," precisely because God is the dancer par excellence. The ancient and mythological origins of the creation of humankind and the world are related to dance:

---

[18] Velasco Rivero, *Danzar o morir*, 329.

There is a Tarahumara legend that refers to how, in the beginning, the earth was soft, and that six ancestors danced *yúmari* to make it firm. According to indigenous explanations, dance is related to both a primitive gift that God bestowed upon men (the earth, fruit, and animals) and to the creation of the Tarahumares by God. In other words, in general, the *yúmari* is related and refers to the ancestors' *ancient mythological times*.[19]

Dance is a communicative language that provides meaning and form to Rarámuri life as a whole. The Rarámuri dance to live and live to dance. If the Rarámuri do not dance, God's wrath is awakened. Many different aspects of everyday life integrate dance as a form of communication with God:

> They dance in order to express gratitude for the harvest, for the animals, etc., 'out of devotion,' 'to pray,' to demonstrate that they believe in and love the Creator. They also dance in order to petition rain (particularly when there is an intensification of drought), a good winter, or the end of an epidemic. Finally, they dance to ask God for forgiveness and dispel threats and punishments. They often claim that God is enraged because the Tarahumares have not behaved as they should, because they do not dance enough.[20]

To make music, the Rarámuri mainly use drums, which they make from goatskin. First, they dance to the four cardinal points successively (east, west, north, south, turning counterclockwise). Then they circumambulate again in order to drink *tesgüino* and offer some to God, so that "God can drink" and dance. If there is food, a third cycle of dances is repeated. After sharing *tesgüino*, they proceed to dance again. Sometimes they make music with wooden flutes, violins,

---

[19] Ibid., 186. The term *Yumari* means to celebrate in order to "prevent the world from dying." See Álvarez Vázquez and Arely Karina, "*Yúmari* el espacio de reciprocidad *rarámuri*," *Arqueología Mexicana* 29, no. 175 (July–August 2022): 70–71, https://arqueologiamexicana.mx/mexico-antiguo/yumari-el-espacio-de-reciprocidad-raramuri.

[20] Velasco Rivero, *Danzar o morir*, 188.

and seed rattles worn around their ankles and calves, also producing rhythmic music accompanied by a very simple step:

> The dance consists of a kind of half trot or skipping movement, which, according to some anthropologists, simulates the way in which deer and turkeys move. My personal impression is that it is more like the movement of a wounded animal (a wounded deer). The dance consists of a back and forth movement along an east-west axis, with the altar and the crosses half way along the trajectory. At the same time, they chant using a rhythmic monotonous intonation.... Those who are present gradually join the dance, not the chanting. The men place themselves on the left and the women on the right of the person who is chanting. A line is thus formed that moves forward, turns around, and moves back.[21]

There is also concentric dancing with the men in the inner circle and the women in the outer circle, moving in the opposite direction to men, and then alternating. Throughout the village, we can also observe dances in a figure-eight formation, as well as dances in processions. While not everyone dances, the spectators nonetheless count themselves as part of the dance. People can join the dances whenever they wish and as often as they like.

In general, there are two important dances: the sword dance known as *matachines*, which is performed only by men during the winter, and that of the "Pharisees," which is performed by both women and men during Holy Week. The dances take place mainly in open spaces, outside the church, in the courtyards of the houses, and in open areas where the dancing processions take place. However, on some special feasts, or in Masses and liturgies during Advent, Lent, and Easter, dances also take place inside the temple. The dancers begin to enter the church in a procession, and once inside the church, they dance toward the center and in front of the altar, then to the four cardinal points. These are performed at the moment of the offering where corn is offered, and during the Eucharist. In general, it is the men who

---

[21] Ibid., 193.

dance; while the women can also dance, their main task is to prepare the food and drink. Mutually dependent, men and women collaborate to establish the order of the cosmos in such a way that the communal harmony becomes a religious experience of Father-and-Mother God through dance:

> Dancing implies accepting the very values of the community. First of all, there is a reference to God as the center of the community and of each individual, and it is a very concrete reference … with his/her paternal/maternal care, his/her demands, and so on. This acceptance is not merely intellectual or willful, to dance is to perform a shared religious experience.[22]

The Rarámuri live to dance. All their religious feasts are expressed with dances rather than words or prayers. Dance constitutes their life and religious experience par excellence insofar as God desires to dance, and desires for the community to dance. However, considering the extreme natural and sociopolitical realities that mark their daily existence, they also dance in order to live. Dancing is a form of resistance to these vicissitudes and severe conditions of life.

Food-Beverage: A Life of Shared Survival

Food and drink are a core component of Rarámuri rituals, either as fasting and abstinence during important liturgical times such as Advent, Lent, and Easter, as feasting where food is shared by all. Unlike the white people and *mestizos* who are perceived to favor eating alone, in private, or in isolation, the vision is for the community to eat and drink together, partaking of the same pot:

> The Rarámuri diet is very basic. It is based on beans, rice, potatoes, squash, corn, and some beef or pork. Despite the simplicity of the food, sharing with others requires a great effort on the part of families. In the Tarahumara Mountain

---
[22] Ibid., 364.

Range, there is a huge problem of malnutrition, especially child malnutrition, which is quite severe. Even cases of infant death due to malnutrition have been reported.[23]

The importance of food traces back to a mythical source. It is said that in ancient times, the *ganokos*—that is, giants that inhabited the Tarahumara Mountain Range—tormented the community, raped the women, and devoured their children. To defend themselves, the Tarahumares killed the *ganokos* with poisoned beans; thus, they were able to live and celebrate their feasts without fear of a horrendous attack. In point of fact, this myth also functions as a symbolic expression of resistance where food becomes a means to thwart and counteract the abuses of the *chabochi* or "white" conquerors. Velasco Rivero notes the parallel between the terrorizing giants and the white colonizers who oppress the people and lands of the Tarahumares:

> The giant summarizes and reflects the behavior of the white people, pertaining to that gigantic and powerful non-Tarahumara culture, . . . who have repeatedly raped Tarahumara women and murdered and devoured their children—either by directly taking their lives, or by taking advantage of their work and striving to assimilate them through political, economic or cultural mechanisms.[24]

Just as the Rarámuri believe that God is pleased by their dancing, they also believe that he desires for them to eat and drink, because God also eats and drinks with them and likes to share their festivities:

> The Creator wants to eat. To feed God is the reason and purpose of every *Yumari*. This is often expressed within a whole symbolism of the struggle between God and the

---

[23] For example, the following cases in the region of Creel, Chihuahua. See Alejandra Sánchez, "Hay 15 niños graves por desnutrición en Creel," *El Diario de Chihuahua*, October 28, 2022, https://diario.mx/estado/hay-15-ninos-graves-por-desnutricion-en-creel-20221028-1986687.html.

[24] Sánchez, "Hay 15 niños graves por desnutrición en Creel."

devil, in which the latter has besieged God (or a saint) behind the clouds, and it is thus imperative that God be fed. It is important to note that in the ritual of offering both food and drink, part of the food and beverage is always tossed up into the air "in order to feed God." Other times, they directly claim that God has given them the harvest, animals, *tesgüino*, and that he likes them to share with him.... "God likes the Tarahumares to gather, dance, eat and drink, and is upset when they do not do so. God likes *tesgüino*, which is like the *spirit* [*iwigá*—breath] of things."[25]

Velasco Rivero includes the testimony of a Tarahumaran from Pawichiki, Chihuahua, who expresses that God and Jesus Christ take pleasure in dancing in the context of a shared meal: "We are going to worship Jesus Christ through dancing because he is going to come to share a meal with us. [...] He will be deeply pleased because God enjoys celebrations in which people dance. God is pleased with the baptized people who pray through dancing."[26]

Rarámuri feasts include drinking large amounts of *tesgüino*, an alcoholic beverage so thick and nutritionally rich that it can be considered as "food." The Jesuit fathers were aware of the local practice of drinking to the point of intoxication, so they attempted to use different means to prevent the Rarámuri from partaking of the beverage. Embedded deeply into the culture since precolonial times, the *tesgüino* custom prevailed despite the missionaries' best efforts to prohibit it. For the Rarámuri, drinking *tesgüino* offers real benefits. It is an economical beverage, made out of surplus corn from the harvest. It helps them deal with cold temperatures at night when celebrations take place outdoors. It encourages socialization because it helps them overcome inhibitions. It is also considered a medicinal potion that can be used for healing and magic.

Food and drink are signs, offerings received from God and offered to God. Thus, they are always associated with religious ceremonies and

---

[25] Velasco Rivero, *Danzar o morir*, 21.
[26] Ibid., 187.

the wider realities of life—cultivation, harvesting, work, healing, birth, and death. Feasts celebrate the sharing of life between humankind, the earth, and God. Meaningfully, the points of encounter can be drawn with a Eucharistic theology where the Paschal meal represents a partaking of Christ's body and blood, a communal feast in which the gestures of breaking and sharing the Divine presence traverses the communicants' daily life and invites them to transform it.

So far, we can observe, along with the Jesuit Pedro de Velasco Rivero, who spent twenty years in the missions of the Tarahumara Mountain Range, that the religion expressed by these communities constitutes a key element of the Rarámuri social, economic, and religious system. We can appreciate that the intersection of dance and food-drink is intrinsic to the lives of the Rarámuri communities, but it is also an imperative to survive the severe climatic, geographical, economic, and political conditions faced by the Tarahumares. Although the missionaries may have always expressed colonial attitudes, it is possible to appreciate the mutual respect and recognition that gradually took place in this new form of Rarámuri-Pagótuame church, which constitutes what could be called "another church," a Third Space that has enabled the Tarahumares and their Rarámuri-Christian traditions to survive. Together with Velasco Rivero, we would like to

> explain why and how—since religion is a key element of the entire Tarahumara social system—this change, far from disintegrating the *Rarámuri* identity, led to a new religion that has been a decisive factor of cohesion and freedom that has created and preserved an economic, political, historical, and artistic environment in which the Tarahumares (unlike other indigenous people in Mexico) were able to survive, preserving their identity.[27]

At this juncture, I wish to invite the reader to join me in a brief journey, a concrete experience of a religious expression inculturation that I witnessed in the Rarámuri-Pagótuame community in the small

---

[27] Ibid., 96.

village of Samachique, Chihuahua. I am referring to the celebration of Holy Week (from Holy Thursday to Easter Sunday) in 2023, in which the intersection between dance, food, and religion is intimately intertwined with these celebrations. In addition, I propose that this immersion exercise can guide us to discern the interesting nature of mutual inculturation of a type of Catholic religious incarnation.

Holy Week in Samachique, Chihuahua

Having read and studied *Danzar o morir* by Velasco Rivero, an enriching, indispensable research source for this paper, I decided that it would be important to have a more direct contextual experience of Rarámuri religiosity. After all, Velasco Rivero published the book in 1983 and it was to be assumed that, since then, there would be some interesting changes or variants that are not reflected in *Danzar o morir*. Over and above this, studying a text on the religious experience of Rarámuri-Pagótuame communities is not quite the same as witnessing firsthand their concrete experiential context. Furthermore, I also found that the recent murder of the Jesuit fathers in Cerocahui, Chihuahua, was a decisive event.[28] Nine months after this violent event took place, the collective trauma can still be felt. This Holy Week, the mission of Cerocahui had to employ security measures, preventing me from attending the celebrations in that community. That said, the community of Samachique, the ministry site of the murdered Jesuit fathers, and also part of the missions of Cerocahui, made it possible for me to perceive both a spirit of vulnerability and resilience among the Rarámuri.

A couple of weeks before I traveled to Chihuahua, I had an unfortunate knee injury. I was advised to proceed with the immersion experience at the Tarahumara Mountain Range as long as I took the necessary precautions and wore a protective knee brace. Deeply invested in living the experience, I gathered the courage to fly from Mexico City to the capital of Chihuahua on Holy Wednesday, April

---

[28] Ibid., 23.

5, 2023. I spent the night in Chihuahua so that I could leave for Samachique early the next day, an eight-hour bus ride. It was the first time I had visited this spectacular area, traveling a winding road with views of rocky mountains and impressive cliffs, surrounded by huge boulders and giant pine forests. The survival challenge of living in this area was evident. Although I had read about the difficult geographical conditions of the Tarahumara Mountain Range, it was not comparable to experiencing it, to actually feel the vertiginous height of the mountains and the imposing geographical milieu.

The weather during the day was moderate, about 20°C, since the less severe springtime was approaching. However, at night, the temperature dropped considerably, to approximately 8°C. Father Enrique Mireles, SJ, a young Jesuit in charge of the Nutrition Clinic at Creel, which is a two-hour bus ride away from Samachique, was the host in charge of the missions in Samachique for this year's Holy Week. While Creel is a highly urbanized city, Samachique is a small village hidden in the most remote area of the mountains, with approximately one thousand inhabitants whose houses are spread throughout the rugged landscape with some rushing streams. The Jesuit fathers in charge of this community were doing missionary work elsewhere, so it was Father Enrique who had been tasked to lead the celebrations in the Samachique community.

In fact, as Velasco Rivero noted, the Jesuit priests play a minimal role in the Holy Week celebrations, leaving it to the lay members of the Rarámuri communities to take the lead in organizing and implementing the Holy Week activities:

> The Rarámuri authorities convene the festivities, decide on the beginning and end, outline the general program and articulate the various parts and even suppress some "liturgical" activities or ceremonies. The priest decides on the prayers and ceremonies, he can propose variants, but he ultimately does not make any definite decisions regarding the whole of the feasts.[29]

---

[29] Ibid., 303.

I arrived at the church on Holy Thursday at approximately 3 p.m. I introduced myself to Father Enrique, who handed me the keys to my assigned room. I was accommodated in a small house in front of the church where volunteers, catechists, and other visitors stay. Because of my injury, I decided that my participation would be discreet—observing, taking photos, and video recording, without being intrusive. Holy Week in Samachique, Chihuahua, begins on the Wednesday before Easter. It is a day of preparation for all the festivities that will take shape on Holy Thursday. For the Catholic Church, Holy Thursday is the commemoration of the Eucharist, with readings on the Last Supper and the reenactment of Jesus' gesture of washing the feet of his disciples. In some Catholic communities, Holy Thursday is celebrated by visiting seven churches.

However, since the early hours, I realized that the Samachique community celebrates in a very peculiar way. There are no prayers or Masses, no foot washing, nor visits to seven churches. Instead, there was ongoing dancing day and night inside and outside the church, as well as in the environs of the village. There were four groups of dancers of around ten people, mostly men of various ages—children, youth, and adults, including some elders. The groups alternated dancing both inside and around the church, and also at several houses and families they visited in the village. For Holy Week, the "dances of the Pharisees" are performed, distinguishing them from the Christian dances. These dances include some pre-Hispanic elements regarding the celebration of the beginning of the agricultural cycle combined with other elements of popular devotion from sixteenth-century Spain. The symbols of Christ's death and resurrection are fused with Tarahumara symbols of sowing and harvesting:

> The Pharisees wear sandals and a *sapeta*, a headdress made of turkey feathers, and carry a wooden sword—sometimes painted with red longitudinal lines—either held in the hand or tied at the waist. In some regions, like Norogachi, they also wear a typical Tarahumara shirt. In addition, their face

and legs are painted white with lime and in the regions in which they do not wear shirts, as in Tewerichi, their torso and back are also painted white. The soldiers wear Rarámuri clothing. They carry wooden spears that sometimes have a bayonet. In some areas, they carry bows and arrows or rifles instead of spears.[30]

Rarámuri traditional clothing.
Image courtesy Ángel F. Méndez Montoya

Velasco Rivero's description written in the 1980s of the Rarámuri clothing and ornaments in general remains the same today. However, it is important to note that the generations of youth do not adopt traditional dress, but wear urban and contemporary clothing with baseball caps, hoodies, jeans, and tennis shoes. This occurs mainly among young men, while the women mostly wear traditional Rarámuri clothing.

[30] Ibid., 267.

Traditional garb for women.
Image courtesy Ángel F. Méndez Montoya

Instead of visiting seven churches, the groups of dancers carry out a dance procession, visiting some houses and families that host the pilgrims and offer them food and drink. Groups of dancing pilgrims carry handmade pine arches to bury in the courtyards of the houses visited. A ritual greeting of the four cardinal points is celebrated, the arches are buried (one arch per house), and an offering of *tesgüino* is made, first tossing some into the air for the spirits and Jesus Christ in honor of these days in which his passion, death, and resurrection are commemorated. The *tesgüino* is kept in large plastic containers; a *jícara*, a small, hand-made bowl of wood or coconut shell, is used as a dipper. Whoever drinks from the *jícara* refills it and, in turn, offers it to another person. In succession, everyone drinks several rounds. Simultaneously, the celebrants dance around the pine arch. The hosts offer the celebrants beans, tamales, corn tortillas, and a squash stew in red sauce.

Tortillas and stew in red sauce.
Image courtesy Ángel F. Méndez Montoya

Meat is avoided until Holy Saturday in order to preserve the Rarámuri tradition of morning fasting and abstinence from meat. Although the traditional Eucharist commemorating the Last Supper is not celebrated, it was clear to me that sharing food, dance, and drink symbolized the Eucharist and Christ's sharing of himself. The homes in which the pine arches are placed sponsored this ritual. The dances occurred throughout the night until dawn. Eucharistic elements were represented on the church altar where food and the tabernacle were placed. Photographs of the Jesuit fathers murdered in Cerocahui, missionaries in these communities, flanked the tabernacle. The passion and death of Jesus that are commemorated on Holy Thursday were here represented by the martyrdom of the Jesuit fathers.

Good Friday began with dances around noon. As in the previous day, groups of approximately ten danced back and forth in the church atrium, inside and around the temple, and in processions visiting the houses. At around three in the afternoon, a procession of about 150 people gathered in the church. Father Enrique interrupted some baptisms in order to preside over the pilgrimage representing the traditional *Via Crucis*. However, in this particular Rarámuri community, instead of the Bible lectures, hymns, and prayers characteristic of the *Via Crucis*—at least in most Catholic villages in Mexico—a procession was made around the church, where pine and flower arches had also been set up. The priest led the celebrants. Next to him, one person carried a crucifix covered with a white cloth, and another person carried an image of the Virgin of Guadalupe. Six women bore a sculpture of the Virgin Mary, also draped in white cloth. At each arch along the way, the priest and those accompanying him knelt down to recite the Lord's Prayer and the Hail Mary. This same gesture was repeated at each arch throughout the procession until the images and crucifix were returned to the interior of the church. Inside the church, the celebrants danced in front of the altar and copal incense was diffused, covering the interior of the temple with a dense cloud of purifying scent. Upon concluding this version of the Stations of the Cross, the rest of the day and night was spent dancing, eating, and drinking until the dawn of Saturday.

Sábado de Gloria, "Saturday of Glory," is the most important and colorful day of Holy Week; it is the celebration of the Eve of Easter. On this day, several important rituals are performed. The rituals begin at noon with the traditional dances of the Pharisees and the Christians. Velasco Rivero describes the several ceremonies that follow these dances:

> The ceremonies of this day—the most colorful rituals—mainly consist in: the defeat of the Pharisees and the death of Judas, the death of the Pharisees, the appointment of the organizers of the feasts for the following year, and the final celebration of food and drink. As in all Rarámuri feasts, the order of these elements can change (except for the final meal) and in some cases they are not all celebrated. The defeat of the Pharisees and the death of Judas are represented. Judas is an

effigy made of straw and "dressed as a *chabochi*," that is, with a hat, trousers, and shirt: often large male or female genitals are placed on the effigy. Although there is almost always a single effigy, there may be two or even three. When there are two, they are male and female. If there are three, a child is added.[31]

Via Crucis, women bearing incense and images of the Virgin of Guadalupe.
Image courtesy Ángel F. Méndez Montoya

In the case of the ceremonies in Samachique, there is also a simulated "struggle" between the Pharisees and the Christians, which Velasco Rivero did not describe in his book. I do not know whether he decided to leave out this information or whether it is something that began to be celebrated after his book was published. Perhaps it is particular to a Samachique ceremony. This struggle begins with a procession to the village's open field. When I visited, approximately three hundred spectators attended and formed a huge circle. The Pharisees stood on one side of the circle and the Christians on the

---

[31] Ibid., 281.

other. The master of ceremonies stood in the middle of the circle with a loudspeaker, animating the ceremony. He called a representative of each group to come to the center to "fight" against each other. The fight consisted of leaning against each other and grabbing the opponent's belt in order to tug him to the ground. Whoever knocked his opponent to the ground would win the fight and gain points for his team. One pair of fighters after another came to the center of the circle. The participants were mostly men of various ages, from teenagers to young and older adults. I was surprised that even women participated in these struggles. The ceremony ended with the verdict, in which the Christians or Rarámuri soldiers always win against the Pharisees or Judas. The triumph of good over evil, of the resurrected Jesus over death and worldly evil, is thus celebrated.[32]

After the fight, the dancers and musicians led a procession of the entire community into the church, dancing, playing music, and spreading incense. Some children and other community members were carrying small boxes and, once inside the church, opened the boxes to free birds that flew around the interior of the temple and finally out into open space. This symbolizes the resurrection of Jesus Christ as a flight for freedom. At the end of the ceremony, people left the church to continue dancing, eating, and drinking *tesgüino* all night until dawn Easter Sunday.

Easter Sunday was quiet. It was a sunny morning with a fresh breeze and an embracing silence. At noon, the church bells called the community to celebrate Mass, which also included dance and music. The Mass was in Spanish interwoven with the Rarámuri language. It was the only Mass celebrated since Holy Thursday. Father Enrique spent these days celebrating baptisms. At the end of the Mass, everybody went home to rest or visited a host family to eat and drink. I left that afternoon to catch the eight-hour bus ride back to

---

[32] I am aware of how the uncritical Christian demonizing of Pharisees has contributed to anti-Semitism. However, as I witnessed it and as it is expressed in their rituals, the Rarámuri tradition is not about condemning a particular religious tradition, less so against the Hebrew tradition. Rather, it is about struggling with issues of the whitening of Christianity by means of colonization and subordination of Indigenous people.

Chihuahua City, where I boarded a flight to Mexico City on Easter Monday. Returning to my everyday life—my academic commitments as a theology professor and researcher at the Universidad Iberoamericana (IBERO), a premier Jesuit university in Mexico—I was left with reverberations of the "running feet," the "dancing feet"; I was still in a state of awe upon remembering the intense experience of passion, death, and resurrection, which does not make use of the spoken or written word, but rather uses the body as a place of prayer and encounter with humankind, the planet, the cosmos, and God.

Running, dancing feet.
Image courtesy Ángel F. Méndez Montoya

Due to my injury, I was unable to participate in some of the dance processions that took place mostly at night. However, on Sunday, on my way to take the bus on the federal highway, approximately three kilometers from Samachique, one of the villagers was driving me to the bus stop to ride the bus back to Chihuahua. While he was driving, he told me that the night before there had been a fight between a drug lord and a Rarámuri youth during which the drug lord had shot the young man's leg. The young man was taken to a nearby hospital in Creel, two hours from Samachique. Apparently, his condition was under control, but his recovery would be lengthy and might cause chronic discomfort. This confirmed the fact that the Rarámuri communities are extremely unprotected in relation to the drug lords, who are mostly white or *mestizo*. Even during the few days that I spent in the community, I noticed the presence of drug lords amid the people. They were always armed, a foreboding presence of violence in the community. I asked Father Enrique if anything could be done about this, but he explained that, for the moment, the Jesuit missionaries had decided not to intervene, considering that the important thing was to remain protected against any act of violence that could have potentially fatal consequences, like the case of the two murdered Jesuits.

The reality of the threatening presence of the drug cartels in the Rarámuri communities is not depicted in *Danzar o morir* because, when the book was published in 1984, it had not yet affected the lives of the Rarámuri. It has now become a very serious problem that affects the life of the Rarámuri communities. Under this lens, Velasco Rivero's title of "dance or die" can be seen to have been prophetic, particularly in these times of neocolonial crime and violence. Living to dance and dancing to survive thus become the driving force of Rarámuri festivities, a quest for the visage of the resurrected in the midst of so much senseless death.

Conclusion:
Toward a Hermeneutic of Inculturation as Third Space

Dancing, eating, and living is an intersection that incarnates the religiosity of the Rarámuri people from Samachique, demonstrating that the Rarámuri Catholic imaginary is creative, crafting its own incarnation of the mystery of the passion, death, and resurrection of Christ (*poiesis*). "Bodily theopoetics" can be envisioned in the expressions of these original peoples, artful geniuses of their own history and narrative, with an in-depth sense of the sacred, creators of an "other" ecclesial space, another theological space and body.[33] The Rarámuri-Pagótuame refer to themselves as those who have been baptized in another space, time, and culture, who do not follow rigid doctrinal patterns, but rather, in their ceremonies, rituals, dances, communal conviviality, and constant struggle to survive, find space to have an encounter with divine grace that may help them to survive, despite the necropolitics of abuse and violence they have faced since the colonization of the original peoples.

Although Velasco Rivero argues that the Rarámuri-Pagótuame are neither autochthonous nor Christian, I consider that they are both, and this other way of being enables us to glimpse the opening of a "Third Space," a religious-cultural expression providing new meaning to the Christian incarnation.[34] This Third Space creates relationships that are not dichotomous or antagonistic, but rather relational and mutually complementary between body and spirit, individual and society, culture and religion, humankind and the planet, as well as the Creation and God. The Rarámuri-Pagótuame expression of Catholicism is not a mere syncretism of superimposed symbols and the hybridization of opposing religions, but rather an occasion that opens up a festive space, a third space in which Christian and Rarámuri imaginaries complement each other, thus creating a festive space that enables them

---

[33] For a more in-depth analysis of the notion of "bodily theopoetics," see Ángel F. Méndez Montoya, *Teopoéticas del cuerpo: la danza, la teología filosófica y las intermediaciones de los cuerpos* (Ciudad de México: Universidad Iberoamericana, 2023).

[34] "Third Space," herein, and for the focus of this article, is an epistemic category mainly inspired by Homi Bhabha, who considers it as an alternative to Western and colonial dichotomies, which leads to a reflection, not only on space, but also on discursive attitudes that reflect an in-betweenness that hybridizes cultures, epistemologies, traditions, and languages, and allows a third space of enunciation in post- and neocolonial times. Homi K. Bhaba, *The Location of Culture* (London: Routledge, 1994). See also Jonathan Rutherford, "The Third Space: Interview with Homi Bhabha," *Identity: Community, Culture, Difference*, ed. Jonathan Rutherford (London: Lawrence and Wishart, 1990), 207–21. Also, Heike Walz, ed., *Dance as a Third Space: Interreligious, Intercultural, and Interdisciplinary Debates on Dance and Religion(s)* (Göttingen: Vandenhoeck & Ruprecht, 2022).

to resist and reexist. The celebrations are thus not a passive acceptance of Christianity, but rather an active reincarnation of deep religious experience communicated through dance, food, drink, and festivity.

The importance of the fundamental salvific aspect expressed by the Rarámuri through dance, food, and drink can be appreciated. This aspect of divine salvation is reincarnated from their own experience of struggle and survival, their search for liberation, in which God intervenes in the community's history and struggles: feasting as a "representation of their own situation and their hope for salvation-liberation."[35] For this reason, in their dances the Pharisees are painted white, representing the white and *mestizo* people who oppress and colonize. The figures representing Judas are finally defeated by the Rarámuri soldiers. Easter is a sign of resurrection and triumph over death and oppression. The dances are processions, but also a pathway to become liberated from the struggle between good and evil, in which good triumphs over evil. The intersection of dance, food, drink, and religion expresses God's intimate communion with humankind as an incarnate, bodily experience of divine salvation-liberation.

Nonetheless, it is always a shared experience, never individual. No words are necessary because the Rarámuri religious expression and experience are intensely corporeal. These "bodily theopoetics" expressed through dance, fasting, and feasting create a specific bodily-dance language that conveys that God is on their side.

Jesus Christ's presence is felt more intensely in Holy Week, and through his *Via Crucis* he identifies with the Rarámuri. Nonetheless, he triumphs over death and announces the resurrection symbolized by the birds that are released in the church on Easter Sunday. The first Jesuit missionaries discovered that the feasts were an important means to convert original peoples. They gradually accepted the Rarámuri expressions, symbols, and practices regarding their experience of the sacred as a possibility of embodying the Christian faith:

> The feasts provided them with the possibility of experiencing the Christian faith in a way analogous and adapted to their

---

[35] Velasco Rivero, *Danzar o morir*, 306.

own religious experience. At the same time, the Rarámuri feasts functioned as a kind of *argument* that encouraged the transition to the new religion.... However, for a fundamentally ritual mentality, the greater complexity and symbolic richness are expressive of a more "convincing," more "coherent" religion and are a valid way of explaining conversion, albeit not the only one.[36]

The feasts preserve the Rarámuri memory and identity, since they do not have any written or engraved historical documents, nor statues or monuments to bind the memory, but the feasts and religious rites are the living "archive" of their cultural reservoir. Action itself is the source and foundation of the Rarámuri religious experience.

The Third Space can be imagined as a specifically Rarámuri church that becomes a challenge for the Catholic Church, calling the Church itself to convert in order to transform colonial practices and recognize that the Rarámuri-Pagótuame are an example of the Rarámuri *ecclesia*. The Rarámuri church thus becomes a sign of hope and salvation, imitating Jesus Christ who saves by aligning with the poor and oppressed. This Third Space is elicited by the ongoing mutual transformation of Christian and Rarámuri values and imaginaries, a fusion between the gospel and culture. There is a process of mutual interaction that does not extinguish the deep religious experience of the Gospel and culture, but rather intensifies it, beyond words and written expression: based on bodily theopoetics that dances, eats, and drinks with God in a way akin to God's celebratory nature.

---

[36] Ibid., 357.

3

Contemporary Inculturational Performing Arts in the Indonesian Christian Church

Marzanna Poplawska

This chapter discusses the contemporary presence of inculturational[1] performing arts (music and dance) in the Christian Church in Indonesia, represented by both Catholics and Protestants.[2] I analyze examples from central Java, north Sumatra, and Flores, demonstrating the significance of local arts—such as Javanese gamelan, Batak and Florenese traditional music and dance—to feelings of being "at home," that is, an Indigenous Christian identity and creative agency that are interlaced with the sense of cultural pride and self-respect. This study was primarily based on field research I conducted in

---

[1] I use the adjective "inculturational" to denote the practices, activities, repertoire, and compositions or songs created in the process of music inculturation. See Marzanna Poplawska, *Performing Faith: Christian Music, Identity, and Inculturation in Indonesia* (London: Routledge, 2020), chapter 7, 195–228.

[2] This study was funded in part by the National Science Center in Poland (research project: 2020/37/B/HS3/03379). I am also very much indebted to the Carmelite community of the Retreat House of Mary Mother of Carmel Tanjung Pinggir in Pematangsiantar, North Sumatra, Indonesia, for their kindness, generosity, physical and spiritual nourishment, help, and care. I am grateful for the opportunity to stay there for several weeks in April and June 2023 to complete this writing and learn more about music inculturation as practiced in North Sumatra.

2002–3. However, it also represents the cumulative insights derived from multiple visits to Indonesia in 1995–97, 2000, and 2010, which gave me the opportunity to be in close engagement with traditional Indonesian cultures, not to mention the contextual frame for sustained thinking and writing on the interrelated issues of religion—Christianity, religious diaspora, and inculturation.

For twenty years I have been engaged in music inculturation in various ways—through research, inclusion of an inculturational repertoire in Gamelan[3] concerts (in the United States and Poland), and keeping in touch with people who practice music inculturation on the ground. While in Indonesia, I attended rehearsals of various church music groups and participated in numerous church services (Protestant and Catholic), weddings of church members, and radio broadcasts. This immersion gave me a deep sense of the community that strives to make their local art and culture an integral part of their worship of God.

In theology, *inculturation* has been theorized by many scholars, including Aylward Shorter and Anscar Chupungco.[4] Over the decades, it has retained its primary theological meaning: "the incarnation of the message of Jesus Christ about the coming of the kingdom of God into a human culture."[5] Aylward Shorter, an anthropologist and historian, warns of undesirable outcomes of cultural blending that may lead "merely to a juxtaposition of unassimilated cultural expressions." Therefore, he calls for "the shift ... away from acculturation," defined as "the insertion of indigenous elements into patterns that are basically Western," and toward inculturation, which is "the creation of indigenous patterns themselves."[6] This "creation of

---

[3] Gamelan is a large ensemble of bronze gongs, key metallophones, drums, flutes, zithers, fiddles, and xylophones. It also includes vocalists (male and female). It is largely used in Java and Bali.

[4] Aylward Shorter, *Toward a Theology of Inculturation* (Maryknoll, NY: Orbis Books, 1988);. Anscar J. Chupungco, *Liturgical Inculturation: Sacramentals, Religiosity, and Catechesis* (Collegeville, MN: Liturgical Press, 1992).

[5] Anton Quack, "Inculturation: An Anthropologist's Perspective," *Verbum SVD* 34, no. 1 (1993): 4.

[6] Shorter, *Toward a Theology of Inculturation*, 266.

indigenous patterns" is key to understanding inculturational practices in contemporary Indonesia. Christian music, dance, and theatrical forms strongly rooted in traditional Indonesian arts constitute a new category and generate new qualities that add to the diversity of Indigenous expressions.

As defined by Shorter, inculturation is a two-way process of mutual enrichment and "the on-going dialogue between faith and culture or cultures," or more fully, "the creative and dynamic relationship between the Christian message and a culture or cultures."[7] In this process, Indigenous people recognize their cultural ideals and in consequence "preserve their culture" and "adapt it [creatively] to a changed [or contemporary] social situation."[8] Indonesian Christians through incorporation of Indigenous arts into their worship actively participate in this dialogic relationship. As an Indonesian priest, Romo[9] Monang Sijabat notes, "It is not about sticking in traditional elements …; it is not about sticking cultural elements into the liturgy. But inculturation … is much more than that.… It is trying to examine the deepest meaning, the spiritual meaning of every traditional activity carried out by the [local] community."[10]

Inculturation in ethnomusicology has been theorized by Jeffers Engelhardt,[11] who outlines its "genealogies, meanings, and musical dynamics." His clear-cut definition of inculturation as "the adaptation or transformation of Christian liturgical expressions and the gospel message under new or changing cultural conditions" embraces the most important facets of this term. Inculturation is understood as "an idea, practice, and process," through which religious ideas and beliefs are being made meaningful for local communities, through the medium of music. The process of inculturation highlights "the intercultural

---

[7] Ibid., 11.
[8] Ibid., 246.
[9] *Romo* (Javanese: "Rama")—father, priest.
[10] Romo Monang Sijabat, OCarm, interview by author, June 13, 2023, Pematangsiantar (North Sumatra).
[11] Jeffers Engelhardt, "Inculturation: Genealogies, Meanings, and Musical Dynamics," *Yale Institute of Sacred Music Colloquium: Music, Worship, Arts* 3 (2006): 1–6.

dynamics of religious translation and adaptation across differences," while drawing attention to contextual similarities and commonalities, and encouraging individual and communal creativity. Engelhardt stresses "the *descriptive* and *critical* [emphasis added] value of thinking in terms of inculturation," for inculturation tackles important issues such as "agency, change, translation, consciousness, experience, and efficacy."

In theorizing inculturation, Engelhardt points to the novel (third) way of approaching it—one that focuses neither on sameness "for the sake of orthodoxy" nor syncretism "as the explanation of new religious phenomena." While concepts of "sameness" may also invoke notions of "purity" (which in full is impossible), syncretism likewise fails as an explicatory tool in defining contemporaneity.[12] The third way concentrates "on the processes and practices of inculturation" rather than on its outcomes, "on the negotiations, translations, and transformations that mediate religious messages in new cultural contexts and illuminate their value and potential." Understood as a process, inculturation never ends; it is ongoing. Inculturation conceived as "performance, feeling, experience, consciousness, embodiment, and efficacy" allows for moving beyond the limiting framework of syncretism. As an antidote to syncretism stands the deep understanding of the meaning of cultural symbols and local practices, which incorporated into the worship do not overshadow the Eucharist that remains in the center of the liturgy.[13]

Theoretically and experientially, inculturation provides a way to move toward a more sophisticated level of cultural analysis: consciousness.[14] The phenomenological approach thus conceptualizes music as a realm of experience, allowing for tackling fundamental issues in the study of music and culture, such as musical meaning, musical interpretation, and "the nature of the performance event."[15] The "localness" that is

---

[12] See Webb Keane, *Christian Moderns: Freedom and Fetish in the Mission Encounter* (Berkeley: University of California Press, 2007), 24, 79.

[13] Romo Monang Sijabat, interview by author.

[14] See Gregory F. Barz, *Performing Religion: Negotiating Past and Present in Kwaya Music of Tanzania* (New York: Rodopi, 2003).

[15] Harris M. Berger, "Phenomenological Approaches in the History of

felt, experienced, interpreted, and comprehended by the local people expands and enhances the expressions of faith, deepening individual and communal spirituality and engagement with the transcendent. Processes of inculturation bring to fore "the agentive, dignifying, and religiously meaningful possibilities" for Christian liturgy and worship. The "performative, feelingful, experiential, conscious, embodied, and efficacious"[16] aspects of inculturation are enacted in multiple ways (often differing regionally and individually) through music composition, arrangement and performance, song and dance, and instrument playing in a way that is intentional and culturally effective (meaningful, relevant, emotive, moving). Through such performative practices, a religious message becomes fully integrated and complete, while faith is articulated in ways that are conscious and full of agency. This agency allows for a local person to choose not only the way of worship but also a new identity that is simultaneously Christian and Javanese/Batak/Florenese.[17]

Performative Resistance

The development of inculturational arts has been based on the realization that being Christian does not exclude being Indonesian. The first Indonesian bishop and archbishop, Albertus Soegijapranata, was known for his motto: "A hundred percent Catholic, and a hundred percent Indonesian!"[18] Discovering that Christianity and Indonesian-ness "are not mutually exclusive has opened the door for conscious efforts to contextualize the church in Indonesia."[19] In the process of inculturation, local Indonesian Christians are in some ways "re-indigenized"; they

---

Ethnomusicology," *Oxford Handbooks Online* (December 10, 2015): 1, 25, https://academic.oup.com.

[16] Engelhardt, "Inculturation: Genealogies, Meanings, and Musical Dynamics," 3.

[17] Romo Monang Sijabat, interview by author.

[18] Scott W. Sunquist, ed., *A Dictionary of Asian Christianity* (Grand Rapids: Eerdmans, 2001), 786.

[19] Sutarman Soediman Partonadi, *Sadrach's Community and Its Contextual Roots: A Nineteenth-Century Javanese Expression of Christianity* (Amsterdam: Rodopi, 1990), 235.

learn what it means to be Javanese, Florenese, Batak, and Christian at the same time, in their contemporary environment. They are both preserving and developing their own identity, which envelops the aspects of ethnic (local), regional, national, global, and individual. In other words, Indonesians—while expanding the depths of their individual and collective identity—are participating in a historical and ongoing process of developing collective (Christian Indonesian) consciousness.[20] What Sumarsam, a Javanese musician and scholar of the gamelan, points out in relation to the adaptation occurring between traditional arts and Islam is also pertinent to the relationships between traditional performing arts and Christianity: the process of adjustment is continuous, "ever-evolving, natural, [and] mutual."[21]

The incorporation of traditional arts in the church may be viewed as a part of a broader context of nationwide relations. Even though the creation of inculturational genres may not have been a political or ideological act at first, it could be considered as such in the context of the relationship of Christianity and Islam (the tensions between minority and majority groups) and the history of Christianity in Indonesia, with its direct colonial associations. In a symbolic sense, music inculturation might be viewed as an act of performative resistance to hegemonic power structures such as the state, or the church itself.[22] When performing Indigenous music, nineteenth-century Javanese Christians resisted colonial-era missionary attempts to eradicate local cultural practice, while twentieth-century Javanese Christians resisted attempts of radical Muslims to conflate religious and ethnic identities into a uniform national identity.[23]

---

[20] See Barz, *Performing Religion*.

[21] David D. Harnish and Anne K. Rasmussen, eds., *Divine Inspirations: Music and Islam in Indonesia* (New York: Oxford University Press, 2011), 341.

[22] Daniel Reed examines a case of Dan people in postcolonial Côte d'Ivoire, who simultaneously proclaim strong ethnic and Catholic identities. He treats it as a case of performative resistance. See "The *Ge* Is in the Church" and "'Our Parents Are Playing Muslim': Performance, Identity, and Resistance among the Dan in Postcolonial Cote d'Ivoire," *Ethnomusicology* 49, no. 3 (2005): 347–367.

[23] See Karel Steenbrink, *Catholics in Independent Indonesia: 1945–2010* (Leiden: Brill, 2015).

The geographical spread and popularity of music inculturation in Indonesia vary according to religious denominations and social strata. While the Catholic Church initiated the institutional efforts in inculturation, Protestant churches followed with contextualization.[24] The focus on contextualization thus varies, as Indigenous music is also incorporated to differing extents. For example, the largest Protestant denomination in Indonesia, Huria Kristen Batak Protestan (HKBP or the Batak Christian Protestant Church), allows for only cautious and restricted use of traditional music,[25] although this has been changing in recent years (see below). Of the Protestant churches in Java, it is the Gereja Kristen Jawa that includes traditional music most methodically and extensively. Other churches do it to a lesser extent; it very much depends on a particular local church congregation. Thus, in a Surakarta church that belongs to Gereja Kristen Indonesia (Indonesian Christian Church), traditional music might be incorporated, for there is a group of people willing to perform it. A local Baptist church (in Surakarta) may also use traditional gamelan occasionally as it happens to own one. In South Sulawesi (Toraja) and Sumba, as both Rappoport and Keane report, inculturation has not yet become popular.[26] Even though the regional churches—Gereja Toraja (Reformed Calvinist Church) in South Sulawesi and Gereja Kristen Sumba—make some efforts toward

---

[24] Contextualization is defined as "communicating the Gospel in understandable terms appropriate to the audience," Gospel.com. Elaborating further, Bruce J. Nicholls, *Contextualization: A Theology of Gospel and Culture* (Vancouver, BC: Regent College Publishing, 2003) states that contextualization of the gospel is presenting it in "forms which are characteristic of the culture to which the gospel is taken." Another source defines contextualization as "meaningful and appropriate cross-cultural transmission of Biblical truth which is faithful to its original intent and sensitive to culture." See "Contextualization: SIM Position Paper," *African Mission Resource Center*, www.africamissions.org.

[25] See Yoshiko Okazaki, "Music, Identity, and Religious Change among the Toba Batak People of North Sumatra" (PhD dissertation, University of California, 1994). Also Yoshiko Okazaki, "Liturgical Music as a Means to Inculturation: An Example from North Sumatra," *Japan Christian Review* 64 (1998): 74–83.

[26] Dana Rappoport, "Ritual Music and Christianization in the Toraja Highlands, Sulawesi," *Ethnomusicology* 48, no. 3 (2004): 378–404; Keane, *Christian Moderns*.

inculturation, for various reasons the process has not yet developed much. Rappoport deems attempts to incorporate traditional elements of Toraja ritual music into Christian service unsuccessful thus far, "as these new hybrid songs mixing traditional features with Christian hymnody are not yet widely sung in churches."[27] Keane observes that the local congregations themselves resisted the introduction of Sumbanese music and dance in the church as well as the efforts to replace the Indonesian and Dutch languages with Sumbanese religious vocabulary, likely because of "poor fit between the local circumstances and a semiotic ideology."[28]

Even though the interest of local communities themselves is fundamental to the development of inculturation, it cannot fully exist without the support and encouragement of the church and clergy. The present generation of priests in Indonesia is well educated (often abroad) and exposed to different traditions and cultures. Very often they work in areas different from their place of birth. Because of that, they always have to adjust, and—although being Indonesian helps—they still have to look for the best ways of communicating with their parish community. Using local languages, culture-based metaphors and comparisons, they explain the Christian teaching in a way that has the power to directly reach people's hearts. Thanks to this, the congregation can understand it much faster and more accurately. Therefore, Indonesian priests have to develop skills in interlocal and interethnic communication in order to be successful. This is a unique feature of the Indonesian church, a result of the multiethnic nature of the Indonesian republic.

In both Java and Flores, inculturational music that uses traditional idioms is generally favored by middle-aged and older generations. The image of traditional arts as "backward," "old-fashioned," and needing "improvement," adamantly propagated by the New Order government, contributed to the fact that young people often reject Indigenous traditions and seek integration with "modern" national culture, which in their eyes is the exact opposite. In this light, the fact that inculturation enhances the appreciation of local cultures among

---

[27] Rappoport, "Ritual Music and Christianization in the Toraja Highlands, Sulawesi," 390.

[28] Keane, *Christian Moderns*, 108–9.

the members of their own as well as other ethnic communities in Indonesia is invaluable.

Inculturational Music

The music that is generated in the process of inculturation can be understood in several different ways. It can be considered a development of regional and traditional music (with specific Christian overtones). Its local features—such as the use of local language, traditional music structures and style, and local instrumentation—bring it closer to *musik daerah* (regional music), though the content is overtly Christian. In this view, inculturational music fulfills the goal of the Indonesian government to "preserve," "process," and adapt tradition to the present-day situation in the pursuit of progress, modernity, and development—goals that had been intensely promoted by the New Order government.[29] Inculturational music also has an intra- and interregional (or translocal) dimension as some of the new Christian compositions—similarly to the modern, non-Christian ones—draw on several local traditions within a single piece of music. Moreover, some songs that incorporate local idioms are performed across Indonesia by different ethnic congregations.

Inculturational music might be a subgenre of *musik baru* ("new music") that developed within the church and uses new, nontraditional techniques (as in the case of Java, especially).[30] The creation of Christian genres based on tradition follows the innovative endeavors

---

[29] Authors writing about Indonesia acknowledge the New Order policies as determinative for arts, and traditional arts in particular, for example: Gregory Acciaioli, "Culture as Art: From Practice to Spectacle in Indonesia," *Canberra Anthropology* 1, vol. 8 (1985): 148–71; Sumarsam, *Gamelan: Cultural Interaction and Musical Development in Central Java* (Chicago: University of Chicago Press, 1995); Lorraine Victoria Aragon, "Suppressed and Revised Performances: Raego' Songs of Central Sulawesi," *Ethnomusicology* 3, vol. 40 (1996): 413–38; Aragon, *Fields of the Lord: Animism, Christian Minorities, and State Development in Indonesia* (Honolulu: University of Hawai'i Press, 2000); Dana Rappoport, "Ritual Music and Christianization in the Toraja Highlands, Sulawesi," *Ethnomusicology* 3, vol. 43 (2004): 378–404.

[30] *Musik baru* is one of the terms applied to new/contemporary compositions or new forms of music in Indonesia.

encouraged by art institutions (for example, ASKI Surakarta and its director, Humardani, in the 1970s) that strived to contemporize traditional arts in accord with the politics of the New Order. In many ways, however, inculturational music remains much closer to the tradition in its use of traditional instruments and genres than many of the experimental creations that fall under the category of *musik baru*.[31]

Inculturational music is a particular branch of yet another broad category, Christian music, with a particular ethnic tinge, as well as a subpart of a developing category of Asian Christian music. In this respect, it pursues pan-Asian goals outlined by I-to Loh on the national level. In any of the above combinations it can be considered one of the Indonesian micromusics, a small musical unit that functions within larger, multiple musical formations.[32]

As Wallach points out in his discussion of various genres of regional music (*musik daerah*), most Indonesians are not interested in the regional music of ethnicities other than their own.[33] This is also true for church music. In the case of the Christian songbook *Madah Bakti*, only some songs from other regions become popular (for example, Javanese *keroncong* in Flores). Each region has its favorite songbook: while *Puji Syukur* is more popular in Java and Sumatra, *Madah Bakti* is more widely used in Flores. Despite the general lack of interest in other ethnic groups' music, some Christian composers are exceptions. They incorporate various ethnic styles, usually for aesthetic reasons, as they search for new expressions and expand the range of their musical language.[34] On

---

[31] See Andrew C. McGraw, *Radical Traditions: Reimagining Culture in Balinese Contemporary Music* (Oxford: Oxford University Press, 2013); Christopher J. Miller, "Cosmopolitan, Nativist, Eclectic: Cultural Dynamics in Indonesian Musik Kontemporer" (PhD dissertation, Wesleyan University, 2014).

[32] Mark Slobin, *Subcultural Sounds: Micromusics of the West* (Hanover, NH: Wesleyan University Press, 1993), 11.

[33] An exception might be Javanese fans of Sudanese pop (Jeremy Wayne Wallach, "Modern Noise and Ethnic Accents: Indonesian Popular Music in the Era of Reformasi" [PhD dissertation, University of Pennsylvania, 2002]). See also Sutton R. Anderson, "Musical Pluralism in Java: Three Local Traditions," *Ethnomusicology* 29, no. 1 (1985): 56–57, for examples of lack of understanding and appreciation for other ethnicities' musics.

[34] The spirit of experimentation and the incorporation of various Indonesian musical traditions is inherent in the environment of ISI Surakarta.

the whole, the core repertoire used in both regions is local.[35] Florenese might be somewhat more interested in using a greater variety of regional musical styles, while Javanese are more committed to gamelan.

In North Sumatra (Medan diocese), the songbook *Puji Syukur* contains a set of additional songs. They were created by local musicians and subsequently approved by the Liturgical Commission to be used in worship. The songs use largely local Toba, Simalungun, and Karo traditional music motifs and rhythms.

Inculturational music encompasses many genres, which constitute "creative responses to the expression of religion through music."[36] Not all of them are equally used. Apart from gamelan music in Java, other traditional forms are also adopted into the Christian context, reworked and transformed in various ways. In Flores, traditional instruments are incorporated into Christian song accompaniment, which is in fact nontraditional as songs in general are not accompanied by music. Some of these efforts are only experimental; others are lasting. Reaching across ethnic and religious traditions to enrich religious expression is generally seen as permissible and even laudable. Therefore, Javanese Christians use forms and instruments associated frequently with Islam (for example, *salawatan* and *rebana*[37]), and Florenese create multiethnic Masses, drawing on music of multiple intraregional communities.

---

[35] Nolan Warden notes a significant role that repertoire plays in formation of identity. He observes that identity's musical aspects "can be changed slowly with the addition or subtraction of new repertoire, created from within a group or added from external sources." See Warden, "Ethnomusicology's 'Identity' Problem: The History and Definitions of a Troubled Term in Music Research," *El oído pensante* 4, no. 2 (2016): 18, http://ppct.caicyt.gov.ar/index.php/oidopensante/article/view/9403

[36] Anne K. Rasmussen, *Women, the Recited Qur'an, and Islamic Music in Indonesia* (Berkeley, CA: University of California Press, 2010), 167.

[37] *Salawatan* has been used in the Catholic Church since the beginning of the nineteenth century. Danan D. Murdyantoro, "*Musik Slaka dalam Ibadat Sabda di Gereja Katolik Ganjuran Bantul*," *Warta Music* 24, no. 3 (1999): 90. Known as Muslim music, it employs a frame drum (*rebana* or *terbang*) and a Javanese double-sided drum (*kendhang*). Salawatan has been practiced in Javanese churches in the Yogyakarta area since 1988.

Catholic Mass, local Javanese community, Pematangsiantar, North Sumatra. Christian/Catholic songs are accompanied by *keroncong* music (Javanese-European/Portuguese hybrid music).
Image courtesy Marzanna Poplawska

Inculturational music is—for the most part—practically oriented. Its specific goal is to be used in Christian church services; therefore, it needs to be relatively simple and accessible to the faithful. Ultimately, a particular congregation is the addressee, recipient, and selector of the repertoire. However, functionality does not necessarily mean lower quality. The work of composers such as Subono and Darsono Wignyosaputro in Java, or Pater[38] Daniel Kiti in Flores, can certainly be counted among contemporary music attainments, forming a bridge between the traditional and modern. Church compositions are quite flexible. Depending upon the competence of the congregation, they can be performed in many different ways: with one or multipart vocals, with varying accompaniment (including prerecorded tapes) or no accompaniment at all, and in various arrangements (gamelan,

---

[38] *Pater*—father, priest (used in relation to SVD priests).

organ). Elements of performance techniques (a conductor) and musical aesthetics (singing timbre) are evidence of selective inclusion of components associated with Western music practice.

The Indonesian language and various local languages (Javanese in Java, a number of ethnic Florenese languages in Flores, and several Batak languages in North Sumatra) are used in texts of Christian compositions. The choice of language depends on the recipients or the audience. While the use of Indonesian language reconfirms the membership of local Christians to the Indonesian national state, the use of local languages empowers the local communities, emphasizing cultural uniqueness.

Composers of Inculturational Music

Many Christian (traditional) music composers, especially in Java, have traditional backgrounds; therefore, their compositions are built on traditional conceptual foundations and infused with traditional aesthetics, sensibility, and spirit. While Christian compositions continue the line of tradition, they also surpass it in search of a distinctive style. Composers in Flores, especially those directly related to the church (priests and ex-friars), more often are fluent in Western music, due to their Christian schooling. They are also more likely to use Western compositional techniques. Similarly, while Western analytical vocabulary is more frequently used in Flores, Javanese music vocabulary persists among Javanese composers. In general, composers creatively negotiate between tradition and modern tastes, advocating for an enduring place for tradition in a contemporary church. To satisfy modern predilections, Javanese composers favor shorter and faster gamelan music forms, which are easier for the audience to comprehend, and are characterized by varying levels of music competency. The time limits of religious services pose an additional barrier for inclusion of longer, more sophisticated compositions (however, such compositions are also created to be performed outside of the typical religious settings). Many of the composers are eager to fuse the local with the global and the innovative, wishing to leave an individual stamp on their compositions.

It can be presumed that the type of compositional methods used by composers of inculturational songs is driven by a communicational striving—the desire to be understood by fellow Christians across regions. In some cases, this is the reason for taking up the tools of Western music: to increase comprehension and acceptance. Western music is seen as a lingua franca. Its omnipresence (especially through popular music) is both threatening to the existence of traditional music and prideful as evidence of the global connection to the "modern" world. Through Western means, composers hope to communicate their ideas to a wider public, especially the younger generation who often appreciate popular music and culture more than local traditions. The aim is both theological and pastoral—to serve the Christian community and to gain more followers—as well as practical: to be understood.

Vocal Music

The multipart singing used in church gamelan compositions is a significant departure from traditional Javanese music and a more discernible influence of Western music (although executed in an Indigenous style). In Flores, multipart singing is less revolutionary. The music of central Flores (Ngada region) traditionally employs several different melodic lines; thus, the concept of multipart singing is not as foreign. Adding extra voices to the traditional Javanese piece transforms it into a completely new whole; the difference is not as notable in Flores, although the local harmony differs from Western. While the Javanese make a point of being clearly innovative with church music (distinct from the traditional gamelan music in many ways), the Florenese strive to maintain close links with local music. Thus, the perception of what is a "new" Christian composition also differs. In Flores, in general, a new inculturated song is one that uses a unique melody and Christian text (while preserving the traditional music idiom), but in Java this is not sufficient. For many Javanese composers, church music has to be dissimilar in character from traditional music and evoke different feelings. Hence, for example, there is more frequent use of a seven-tone *pelog* scale in church compositions than a five-tone *slendro*, and avoidance of solo vocal parts (*sindhen*) in favor of choir only. Both the *slendro* scale and *sindhen* parts have strong traditional connotations.[39]

The songs created in the inculturational process in Flores overall maintain strong links with the traditional repertoire. In general, Western music and traditional music are blended together through the use of compositional and arrangement techniques, a broadened notion of musical accompaniment, and performance practice. Through music experiments, guided by differing aesthetic principles, composers approach inculturational composition in various ways. While music and religious songs are the major arenas of inculturation, traditional dance and selected rituals also become the subject of inculturational experimentation.

Among composers of inculturational songs are priests of diverse musical backgrounds, lay musicians with traditional and Western music backgrounds (some with seminary education), and friars. In general, composers of church vocal compositions deal with traditional material in two ways: (1) a song can be taken straight—appropriated in its entirety, with religious text exchanged for the original, or (2) only some traditional motifs are used with new text.

The text of the song has a primary function of communicating the religious content. The text is the essence of the song, and especially enhances songs of limited melodic ambitus or range. This is true for traditional and religious songs alike.[40] Some traditional songs (for example, those featured in *reba* or the harvest celebration) are very simple melodically, based on only two or three notes. They have many verses but employ the same melody throughout.

---

[39] Both scales or tuning systems are featured in traditional gamelan music. However, originally *slendro* was used exclusively in the traditional shadow theater performances, which may explain its association as more typically Javanese, at least for musicians. A seven-tone *pelog* is closer in terms of intervals to the Western diatonic scale.

[40] Pater John Ghono, SVD, interview by author, April 26, 2003, Mataloko (Ngada/Flores).

There are three main sources for the song lyrics: the book of Psalms; the texts of existing prayers; and the original texts of traditional local songs, which can inspire the composer. Original texts that are suitable can be used successfully in religious songs.[41] They may contain symbols, aphorisms, teachings, and valuable advice. Such qualities can be adopted to enrich the religious service.

Some composers are convinced that there is no reason to alter or transform a regional song if it is already "good." Traditional songs have their own unique value; altering them would degrade and destroy them.[42] Therefore, usually the entire melody of a traditional song is taken, as the melody itself is considered neither secular nor sacred. Even though any melody can be used as a church song, the song should not elicit "wrong" or undesirable associations.

The connection between the church song and its prototype is very important for local people, though perhaps less important to people outside of a given tradition, who lack associations with the original song. The situation when a Ngada song is sung by a Javanese or Batak person will be different from the situation when people of Ngada sing that song, for the Ngada locals have "a very different concept, a very different idea," a different awareness, because "they know its background."[43] It becomes apparent that in the Indigenous areas, songs of a given ethnic character are perceived and understood on several cognitive levels, thus more fully and deeply. This complex web of meanings and connotations is usually inaccessible to outsiders.

When a traditional song becomes a church song, it is usually given a new context. However, as referenced above, some connection with the previous (traditional) context is maintained; therefore, the original context is to some extent preserved. The linkage with original context evokes more emotion, and the songs sung in the church are experienced more fully and profoundly. Thus, singing itself becomes

---

[41] Ibid.

[42] Pater Petrus/Pit Wani, SVD, interview by author, April 6, 2003, Ledalero (Maumere/Flores).

[43] Ibid.

more meaningful. Songs that connect singers with their own tradition touch their hearts, hold special meaning for the performers, and enrich their spiritual experience.

Catholic Mass on Palm Sunday, Wolowea, Raja-Nage region, central Flores.
Image courtesy Marzanna Poplawska

Instruments in the Church

In general, the inculturation process in central Flores (Ngada) introduced a new element: instrumental accompaniment for singing, not typically found in traditional music. Instrumental music and vocal music in Ngada are traditionally never performed together. The instruments most often used in the church are *gong gendang* (gongs and drums) and *foi* (flute).

Through the use of instruments, experimenters were able to create a certain "uniqueness of inculturation." Consequently, the performance context and practice have changed. It is significant that this change occurred through the conscious efforts of Indigenous people striving for creative modification. Their actions can be seen as a creative experimentation with their regional musical and cultural heritage. Therefore, inculturation brings about change that is not destructive (to the original musical and cultural context) but creative, experimental, and enterprising.

Along with instruments, traditional tempi and rhythms appear in church compositions. The innovators try to integrate the instruments with vocal music and construct a meaningful whole out of varying elements. It seems that as long as all the elements originate from tradition, this practice is acceptable. The religious community enjoys the experiments, receiving them positively, and thus approving of the use of traditional instruments in the church. The sound of traditional instruments and music motivates and inspires prayer.

When instruments are used to accompany songs, the playing technique changes. This is the case with gong gendang and foi, for example. Gong gendang has to adapt itself to the vocal part; it has to follow the ambitus of a given song, the melody line, and its movements. However, when played on its own, it is free of the restriction of the vocal melody.

In their musical projects, composers have to work within the instruments' limitations. Even using a flute is challenging: "they cannot all [play] in C or G, [or] E. Thus, we have to make so many flutes, try all."[44] Also, the narrow melodic range typical of Ngada songs may be limiting, as it provides fewer compositional possibilities.

In terms of instruments and their use in the inculturational process, local musicians bring up and discuss an important issue. Some instruments initially came from Europe but were later adopted, used in the church, and currently are considered almost *asli* (original or Indigenous). One such instrument is the recorder. As Pater John Ghono admits, "The flute, which I usually use, is a recorder. Its sound, although it is a modern instrument, is familiar to people here. That is, when played, people feel like it is something original [local]."[45]

Another priest, Pater Dan Kiti, points out that even the organ (a Western instrument) has already become a part of Florenese culture,

---

[44] Ibid.
[45] Pater John Ghono, SVD, interview by author, April 26, 2003, Mataloko (Ngada/Flores).

and people feel that it is inherent to it. The organ came to be a local presence in the same way the Catholic religion did. It is no longer perceived as a foreign instrument.

In North Sumatra, in the Karo area, a keyboard has become an integral part of local culture—in both traditional and church music. Karo musicians use a particular model of keyboard, which is recognized as "kibort Karo," that is, a Technics KN2000, and nowadays newer models—the KN2004 and KN2006—as well as the Yamaha PSR. The sound of other kinds of keyboards (for example, Roland) are not appropriate (they "don't agree with the aesthetics/feeling of Karo people"). The keyboard samples Karo traditional instruments such as *kulcapi* (a small guitar), *sarunai* (an oboe), or *keteng-keteng* (a drum). The keyboard was introduced to traditional Karo ensemble *gondang* in the 1990s by Jasa Tarigan, an accomplished *kulcapi* player. Nowadays, the keyboard is recognized as distinctively Karo, and without it *gondang* even loses its Karo identity for local people.[46]

These preceding observations demonstrate the difficulty of evaluating, judging, and labeling what is local and what is not local among not only instruments but also other cultural aspects. Clearly, some practices, instruments, and songs have been domesticated over time and at present are considered a local property. Indigenous people adapted elements they found useful and appealing that were not counter to their traditions; consequently, they began to consider them as a part of their own culture and community. The domestication process generally happens gradually over time as the changes are socially accepted. Contacts with Europeans also played their part in the processes of change and innovation.

Javanese Gamelan

Gamelan is employed in both Catholic and Protestant churches in central Java, as well as other parts of Java and in Bali. Both denominations have their own sets of songs used in worship.

---

[46] Bapak Brevin Tarigan, interview by author, May 4, 2023, Medan (Sumatra Utara).

Procession for the holiday of the Sacred Heart of Jesus,
Catholic Church, Ganjuran, Yogyakarta, central Java.
Image courtesy Marzanna Poplawska

Religious vocal compositions or hymnody in the Protestant church are called *Langen Sekar* (LS). The name was coined by a Javanese musician and composer, Bapak[47] Darsono Wignyosaputro, a founder and the foremost composer of *Langen Sekar*. The name refers to traditional Javanese art and culture, emphasizing the fact that LS is a part and continuation of it. The word *langen* means pleasure or enjoyment; combined with *sekar*, it indicates a particular kind of art: chanted or sung classical poetic verses.[48] Therefore, LS can be interpreted as vocal art.

LS has already acquired a lasting place in the Christian celebrations in Protestant churches in Java. However, it is used for

---

[47] *Bapak (Pak)*—father or Mister, a respectful form of addressing an older man.

[48] Elinore C. Horne, *Javanese-English Dictionary* (New Haven, CT: Yale University Press, 1974); Bapak Cipto, interview by author, July 26, 2002, Surakarta (Java); Bapak R. B. Soewarno, interview by author, October 11, 2002, Surakarta (Java).

only bigger events such as sacrament celebrations (e.g., baptism and confirmation), Easter, and Christmas. Most of the churches have to struggle with the absence of gamelan; paradoxically, gamelan is rare in its native land. To overcome this deficiency, LS instructors usually use recordings with instrumental accompaniment to which the LS group and congregation sing. Even for bigger church holidays, there might not be live gamelan; the churches have neither sufficient financial means nor the physical space. Interestingly, the initial idea of composing church songs with gamelan accompaniment was affirmed when Darsono Wignyosaputro heard a sermon based on Psalm 150 delivered by a Protestant clergyman. The text of Psalm 150 refers to praising God with instruments that are, or could be, interpreted as gamelan instruments. Thanks to Psalm 150, Wignyosaputro realized that Western instruments are not the only instruments suitable for Christian worship. The accompaniment of LS songs has strong traditional components: the full gamelan orchestra and the traditional short forms of *ladrang* and *ketawang*.[49]

Church songs by Wignyosaputro are all in the Javanese language; none use the national Indonesian language. Most of the songs are written in *pelog*, employing all three modes of the scale; only a few are in *slendro*. Wignyosaputro explained that the feeling of *slendro* is too close to traditional Javanese songs. His goal was to compose songs that are perceived as aesthetically distinct from traditional Javanese songs. This distinctiveness is his compositional credo, which contrasts with that of church music composers on the island of Flores in eastern Indonesia, who strive for traditional-sounding religious songs with a feeling of similarity and familiarity. The notation of songs includes vocal melody (or melodies), corresponding text, and main instrumental melody, that is, *balungan*, which is essential to the songs' accompaniment.

The majority of Wignyosaputro's compositions have unique lyrics and melody. To create the text, Wignyosaputro uses elements of Javanese poetic forms. Thus, although the text follows the structure

---

[49] *Ladrang* contains thirty-two beats per cycle; it is probably the most common form of Javanese gamelan pieces. *Ketawang* contains sixteen beats per cycle. All beats are divided into units of four (equivalent of Western 4/4 meter).

of traditional Javanese verse, the contents and the melody of the song are his original creation.

The presence and character of vocal parts is an essential criterion for the distinctiveness of LS songs. Wignyosaputro revealed that "if there are no vocal parts, then [the piece] is like traditional gendhing." While the form of the piece, its instrumental structure (*balungan*), and the way of execution (*garap*) are traditional, the vocal melody lines make the LS unique.

Most songs composed by Wignyosaputro have two singing parts; however, some have three, or just one. Singing groups may choose to use one or more vocal parts depending on their abilities. The vocal parts are sung by women and men separately. The range distribution of the vocal parts does not equal that of a Western choir. This is similar to the traditional practice, where *gerong* and *sindhen* parts[50] may not differ much in terms of pitch.

In composing the second and third voices, Wignyosaputro mainly used the rules governing Javanese gamelan in terms of voice leading and constructing harmonies. Some vocal parts can also assume a traditional form of *gerong* (in terms of melody lines and rhythm). Another compositional method is canon.[51]

Batak Traditional Music

In North Sumatra, where several groups of Batak reside (including Batak Toba, Karo, and Simalungun), traditional music, songs, and dance are still being used in the Catholic churches. Even when organ is featured in worship, it also makes use of traditional *gondang* music in terms of melodies and timbres. Therefore, *gondang* music secured a lasting place for itself in the Catholic churches in this area.

Nowadays, the *gondang* music and dancing (*manortor*) during the liturgy are common. As Romo Monang Sijabat, a Carmelite priest, affirms, "This is our identity, our heritage that we must bring into the

---

[50] *Gerong* is a male unison chorus, and *sindhen* is a female solo vocalist.
[51] Wignyosaputro mentioned that the canon technique gives an impression of bells (associated with church and worship).

church." Most people already understand that. Romo Monang, himself a Batak Toba—through research that involved talking to local elders and specialists on Batak Toba customs (*adat*) and philosophy—came to create a special inculturational thanksgiving and petition service related to the harvest thanksgiving ceremony. He also employed elements of this service in the wedding and death ceremonies. His initial interest was in the ways that Batak people traditionally prayed, gave thanks for their crops, and asked for blessing for the new ones. His goal was to create a service in which people give thanks and ask for blessings in accordance with their local identity.

A Catholic church of traditional Batak Pakpak architecture, Sumbul, Pegagan, Dairi, North Sumatra. Copyright © 2023 Romo Lucianus Meo Wio, O. Carm

Romo Monang used traditional music, instruments, and cultural symbols as a means of thanksgiving prayer and supplication. Thus, in his case, music serves as more than just an accompaniment to songs and embellishment of Catholic ritual and liturgy. It is not just the outer packaging that he used (traditional clothing, instruments, dancing), but the inculturation process at play involves a deep analysis of local symbols that are subsequently employed in the church ceremony.

Romo Monang researched the meaning behind each instrument and different styles of traditional *gondang* music as well as dance movements and traditional Batak offerings. One of the *gondang* styles can communicate the request for forgiveness (*gondang pangelekan*). This request is only sounded by *gondang* and accompanied by tor-tor dance movements that are executed by the priest and the congregation. The words "God have mercy on us" are omitted; the priest kisses the ground, requesting forgiveness without words; then he gives a general absolution.

A wedding celebration of a family from Perdagangan Catholic parish, North Sumatra. Author is fourth from left in the row.
Image courtesy Marzanna Poplawska

The ritual is practiced every year, after the harvest and before planting new crops. The congregation members continued doing it, even after Romo Monang moved to another parish. "This is us, this is our identity, let's not lose it," they say. Through the practice of this special thanksgiving ceremony that fuses Christian thought with Batak manners, people's faith increased, enhancing family and communal prayer, the feeling of togetherness, generosity, and responsibility for their community. This case shows that it is possible for the liturgy to be "hypostatically united with the traditions and culture of the local church"; therefore it indeed can be truly incarnated.[52]

---

[52] Anscar J. Chupungco, *Liturgical Inculturation: Sacramentals, Religiosity, and Catechesis* (Collegeville, MN: Liturgical Press, 1992), 18.

Dance

Components of local dances are incorporated into Christian services on a much lesser scale than music. Supriyanto lists processional and offering dance as forms of new choreographies that have been integrated into the Catholic Church in central Java.[53] The history of dance in the church traces back to the 1970s. The occasions on which dance becomes a part of a Mass are especially festive: Christmas, a confirmation led by an archbishop of Semarang, and the holiday of the Sacred Heart of Jesus, which is celebrated on the last Sunday of June in Ganjuran. In 1989, dance was a component of the Mass during the visit of Pope John Paul II in Yogyakarta; during that celebration, some two hundred dancers were featured.[54]

In central Java, Christian elements are featured in human-actor dance theatre—*wayang wong*—and popular (folk) theatre—*kethoprak*. *Wayang wong* combines characteristics of both dance and puppet theatre, for the actors-dancers impersonate shadow puppets. According to Supriyanto, Javanese dance appeared in the Catholic Church when Bagong Kussudiarjo, a leading Javanese choreographer who became Christian in the 1960s, created the first Christian dance dramas: *Kelahiran Kristus* ("The Birth of Christ," 1968) and *Aleluyah* (1970).[55] The musical accompaniment to these dramas was authored by Ki Wasitodipuro (Wasitodiningrat), a renowned musician and composer, who collaborated with Bagong Kussudiarjo for almost a decade in Yogyakarta. *Kelahiran Kristus*, a three-hour dance drama enacting the life of Jesus Christ, was commissioned by a Catholic church in Yogyakarta and performed several times between 1968 and 1989.[56] At first, some people opposed the dancing by the character of Jesus; they thought it inappropriate.[57] In

---

[53] Mathias Supriyanto, *Inkulturasi Tari Jawa* (Surakarta: Yayasan Citra Etnika, 2002), 202.

[54] Ibid., 118.

[55] Ibid., 201.

[56] Nyoman I. Wenten, "The Creative World of Ki Wasitodipuro: The Life and Work of a Javanese Gamelan Composer" (PhD dissertation, University of California, 1996), 305.

[57] Supriyanto, *Inkulturasi Tari Jawa*, 201.

terms of dance movements, Jesus and Mary were portrayed as refined characters—Bima and Sumbadra (or Sinta), respectively—and Herod as coarse Rahwana or Prabu Baladewa.[58] Christian *wayang wong*—similarly to Christian shadow theater[59]—draws heavily on traditional patterns. The music for *Kelahiran Kristus* is written in the *pelog* scale, which for Wasitodipuro resembled a Western scale. The piece incorporates bells (*lonceng*), three-part vocals, canon, and stylistic characteristics of Balinese and Sundanese music. One of the pieces from the drama, "Gendhing Ratri Suci" in *pelog nem*, is the Christmas carol "Silent Night," arranged for gamelan. The playing technique of some slab (key) metal instruments evokes Western or European aesthetics: *gender* and *slenthem* resemble an organ, and the *demung*, a church bell.

Dance dramas are usually performed outside of the church. They feature a range of themes, depending on circumstances. For example,

- The story of Easter
- The story of the conversion of eastern Indonesia, featuring Francis Xavier, one of the most prominent Catholic missionaries, who traveled to Asia, including India and Moluccas
- A story based on the elements of the Hindu *Bhagavad Gita*[60] (for the ordination celebration of a Protestant pastor)
- The story of Deborah, the Hebrew judge of the Old Testament;
- "Yudas Iskariot"—the story of Judas, who regrets denouncing Jesus
- A story of the struggle between Goliath and David

---

[58] Ibid., 99, 101. Bima is the second of the Pandawa brothers; Sinta is the heroine of Ramayana and wife of prince Rama; Rahwana is the demon-king, a villain from Ramayana; Prabu Baladewa is the brother of Sumbadra, king of Mandura.

[59] See Marzanna Poplawska, *Performing Faith: Christian Music, Identity, and Inculturation in Indonesia*, and Poplawska, "Wayang Wahyu as an Example of Christian Forms of Shadow Theatre," *Asian Theatre Journal* 21, no. 22 (2004): 194–202.

[60] The *Bhagavad Gita* is a Sanskrit epic, a part of the Mahabharata. It contains a conversation between Arjuna and Krishna, who reveals his identity as the Supreme Being Himself.

- The mystery of Christ's birth (St. Mary's annunciation)
- The ministry of Joseph in Egypt, and the attempted seduction initiated by the wife of Potiphar

Performances of Christian folk theater *kethoprak* are much rarer than Christian shadow theatre. The Christian *kethoprak*, like other theatrical forms, maintains the traditional structure. Stories come from both the Old and New Testaments.

In Flores, even though dance is an important element of the culture, in the church it is used only occasionally and merely for certain parts of the Mass. Most often there is dance for the entrance, as well as for the Gloria and the Sanctus. For major celebrations, dance is featured in the offering (although instrumental music frequently takes its place); also, the closing may introduce dance.[61] Dance is commonly used for various processions during religious feasts. It is treated as a tool in making the church ceremonies more culturally familiar as well as more elaborate and thus more exciting for the attendees. Inculturational dance is heavily based on traditional dance, making an extensive use of its characteristic motifs and sequences of movements. The elements of traditional dance are further developed in the process of adapting it for Christian services. This also includes the traditional dance attire, which may be adjusted and transformed as needed.

Romo Krisna—who, like many Indonesian priests, has experience working in various areas (Java, Flores, and North Sumatra)—makes a continuous effort to adjust to changing cultural circumstances. While working with candidates for priests in Flores, he developed the *gawi*-style meditation, which was inspired by movements of the Florenese *gawi* dance intended for older people. Even though the music accompaniment remains the same, the movements for elders are much slower and more contemplative. Therefore, *gawi*-style meditation is executed while standing, with music accompaniment and slow, meditative movements of the feet only (as in the traditional dance). As Romo Krisna asserts, just looking at this kind of meditation is very moving.

---

[61] Bapak Ferdi Levi, interview by author, April 29, 2003, Ende (Flores).

The criteria of suitability for a Christian service are applied to dance in the same way as they are to songs. Many traditional dances are "suitable, good, not contradictory, noble, glorious";[62] thus, they can be used for religious services without any problem. The types of dances that are not suitable and do not symbolize Christian spirit are erotic dances (the erotic element would be a sign of disrespect, ill manners, and even funny), and dances that consist of jumps, which "disrupt the atmosphere of religious service, morality, religion."[63] The dance has to fit with the atmosphere of religious service.

Conclusion

What is the future of inculturation, and music inculturation in particular?

In North Sumatra, with the new translation of a Eucharistic rite for the Roman Catholic Church authorized by the Bishops' Conference of Indonesia, new guidelines for the marriage rite also followed. They constitute a certain setback in employing traditional culture in the Catholic Church. According to the prescriptions, traditional symbols still can be present in the liturgy, but not employed or utilized in a special way. Thus, it is still possible to bring to church traditional cloth *ulos* or rice that usually is used for blessing, but these objects cannot be a part of the liturgical rite as such. They can be used after the Mass has ended.

On the other hand, the Batak Protestant Church (HBKP) recently opened up to traditional music, which since about 2010 has been increasingly used in worship. Nowadays, almost every church makes use of traditional music to some extent. Many young people play *kulcapi*, and its acceptance by the church is probably one of the factors in its increasing popularity.[64] Even though artists make an effort to uphold traditional music, the support of the church is crucial to

---

[62] Pater Daniel/Dan Kiti, SVD, interview by author, May 3, 2003, Ledalero (Maumere/Flores).

[63] Ibid.

[64] Bapak Brevin Tarigan, interview by author, May 4, 2023, Medan (Sumatra Utara).

its endurance and preservation in contemporary settings. Numerous adolescents learn various kinds of music through the church; therefore, it is important for traditional music to also be present there. Most of HBKP churches hold an annual thanksgiving celebration of harvest (*kerjarani*)—one of the major traditional feasts. People bring crops to the church, and traditional music is always sounded on that occasion.

Though it is difficult to foresee the future of inculturation, a positive stance might be assumed. Even though the social changes that affect traditional music are inevitable, it still occupies an important space in the individual and communal life of local people.

For Romo Monang and many other Indigenous people, there is no clash or divergence between the Christian message and local culture. They come to the church as Catholics who are still Batak people; they pray, while bringing in their own symbols and music.[65] "We are religious people, truly religious people, but we are also people with customs," affirms Romo Monang. For him and others, the real inculturation is the "Catholic prayer in a Batak way." People come in their *wholeness*, and the Church—by accepting them as *wholes*—becomes present in the rhythms and struggles of their lives.[66]

> Inculturation purifies the culture that is already pure, so that it becomes part of the Church and belongs to the Church, which can be used to increase and grow the faith of the people, appropriately to the context.[67]

Inculturational music represents both top-down and bottom-up flows. Encouraged by the contemporary church and allied institutions, it is also desired by individuals and whole communities. Inculturational music is the result of the creative energy of local people who, either through institutions or on their own, strive to integrate their religious and cultural or musical worlds. The agency of the people is central to the development of inculturation. Through their own initiatives and actions, they shape the inculturation process, and in consequence they

---

[65] Romo Monang Sijabat, interview by author.
[66] Ibid.
[67] Ibid.

shape the Church itself, so it is becoming "the Church *of* a particular locality."[68]

The many Christian genres in Indonesia have been developed in order to bring traditional components into Christian worship. Their adaptation to Christian needs follows the creativity and proverbial ability of the Indonesian people to adopt and adapt various cultural forms and influences to their needs and their Indigenous milieu. Although directed by various motivations (Christian zeal, regional cultural "patriotism," artistic curiosity), the Christian forms contribute to the richness of Indonesian arts, being a testament not only to the adaptability and flexibility of Indonesians but also to their partaking in global creative processes. Through their involvement in creating Christian globality, Indonesian people contribute ingeniously to the world Christian heritage. They also demonstrate that Christianity is neither monocultural nor monotonous.[69]

---

[68] Chupungco, *Liturgical Inculturation*, 17.
[69] Pope Francis, *Evangelii Gaudium*, apostolic exhortation (2013), section 117, www.vatican.va.

Part II

Method and the Lessons of History

4

CEREMONIAL GENIUS

Australia's First Peoples and Liturgical Inculturation

Carmel Pilcher

The ceremonies brought us together on a religious group basis. They impressed on me the fact and the satisfaction of a communal worship, a worship in language and song and dance and action that is meaningful to all. I long for the day when our deep Aboriginal ceremonial instincts can find genuine expression in our Christian celebrations, when these celebrations will no longer be foreign but truly ours.[1]

Dr. Miriam Rose Ungunmerr-Baumann, celebrated elder, educator, and artist from the Ngan'gityemerri language group and living in Daly River in the Northern Territory, spoke these words as part of an address to Catholic Women in Darwin in 1986. I believe they echo the voices of many First Nations Australian Catholics to this day. From the outset I acknowledge that my contribution to this discussion is from the perspective of a white non-Indigenous Australian Catholic who continues to be a student of religious ceremony as expressed in

---

[1] Miriam Rose Ungunmerr-Baumann, "Autobiography Reflections: Address Given to the Catholic Women's League, Darwin, NT," *Nelen Yubu Missiological Journal* 28 (Spring 1986): 18.

ritual and symbol.[2] While I cannot trace my ancestry back to the first Europeans who claimed this land for Britain in 1770, I do acknowledge with deep regret that I am part of its shameful history of colonization.

The scope of this study will be restricted to the story of liturgy and culture in two Catholic dioceses: Broome and Darwin, where Aboriginal and Torres Strait Islander peoples continue to live culturally in remote communities. While acknowledging the missionary efforts of other Christian traditions, their situation is different from our own and it would be difficult to adequately address their attempts at liturgical inculturation in the space of this chapter.[3]

Here I trace developments in the liturgical life of First Nation Catholics in Australia from the early missionary attitudes of "cultural domination" and "assimilation" to later "adaptation" and eventually "inculturation." The burgeoning of the social sciences and the liturgical reform brought about by the Second Vatican Council (SC 37–40) were key factors in this shift. Missionaries learned from anthropologists, sociologists, and linguists that the ancient inhabitants were not ignorant savages but deeply spiritual people with a strong ceremonial life. The liturgical reform enkindled Catholic worshipers to exercise their baptismal priesthood as fully active and intelligent participants in the liturgy, a departure from simply being passive spectators and observers at Mass.

Our study begins with a brief account of pioneer missionary encounters of evangelization of the original inhabitants. Later, as a result of the liturgical reform, church leaders recognized that major changes—including not only the vernacular but also cultural elements—would be needed if the newly baptized were to participate intelligibly in the liturgy. We rely largely on the methodology of Anscar

---

[2] I am indebted to several First Nation people who were invited to comment on this book chapter. I am particularly grateful to First Nation Catholic elder and Quandamooka woman Evelyn Parkin.

[3] For example, the Uniting Church of Australia, Anglicans, and Lutherans, among other Christian churches, have continued to serve First Nations people in mission areas in Australia. Only the Catholic Church continues to have no Indigenous ordained ministers.

J. Chupungco, OSB—expanded in the next section—as a useful framework for our exploration and analysis of the examples cited.

However, following the national referendum in 1967 where First Nation people were recognized for the first time as Australian citizens, many returned to their own lands and traditions. This empowered newly baptized Catholic Aboriginals who were steeped in ceremony to bring their own foundational stories and rituals into conversation with the Roman Rite. In this way, they became co-creators, equal partners with church leaders in the preparation and celebration of the church's liturgy, in a process that we identify as "interculturation."[4] If we stay with a method proposed by Chupungco where cultural elements from the local culture are integrated into the Roman Rite, we run the risk of church dominance that denies the unique contribution of First Nation Catholics to enrich the celebration, as recent experiences in Canada show.[5] We argue that when the Catholic Church becomes open to engaging as equals in a process of interculturation, the ceremonial genius of Australia's First Nation peoples will enrich the celebration of the Roman Rite for Australian Catholics.

Liturgical Inculturation

Culture

It is necessary at this point to define various terms of importance to the discussion. Scholars continue to promote various understandings of culture. Aylward Shorter provides a succinct definition: "Culture is ... essentially a transmitted pattern of meanings embodied in symbols, a pattern capable of development and change, and it belongs to the concept of humanness itself. It follows that if religion is a human phenomenon or human activity, it must affect, and be

---

[4] Term attributed to Bishop Joseph Blomjous. See Aylward Shorter, *Toward a Theology of Inculturation*, special ed. (Eugene, OR: Wipf & Stock, 2006), 13.

[5] See Carmel Pilcher, "A Missed Opportunity: Recent Papal Liturgies in Canada," *La Croix International*, August 16, 2022, https://international.la-croix.com.

affected by, culture."[6] Ongoing archaeological evidence indicates the presence of humans on the continent now known as Australia at least as far back as sixty-five thousand years, making Aboriginal and Torres Strait Islander peoples one of the longest-surviving cultural groups on Earth.[7] The survival and resilience of Australia's First Peoples is testament to a lifestyle that was highly structured, marked by regular ceremony, and able to exist in harmony with a vast continent amid often harsh climatic conditions. The cultural traditions of Australia's First Nations of such longevity are therefore to be highly respected and carefully studied.

Gospel book. Kalumburu dancers and digeridoo player.
Copyright © 2016 Diocese of Broome

One cannot speak of an Australian Aboriginal culture, just as one cannot speak of a non-Aboriginal Australian culture. However, essential characteristics can be identified—for example, that First Nations Australians see themselves in relationship, not only with each other, but through their connection to country, to the flora and fauna, and to the spirit world of their ancestors.

---

[6] Shorter, *Toward a Theology of Inculturation*, 5.
[7] "Australia's First Peoples," Australian Institute of Aboriginal and Torres Strait Islander Studies (AIATSIS), https://aiatsis.gov.au.

Ceremony

Culture is ever evolving. Australia's First Peoples had a continuous cultural tradition over tens of thousands of years, expressed and nurtured through their customary ceremonies. To an outsider it is difficult to describe these Indigenous ceremonies. All Aboriginal and Islander nations marked rites of passage—birth, initiation, death, and other significant events—with ceremonies that may be performed in secrecy and great seriousness, or in more social contexts. Ceremonies that are widely social might take weeks or even months to prepare and celebrate. Such ceremonies were, and still are, an important part of their identity; they serve the purpose of reinforcing relationships with land, flora and fauna, as well as each other, and enforcing law that determines the values and behaviors of the clan or group. The ceremony itself was never entirely fixed and was influenced by external factors. For example, anyone observing a traditional ceremony in Darwin after World War II would see the dancers imitating the planes that continuously bombed and decimated their city and surrounding areas.

Pioneer Catholic missionary John Leary, MSC, suggests a way to differentiate traditional ceremony and ritual. "For the indigenous people the economy was based on the spiritual, on ceremony and ritual. They saw correct ritual as the means by which their needs were provided. So they hunted and collected what was produced through ritual."[8] Their daily lives were intertwined, expressing an innate connection between occasional formal ceremony, expressed in particular songs, dances, and stories, and their daily regular ritual action such as hunting and gathering.

Just as there are various layers of culture that are characteristic of First Nation Australians, so there are various studies of liturgy and culture. Various terms and theories have been proposed—assimilation, adaptation, enculturation, acculturation. Our discussion of liturgy and

---

[8] John Leary, MSC, "Fifty Years with Traditional Aborigines," *Compass: A Review of Topical Theology* 37, no. 3 (Spring 2003): 6.

culture will be governed by the lens of inculturation as adopted and developed by Anscar Chupungco.

> It [liturgical inculturation] is a process whereby pertinent elements of a local culture are integrated into the worship of a local church. Integration means that culture influences the composition and proclamation of prayer formularies, the performance of ritual actions, and the expression of liturgical message in art forms. Integration can also mean that local rites, symbols, and festivals, after due critique and Christian interpretation, are assimilated into the liturgical worship of a local church.[9]

Liturgical inculturation is the bringing together of the culture, in this case Indigenous Australian, into dialogue with the Roman Rite, resulting in elements of culture becoming assimilated into local liturgical worship, and the local culture having similarities with the church's liturgy.

A Methodology for Liturgical Inculturation

Chupungco believes that it is not possible to make liturgical inculturation "work" without a clear methodology. He suggests three methods that can operate in combination, which we briefly offer here and are pertinent to our discussion.[10]

The first method is *creative assimilation*. Chupungco credits the beginning of this activity with ancient church leaders, who creatively integrated various elements into the liturgy. These would have been familiar to local worshipers, perhaps as household rites, or even religious ceremony, such as mystery rites. He makes the point that these cultural elements were reinterpreted in light of the Scriptures. In describing this process, he cautions that it can be fraught with problems, where ritual elements seemingly comparable are actually

---

[9] Anscar B. Chupungco, OSB, "Methods of Liturgical Inculturation," in *Worship and Culture: Foreign Country or Homeland?*, ed. Glaucia Vasconcelos Wilkey (Grand Rapids: Eerdmans, 2014), 263.

[10] Ibid., 264–75.

incompatible with the Christian message. A careful study is needed that assumes a clear understanding of the meaning of each.

The Roman Rite is characterized by simplicity and austerity, and is not always helpful to cultures who express ceremony differently. Aboriginals and Islanders who were so familiar with their own rich communal ceremonies found it hard to make connections and to feel at home in the church's worship. Traditional ceremony included everyone in the ritual actions of singing, dancing, and art, including body painting. Even though the liturgical reform of Vatican II restored participation to all worshipers, the ordained presider and word, rather than action, continue to dominate.

The second method Chupungco identifies is *dynamic equivalence*. He states, "While creative assimilation starts with what one's culture can offer and hence can be added to Christian liturgy, dynamic equivalence starts with what exists in the Christian liturgy and how culture can further develop its *ordo*, or shape."[11] Dynamic equivalence begins with the Church's liturgy; principally but not solely, its focus is the liturgical texts. For the most part, it concerns translation of texts, but it also covers structure or ritual action.

For centuries the Latin language has been associated with the Roman Rite of the Catholic Church. In 1965, when the Vatican Council fathers approved the use of the vernacular in the Roman liturgy, principles of translation were determined. The major aim of *Comme Le Prévoit*[12] was to offer a way to enable translators to communicate the texts of the liturgy in local language that the participants could understand. The instruction was to begin with the meaning of the text, rather than individual words or phrases. It acknowledged that languages are made up of particular thought patterns, with their own idioms and forms of expressions, as well as vocabulary and style. Therefore, literal word-by-word translations in the liturgical text were inadequate.

Before colonization, Aboriginal people living across such a vast continent had hundreds of languages. In one mission station—set up

---

[11] Ibid., 266.

[12] "*Comme Le Prévoit:* On the Translation of Liturgical Texts for Celebrations with a Congregation," Concilium for Constitution on Liturgy, January 25, 1969.

to protect Aboriginal people who were driven from their lands—there might be multiple languages spoken. This provided a challenge to the European missionaries and of course for newly baptized Aboriginals and Islanders who were required to follow the Catholic rites in Latin. After the Second Vatican Council, the Roman Missal was translated into the vernacular. In Australia this meant English, a language associated with the colonists. Most missionaries were not linguists, and although many of them mastered local languages, it was another task to translate liturgical texts into local languages that were at the time only in an oral form, and therefore not written. Furthermore, in Indigenous societies with highly complex social structures that valued continuity and connectivity, certain practices and even language terms were considered taboo. In this study, we discuss one significant example of dynamic equivalence of the text of the Roman Rite for a local community, instigated by Pallottine missionary Fr. Kevin McKelson and spread to other groups.

Chupungco identifies a third tool for liturgical inculturation, that of *organic progression*. This he describes as "supplementing and completing the shape of the liturgy established in the official edition."[13] While the Roman Church offers the possibility of organic progression of the rites, it guards against discontinuity. The Constitution on the Sacred Liturgy speaks of preserving "the substantial unity of the Roman Rite" (38), and its interpretation has provided a sticking point for scholars and official church authorities.[14] Chupungco offers a number of steps that accompany a study of the typical edition of the Roman Rites. These include consideration of historical, linguistic, and theological aspects of the texts as well as the pastoral needs of the local worshiping community. This more sophisticated approach requires the particular skills of qualified liturgists and theologians.

We are indebted to scholars such as Chupungco, who made liturgy and culture their lifework. However, I would agree with Eva Solomon,[15] an Anishinaabe Canadian, that because inculturation

---

[13] Chupungco, "Methods of Liturgical Inculturation," 273.

[14] See Shorter, *Toward a Theology of Inculturation*, 191–95.

[15] Eva Solomon, CSJ, SSM, *Come Dance with Me: A Medicine Wheel Practice of*

is a term with limitations, at least for many Indigenous people, it is "suggestive of a colonialist attitude." I would add that as applied to liturgical inculturation, it favors the Roman Rite as superior to Indigenous ceremony. Solomon would propose that, in the current context, interculturation is the way forward, accepting Shorter's definition: "Interculturation is carried out in partnership by individuals who represent different cultures."[16]

Interculturation as a dialogue between two cultures, both individual and communal, must be approached as a partnership of equals. "Interculturation is indeed both an individual and communal as well as a theological and cultural matter and is true partnership that implies a dialogue of equal partners." In contrast to inculturation, Solomon explains, "The interculturation process, by distinction, enriches and radically transforms the dialoguing individuals and communities through an encounter with the person and Gospel of Jesus."[17] I agree with Solomon, who invites us to move beyond liturgical inculturation to interculturation; "an expansiveness" is possible, "rather than the narrowness and divisiveness that 'insertion' envisages."[18] The process of interculturation is lengthy and will take time to develop. But crucially, it must begin with an understanding of an equal partnership, bringing the church's liturgy into conversation with Australian Indigenous culture. For this to even be possible, awareness raising and formation will be needed among Catholic dialogue partners.

Evangelization, Assimilation and the Pioneer Catholic Missionaries

Catholic missionaries did not effectively begin evangelizing Aboriginal and Islander peoples in the Kimberley and northern Australia until the second half of the nineteenth century. At the time, colonial

---

Anishinaabe Catholic Interculturation of Faith, vol. 1 of *New Paths for the Churches and Indigenous Peoples* (Montreal, QC: Novalis Publishing, 2022), 74.

[16] Shorter, *Toward a Theology of Inculturation*, 14.
[17] Ibid.
[18] Ibid.

policies by government and churches were determined to assimilate the "natives." They turned a blind eye to the extensive genocide of Aboriginal peoples that took place in many parts of the vast continent. It can be said that the British who colonized Australia were advancing their own interests; in fact, they saw the far-flung land as an ideal place to deposit convicts and other felons. As for the local inhabitants, where possible, they were exterminated. Multiple records of massacres now exist, where Aboriginal people were simply herded together and shot dead, the murderers justifying their atrocities by deciding that the Native peoples were not fully human.[19] With the intention of colonizing them, government authorities with the collusion of church leaders stole generations of children from their parents and families in a practice that continued well into the twentieth century.[20]

Some mission stations offered places of shelter and refuge to displaced peoples literally fleeing for their lives from European settlers who had taken their land. The European missionaries encountered people whose way of life could not be more different than their own. While at least church leaders believed the local people to be their equal in the eyes of God, they were convinced that the "native" people would never survive colonization, including recovering self-determination, without adopting a European lifestyle. This resulted in Christian missionaries following the church policy that at the time was "cultural domination." Shorter describes this as "the unwelcome transference of foreign cultural traits: symbols, meanings, values and behaviour, from one culture to another."[21] Catholic missionaries understood the Christian message and a European lifestyle to be synonymous. In the words of pioneer Jesuit missionary Donald MacKillop, "Religion is

---

[19] For insights into these atrocities, see John Harris, *One Blood: 200 Years of Aboriginal Encounter with Christianity: A Story of Hope* (Sutherland, NSW: Albatross Books, 1990).

[20] "Bringing Them Home," National Inquiry into the Separation of Aboriginal and Torres Strait Islander Children from Their Families, 1997, https://bth.humanrights.gov.au/.

[21] Shorter, *Toward a Theology of Inculturation*, 8.

primarily our intention, but in a manner secondary in our practice because we recognise that we must first civilise the blacks before we can Christianise them...."[22] Before the "natives" could be evangelized they needed to be "civilized," and that meant taking on European ways, including dress, mannerisms, food, manual work, building houses, and farming the land. And without full "conversion," Aboriginal and Islander people were unable to experience eternal salvation.[23] While some missionaries expected that Christianity meant a complete suppression of former cultural identity, including language and ceremony, other pioneer missionaries learned local languages.

Bishop John O'Loughlin MSC

In 1949, John O'Loughlin, MSC, was ordained bishop for the Darwin Diocese.[24] Like his predecessor and missionaries before him, the bishop was of the opinion that Aboriginal people needed to be completely assimilated into Western culture. This is evident in his paper "Christianisation as an Essential Part of Assimilation,"[25] where O'Loughlin describes the "missionary endeavour" as preaching the gospel to the "pagans" and that the newly baptized must accept, among other practices, different "forms of worship." It would seem

---

[22] Cited in Martin Wilson, MSC, "Missiological Reflections, Occasional Address, Gsell Centenary 1906–2006," Nungalinya College, Darwin, August 14, 2006, 5 (accessed from the Catholic Diocese of Darwin archives). For a fuller account of the Jesuit mission, see Harris, *One Blood*, 461–80.

[23] Gideon C. Goosen, "Christian and Aboriginal Interface in Australia," *Theological Studies* 60, no. 1 (1999): 72.

[24] Bishop John O'Loughlin (1911–85) served the Diocese of Darwin, which covers almost all of the Northern Territory (the north to central area of Australia), an area of almost 1.5 million square kilometers. Vast distances and major differences among the tribes of Aboriginal and Torres Strait Islander tribes provided significant challenges for the bishop and his missionaries.

[25] Bishop John O'Loughlin to the Missions/Administration Conference, 1957. The address is quoted in full in Peter Hearn, MSC, *A Theology of Mission: An Analysis of the Theology of Mission of the Catholic Diocese of Darwin in Its Ministry to Aboriginal People during the Episcopacy of John O'Loughlin, MSC, 1949–85* (Kensington, NSW: Nelen Yubu Missiological Unit, 2003), 351–56.

from his address that the bishop judges aspects of the way of life of the Aboriginal person to be immoral and therefore contrary to the gospel message. In his opinion, "The natives' religion properly so called, which we would regard as a conglomeration of magic and superstition, is a hindrance not only to his acceptance of the Christian Faith, but also to his assimilation."[26]

Bishop O'Loughlin continued the practice of his predecessors, suppressing traditional ceremony, including initiation rites, for anyone wishing to become Catholic. He dismissed traditional ceremony as "magic" and was confident that the "pagan aboriginal," who by his observation was experiencing the "loss of tribal organisation and belief," offered an opportunity for Christianity. While many Aboriginal and Islander peoples adopted the gospel message because of the genuine care and compassion offered them by the early missionaries, some, like O'Loughlin, believed they were evangelizing in a vacuum, deciding that First Nations peoples had neither religion nor spirituality. However, this attitude was to change with the influence of the burgeoning of the social sciences.

From the earliest times of Australian colonization, anthropologists, sociologists, and linguists lived with Native peoples, observing, analyzing, and recording their tribal culture. Scientists discovered societies with highly sophisticated structures and organization where relationships determined which clans could interact with whom, and how these relationships affected their connection to the environment. Over time, as they built trust, European scholars were invited to observe traditional cultural ceremonies that not only marked significant moments in their lives but, as they learned, were intertwined with the law and ensured continuity with the spirit world.[27]

---

[26] Ibid., 354.
[27] These scholars included R. M. and C. H. Berndt, T. G. H. Strehlow, W. E. H. Stanner, and P. E. Elkin. While all are European or early colonists, their studies are significant, observing cultural expressions of Indigenous peoples at a time when they were yet to be influenced by white settlers or missionaries.

Bishop John Jobst, SAC

While John O'Loughlin was leader of the Darwin Diocese, German Pallottine John Jobst was bishop of the neighboring Broome Vicariate.[28] Early in his leadership, Bishop Jobst sought the advice of anthropologists and linguists to better understand the Aboriginal people under his care. Interested to know if new Aboriginal Catholics could continue to engage in traditional ceremonies, he initiated a meeting with Fr. Ernst Worms, Dr. Petri, and a certain Dr. Micha, a visiting ethnologist. He was assured by the sociologists that with the exception of those standards and practices that were incompatible with Christian values, "Aborigines could adhere to their traditions, mythology, their initiation rites and their law when they accepted the Catholic faith."[29] Bishop Jobst was one Christian missionary who valued the work of social scientists.

Ernst Worms and Helmut Petri

His compatriot German Pallottine Fr. Ernst A. Worms (1891–1963), well respected as both a missionary and anthropologist, served in the area known as the Kimberley in the Broome Vicariate, to the west of Darwin and the Northern Territory. Worms and his colleague Dr. Helmut Petri wrote a definitive work that contradicted understandings that Aboriginal people were simply pagan with no spirituality. The two anthropologists provide insights into an Aboriginal worldview that included detailed descriptions of the variety of sacred objects, music, stones, images, as well as sacred beings used in traditional ceremony. They tell us,

---

[28] German-born Pallottine Bishop John Jobst (1920–2014) was ordained bishop in 1959. The Kimberley Vicariate (now Diocese of Broome), which bounds the Diocese of Darwin, is situated in North West Australia, covers 773,000 square kilometers, and at the time included four mission stations, and in total about eighteen hundred Catholics.

[29] Margaret Zucker, *From Patrons to Partners and the Separated Children of the Kimberley: A History of the Catholic Church in the Kimberley, WA*, 2nd ed. (Fremantle: University of Notre Dame Australia Press, 2005), 119.

> For making the objects the Aborigine regards every material to be suitable and holy, be it wood or stone, bone or hair, bark or grass, shells or fruit. When used in ceremonies with song, proclamation, and drama, the decorations and traditional motifs on the sacred objects express in an original way the Aborigine's beliefs, religious sensibility, and attitude towards life.... His creative talent, marked by strong regional characteristics, invents ever new variations of liturgical objects from which—with even greater certainty—an even closer contact with the spiritual world and his natural environment is expected to come.[30]

Throughout their account they discuss in detail what they understand to be the meaning of various ceremonies that mark life moments, including initiation and funerary rites. For Catholic missionary Worms and his colleague Petri, Aboriginal cultures were both spiritual and religious, and deeply connected to the activities of the spirit beings and their ancestors in a continuous presence brought about by sacred objects and ceremony.

Ronald and Catherine Berndt

This was also the opinion of social anthropologists Ronald and Catherine Berndt, who traveled to many remote communities for more than four decades, and who wrote a seminal work titled *The World of the First Australians*. In their understanding, "Myth and ritual not only provide the members of an Aboriginal community with a framework through which to perceive their world. They are also an assertion that human life is important, that it has meaning, that it makes sense."[31] In other words, it was the informed opinion of the Berndts that the entire value structure and existence of the

---

[30] Ernest A. Worms, SAC, and Helmut Petri, *Australian Aboriginal Religions*, rev. ed. from the original German (Kensington, NSW: Nelen Yubu Missiological Series 5, 1998), 6.

[31] R. M. and C. H. Berndt, *The World of the First Australians: Aboriginal Traditional Life: Past and Present*, 4th ed. (Adelaide: Rigby Publishers, 1985), 287.

Aboriginal and Torres Strait Islander peoples was centered on their ancient songs, dances, and stories that continued over the centuries to be celebrated in ceremony.

The Berndts saw ceremonial life as central to the essence of the Aboriginal community: "Virtually all Aboriginal religious ritual focused on life. The Dreaming was of contemporary relevance: the past, the present and future were regarded as a continuing and uninterrupted stream."[32] The past became present in ceremonies marking tribal life and celebrating relationships that were never only about people, but bound up with the life-giving force of the land, the sea, and all creatures.

W. E. H. Stanner

Eminent anthropologist W. E. H. Stanner[33] expressed it this way: "All rites … were concerned in one way or another with the most precious good of all, life itself, and more particularly with the continuance of life."[34] In the same paper, Stanner offered a series of propositions to argue that Aboriginal rites (ceremonies) have strong religious elements. While he cannot justify that Aboriginal ceremony is prayer or worship, he does believe, "There is a half-explicit concept of men co-operating ritually with unseen powers at holy places and on high occasions, to further life-pattern believed to have been ordained by its founders, and of doing so under an assurance of a continuing flow of benefits."[35] This "economy of ritual" ensures that when the community cooperates with "unseen powers" it ensures a continuing favorable possibility of life and well-being. Stanner believes this to be liturgical in character, "in that they were organized works of public—

---

[32] Berndt and Berndt, *The World of the First Australians*, 302.

[33] Martin Wilson, MSC, says of Stanner, "There would be few anthropologists who have enjoyed a relationship with one mission as long as he with Port Keats and one characterised by such a degree of mutual respect at that." *Nelen Yubu* 13 (September 1982): 3.

[34] W. E. H. Stanner, "Some Aspects of Aboriginal Religion," Charles Strong Memorial Trust Inaugural Lecture, Australian National University, *Oceania* (1976): 26.

[35] Ibid., 28–29.

as distinct from private—duty, deference and even reverence towards or faith in, an otherworldly provenance of human well-being."[36] He goes on to state that, in his understanding, while Christian liturgy is about salvation, the Aboriginal "economy" also ensures continuity of life whereby "souls" (we might say the spirit) lived on in country and clan, thus bringing about connection with the Dreaming.

Stanner compares the Aboriginal tribal ceremony with Christian liturgy: "The ritual uses of water, blood, earth and other substances, in combination with words, gestures, chants, songs and dances, all having for the Aborigines a compelling quality … a sacramental quality."[37] Stanner's conclusions, drawn after a lifetime of observing, studying, and working with the Aboriginal communities of Port Keats (now Wadeye), offered Christian missionaries significant insights into the integrity and depth of Aboriginal traditional ceremony and religion.

Martin Wilson, MSC

Missionary priest and sociologist Fr. Martin Wilson, MSC,[38] in a paper titled "Aboriginal Religion and Christianity: Ideological Symbolism, Ritual Sacramentalism," asked, "What sense can a Christian make of Aboriginal religion?" Wilson's intention was to refute the notion that First Nation peoples either had no religion or that their religion was "pagan." He set out to provide "an investigation of the congruence between Aboriginal religion and Christianity on a twofold dimension: (1) as systems of belief about the religious character of the world, and (2) as systems of ritual action whereby human society has access to the world's founding power or powers." Wilson asked a further question: "What religious significance do Aboriginal myths and

---

[36] Ibid., 30.
[37] Ibid. See also n15.
[38] Martin Wilson (1930–2022), Catholic Missionary of the Sacred Heart (MSC), who served in the Darwin Diocese, was a revered sociologist, educator, and writer. To him we are indebted for the publication of the journal *Nelen Yubu*, which included eighty-one editions, 1978–2002.

rituals (ceremonies) have for Christians, whose faith is set by God's revelation in and through Christ?" He proceeded to address the issue of belief by exploring Aboriginal mythology and ideological symbolism expressed in what he termed "narrative metaphor," that when understood finds a comparison in Jewish mythology and history in the Christian tradition. He proposed that both could be used beside each other in evangelizing the Aboriginal people to accept Christianity.

In his explanation of "ritual sacramentalism," Wilson provided examples of traditional Aboriginal ceremonies from the studies of Stanner, Elkin, and Strehlow, all of whom, he informs us, use the term "sacrament" to interpret their ritual meaning. Wilson was prepared to apply their conclusions regarding Aboriginal ceremonial sacramentality to Christian sacrament, which he describes as "a sacred visible sign which effects what it symbolizes." While Wilson was quick to caution that "like any other culture, Aboriginal culture must be deeply challenged by Christianity," his message is clear to those who supported the practice of suppressing traditional ceremony for the newly baptized: "It is a great shame to tell an Aborigine that he must abandon all that as pagan nonsense if he wants to become a Christian."

Wilson concludes his study with a logical consequence: "If what I propose in terms of ideological symbolism and ritual sacramentalism is true, it has to be maintained that Aboriginal religion is not only authentic but bears a remarkable congruence with Christianity especially as a system of ritual action."

Stanner talks of Aboriginal ceremonies as being characteristically sacramental liturgy. Wilson takes this one step further and argues that both Aboriginal religious ceremonies and Christianity share systems of ritual action that are similar in many aspects, and can rightly be called sacramental as well as spiritual. Wilson, of course, had his detractors, notably fellow missionary Fr. Dan Donovan, but the insights are informed by social scientists at the time and brought about a shift in understanding and appreciation of Aboriginal and Islander spirituality and ceremony.

An Australian Aboriginal Liturgy

The Second Vatican Council opened possibilities for missionaries to adapt the liturgy to the needs of Aboriginal and Islander Christians.[39] While still in Rome attending the Council, Bishop John Jobst was moved to exclaim, "We have incorporated into our liturgy ... next to nothing of the Native's culture, hence religion presented to them, particularly the liturgy, will always be alien and foreign to them."[40] He urged his priests to study traditional culture with a view to enriching the church's liturgy.[41]

In 1970 Pope Paul VI became the first pope ever to come to Australia. During this momentous visit he assured the "descendants of Australia's original inhabitants" that "We know that you have a lifestyle proper to your own ethnic genius or culture—a culture which the Church respects and which she does not in any way ask you to renounce."[42] This important affirmation from a pontiff both acknowledged that Aboriginal and Torres Strait Islander Australians had a unique "ethnic genius" and also encouraged them to bring their rich cultural expression to the Catholic faith.[43]

The organizers of the fortieth International Eucharistic Congress, held in Melbourne in 1973, were similarly inspired both by Jobst and

---

[39] Especially the Constitution on the Liturgy 37–40 and other documents that address faith and culture, including *Gaudium et Spes*, *Lumen Gentium*, *Evangelii Nuntiandi*, and *Redemptoris Missio*. While we agree with Shorter's summation that because the liturgy was the first area decided upon, it was out of step with developments in theology expressed in later documents, it did at least open the door to liturgical inculturation. Shorter, *Toward a Theology of Inculturation*, 191.

[40] At the time Fr. Peile was studying various social disciplines—anthropology, ethnology, and sociology of the Aboriginal people. Letter from Bishop John Jobst to Fr. Anthony Peile, SAC, November 5, 1964, Archives of the Diocese of Broome.

[41] Letter from Bishop Jobst to Fr. Kearney, December 7, 1964, Archives of the Diocese of Broome.

[42] Pope Paul VI, "Address to the Promoters of Human and Social Activities, Sydney, Australia" (December 2, 1970), www.vatican.va.

[43] John Paul II referred to the speech of Paul VI in "Address of John Paul II to the Aborigines and Torres Strait Islanders in Blatherskite Park" (November 29, 1986), www.vatican.va.

Paul VI. Consequently a "Mass for Aborigines" was one of a series of liturgies that was celebrated during the Congress.[44] In preparation for the celebration and at the invitation of Bishop O'Loughlin,[45] Church leaders, including First Nation elders, were invited to Darwin for a two-day meeting that included twenty-six Indigenous people from every Australian state.[46] Fr. Hilton Deacon (later bishop) from Melbourne, concluded, "Aboriginal representatives ... were unanimous that they wanted their own liturgy. They had pointed out that tribal communication depended greatly on dance and symbol and not words."[47] Deacon went on to explain, "At Mass they felt no sense of identity." It seems that Bishop John Jobst was right to surmise that Aboriginal Catholics experienced the liturgy as "foreign and alien."

Archbishop Annibale Bugnini, the great liturgical reformer, recounted that the liturgies were prepared by the National Liturgy Commission, in "complete co-operation" with the Congregation for Divine Worship.[48] The introduction to the Mass in the official order of service explains its uniqueness:

> The Holy Father in his statement to the Aborigines during his visit to Sydney in 1970 makes the point that there was much in Aboriginal culture which required preserving. We understand this to mean that cultural patterns, thought patterns and social structures be preserved wherever possible

---

[44] For more about the Aboriginal Mass, see Carmel Pilcher, "An Australian Aboriginal Mass," *Worship* 90 (March 2016): 151–69. Also, "This is but a beginning: An Australian Aboriginal Mass," *Questions Liturgiques/Studies in Liturgy* 96, nos. 3–4 (2015): 129–48. A seventy-minute DBD-R video of the Mass in its entirety is available from ABC TV archives (Australia), "Divine Service Aboriginal Liturgy 40th International Eucharistic Congress," May 6, 1973.

[45] Bishop O'Loughlin to Fr. Brian Walsh, Archdiocese of Melbourne Archives (November 1971).

[46] Cited in a news release prepared by Michael Costigan from the Eucharistic Congress Secretariat in 1972. Catholic Archdiocese of Melbourne Archives.

[47] See "Aborigines Want Their Own Liturgy," *Catholic Weekly*, June 22, 1972, 10.

[48] Archbishop Annibale Bugnini, CM, *The Reform of the Liturgy, 1948–1975* (Collegeville, MN: Liturgical Press, 1990), 920–922.

so long as they are in keeping with the basic principles of the Christian ethos. Consequently, this liturgy is an attempt to express the Eucharistic Act in cultural and thought patterns of the Aboriginal peoples.[49]

The Aboriginal Mass included Aboriginals and Islanders from all over Australia. Representatives from Port Keats (Darwin Diocese) and Kununurra (Kimberley) sang and danced, and others also chanted during the Mass. In his introductory remarks, Fr. Hilton Deacon shared the hope that "this is but a beginning."

The Australian Aboriginal Mass was a serious attempt to enhance the liturgy with the richness of Aboriginal and Islander culture. It was an attempt at liturgical inculturation with texts that were translated by Church authorities, using the Church's guidelines that called for dynamic equivalence. Song, dance, mime, and art were added to or replaced existing rites in what Chupungco would term "creative assimilation." Although the whole of the nation's imagination was spurred by this event, it was the missionaries and First Nations Catholics who saw this celebration as official church approval for combining elements of traditional myths and ritual elements of ceremony into the church's liturgy.

Liturgical Inculturation in the Kimberley

Even before the Congress Mass, missionaries and their communities had begun bringing the process of liturgical inculturation to the local community. Rome was aware that "There was a special Eucharistic Prayer composed by local missionaries and approved by the congress. Later on, the bishops working with the tribes obtained permission to use this Eucharistic Prayer regularly in Masses celebrated among the aborigines."[50]

---

[49] *Liturgies and Programme, 40th International Eucharistic Congress 1973*, 103, Archdiocese of Melbourne Archives.

[50] Bugnini, *The Reform of the Liturgy*, 921. See also *Eucharisties de tous pays. Celebrations*, Centre National De Pastorale Liturgique (Paris: Diffusion Cahiers Du Livre, 1975).

The La Grange Mass—Texts

The Eucharistic Prayer, and indeed, the texts of the Aboriginal Mass, were largely the work of Pallottine missionary and colleague of Bishop Jobst, Fr. Kevin McKelson, a skilled linguist, who served in the Kimberley from 1954 to 2006.[51] While McKelson had already translated hymns and devotional prayers into the languages of the local people, the Second Vatican Council gave him the impetus to go further. McKelson was guided by a statement in the Decree on the Church's Missionary Activity: "The faith should be imparted by means of a well-adapted catechesis and celebrated in a liturgy that is in harmony with the character of the people."[52] The need for the celebration of worship that was intelligible to participants was the driving force for McKelson's work. In his own words, "I have over the years taken the cultural situation of the aboriginals seriously while trying to remain true to the basic principles of Eucharistic celebration."[53] He offered several principles that underline his liturgical work. We mention four here that are key to this discussion. In a traditional Aboriginal ceremony, McKelson informs us, all participate. Because there is no passive participation, this should flow into the Church's liturgy. Aboriginals use few words in their ceremonial songs, and these are constantly repeated. McKelson suggests the use of Aboriginal melodic forms to accompany doctrinally truthful liturgical texts, which, he adds, should ideally be composed by the community. Aboriginal language is not primarily oriented toward abstract ideas.

Most of McKelson's work in liturgical inculturation took place at the La Grange Mission (later Bidyadanga). There the pastor had

---

[51] The entire collection of Kevin McKelson's work is available from Australian Institute of Aboriginal and Torres Strait Islander Studies (hereafter AIATSIS), Canberra ACT, AIAS033.130717.

[52] Decree on the Church's Missionary Activity *Ad Gentes Divinitus*, December 7, 1965, 19. *The Basic Sixteen Documents: Vatican Council II—Constitutions, Decrees, Declarations: A Completely Revised Translation in Inclusive Language*, ed. Austin Flannery, OP (Northpoint, NY: Costello Publishing, 1966).

[53] K. McKelson, "Cultural Adaptation in Liturgy," 1, AIATSIS, AIAS033.130717.

long observed and studied the local people, who came to the mission from five tribal language groups: Karajarri, Nyangumada, Yulbaridya, Dyuwaliny, and Mangala. McKelson translated the Mass of the Roman Rite into these five languages.[54]

McKelson began his translating task by sitting with the local elders, especially Tommy Dodds, and working through the texts of the Mass with them.[55] The linguist, McKelson, knew that certain English words and concepts were culturally taboo. He was also familiar with the thought patterns expressed in the Indigenous languages. European languages, such as Latin and English, often expressed abstract ideas, while Aboriginals were concrete thinkers, usually communicating in ceremony through story and ritual action. This combined with the limitations of local vocabulary meant that some Roman terms— for example, the term "holy"—had no equivalent in the traditional languages. After pondering an alternative that could be used, "truly good" became its equivalent. "Forgiveness" was also a foreign concept in Aboriginal life, but expressing sorrow was very important. In the Penitential Rite, or confession of sins, McKelson reworked the text to reflect their experience and understanding: "Sometimes we do not love God, other people or ourselves. Let us remember our wrong and tell God we are sorry," to which all replied, "We have done wrong, we are sorry, help us Father not to sin again."[56]

As he worked through each section of the texts of the Roman Mass and his faith community gave their approval, McKelson progressed to

---

[54] Over time McKelson translated the Mass texts into each of the languages spoken by the people and rotated these each Sunday. A copy of these translations is available from the Bidyadanga Catholic Community and also AIATSIS, AIAS033.130717.

[55] Tommy Dodds must have been of particular assistance because he is the only Aboriginal named by Kevin McKelson in his unpublished notes. McKelson's notes indicate that he constantly consulted and observed those in his mission station for advice and to learn their customs and laws. AIATSIS, AIAS033.130717.

[56] Father Kevin McKelson, SAC, "Introduction to the Aboriginal Mass, The Missa Indigena," 58, unpublished manuscript, with subtitle: "Last reading 20 September 2007, Draft only," AIATSIS, AIAS033.130717.

the next step. The languages he was working with were oral and had never been recorded. So, with the help of other colleagues, McKelson transcribed the now Indigenous liturgical texts. Once they were written, McKelson led the Sunday Mass in the vernacular of his assembly, choosing a different language in turn each week.[57]

It was only later that McKelson translated the Mass texts into simple written English. The "La Grange Mass," as it was first known, became the unofficial English text, and indeed provided the texts for the Congress Mass, which soon spread to Catholic mission communities across the continent. Because the La Grange Mass began its existence not in English or Latin but in Indigenous languages, each local community could take the English version and reverse the process, writing in their own local languages.

McKelson regularly consulted with colleagues, social scientists, and liturgists, in Australia and overseas, including Anscar Chupungco, and continued to refine the texts.[58] As La Grange/Bidyadanga Aboriginals became more exposed to Europeans and others living in the neighboring town of Broome, they also became more familiar with the English language. McKelson adapted the texts accordingly, although never radically. It was McKelson's conviction that "a naïve return to the cultural heritage of the past would be just as harmful as the ignoring of culture itself."[59]

Over the more than four decades that McKelson developed the Missa Kimberley—it had become his lifework—he was never satisfied,

---

[57] This last piece of information was told to me by elders Maureen Yanawana and Madeleine Jadai from the Bidyadanga (formerly La Grange) Mission.

[58] McKelson's consultants included Fr. Ernst Worms, Dr. H. Petri and Dr. Gisela Petri Oderman, whom he acknowledged as having influenced him profoundly. He met with the prefect for the Congregation of Worship and the Sacraments, Cardinal James Knox (Archbishop of Melbourne during the Eucharistic Congress), while in Rome in 1978. Anscar J. Chupungco, OSB, offered encouragement and suggestions in correspondence to Fr. Kevin McKelson, June 9, 1978, Broome Diocesan Archives.

[59] Kevin McKelson, "A Case for Enculturating the Liturgy," revised October 1979, unpublished manuscript, Broome Diocese Archives.

continuing to seek advice concerning a particular word or phrase. Not only did he see the need to accommodate the local community's full participation, but he hoped his attention to liturgical form and accuracy would lead to official ecclesial approval.[60] In later years he decided, "Strictly speaking my role should have been that of a scribe listening to what the local Catholics have to say and writing it down.... My efforts can only be regarded as second best."[61] However, his careful and ongoing collaboration with his community surely offers an example of liturgical inculturation, based both on the exacting principles of translation according to dynamic equivalence and his wish to ensure that Aboriginal Catholics can fully and intelligently participate in the church's liturgy.

Cultural Adaptations in the East Kimberley
—Ritual Actions

While Fr. Kevin McKelson focused principally on liturgical texts, Aboriginal elders took the lead in preparing church worship in other areas of the Kimberley. Fr. Werner Kriener, SAC (1920–2014), writes of a retreat held in 1982 at Gregory Well that he believes brought about the birth of serious Aboriginal involvement in the liturgy. He describes how the men who participated "discovered God at night and in turn God gave them new spiritual thoughts. They composed a whole range of 'Junbas' which they would use at Mass. There was great enthusiasm. This was the birth of their own liturgy."[62] Fr. Kriener saw this as a watershed moment, not just for his own community but others as well, as Aboriginal Catholics felt empowered to become actively involved in bringing their culture to the church's official liturgy.

---

[60] This hope continues. The Mass has been celebrated continually in the Broome Diocese and beyond. It has been published as *The Missa Terra Spiritus Sancti, the Mass of the Land of the Holy Spirit* (MLHS), Liturgy Brisbane, Queensland, 2018.

[61] Kevin McKelson, "Adaptation of the Mass 1990," Diocese of Broome Archives.

[62] Story told in song and dance, Werner Kriener, SAC, "Inculturation of the Liturgy in the East Kimberley," *Nelen Yubu* 58, no. 3 (1994): 12.

A festival to mark Pentecost brought together communities from the Eastern Kimberley for a weekend each year. Rich elements of traditional ceremony were included in the various liturgies and celebrations. Each community prepared a different segment of the ceremonies back in their own places, including artwork, songs, and dances. The men performed a fire ceremony that depicted an original myth, but in the context of Pentecost, this reflected the continuing activity of the Holy Spirit in the ancient ancestors.[63]

Josephite Clare Ahern, an Irish missionary, describes a blessing of water by women at the beginning of the Eucharist during the Pentecost festival. We are told that the women, accompanied by the singing of the men, called down blessings on the water as they danced around the altar and then sprinkled all in the assembly. Ahern remarks that this ancient ceremony "had often been used before their own ceremonies or before they entered a place sacred to their traditions." For a desert people, water holes were a life source and sacred.

Art also found its place in the Christian liturgy. For the worshipers, some traditional myths readily connected to the Scriptures, and local artists illustrated these in painting and storytelling. Again, from Clare Ahern:

> There, amidst the smoke and stars, the artists were called upon to explain the meaning of their Pentecost art. Proudly confident that their large paintings in tempera colours and on three-plywood carried a powerful message, Junee Sturt and Sambo Gordon of Red Hill explained in Djaru and English its meaning. They spoke of earlier Aborigines and their secret with the firesticks and now the Aboriginal awareness of the Spirit. They drew Aborigines, firesticks, caves, snakes, trees and the Spirit.

---

[63] At the suggestion of one of the Christian Aboriginal elders, George Stuart, from Red Hill, a number of communities traveled to one place in the Eastern Kimberley each year to celebrate the festival of Pentecost. For a detailed description of one such festival see Clare Ahern, "New Hope on the Pentecost Road," *Nelen Yubu* 25 (Summer 1986): 17–24. What follows is from that account.

The art depicted ancient and Christian symbols. Ahern realized, "The story of Pentecost, for the Aborigines present, was not an isolated event or one that began with Christ's coming. It was tied to their past and all their stories." An ancient people continued to be deeply connected to the activities of the spirit beings and their ancestors in an unbroken presence. Their story now included Christ and the Triune God. Missionary Colleen Kleinschaffer recounted another story: "The Bishop was also suitably adorned with a special mitre made from cardboard decorated with ochre painting, human hair and flowers. A staff topped by a spirit bird and a clay pectoral cross hung by human hair string completed the Episcopal attire."[64] It is no surprise that a people imbued with ceremony, who had recently returned to their traditional lands and lifestyle, would bring familiar ritual elements into their newly adopted Roman Rites. This also included ritual guidance to presiders, where at one celebration of baptism "the priest was instructed to roll up his sleeves, put his arms in the drum (water container) and pour the water with his hands, over the heads of the baptized."[65]

Two important conclusions can be drawn from these reports: (1) First Nation Catholics felt empowered to prepare and lead liturgy: "We will show you Sisters, we will show you the proper Aboriginal way."[66] (2) Traditional Aboriginals understood Christianity not as a rupture to all that went before but an event in continuity with the dreaming and the action of their ancient ancestors that now includes the creator Spirit and Christ, who continue to be involved in the present, expressed through the Church's ceremony. This expands Chupungco's definition of liturgical inculturation to a clear sense of intercultural liturgical decision making.

---

[64] For a detailed account of this ceremony with other examples, see Colleen Kleinschaffer, "Fresh Shoots of the Mulan Tree," *Nelen Yubu* 23 (Winter 1985): 17, 18.

[65] Recounted by Ahern in "The Chase and the Kandat Djaru," *Nelen Yubu* 26 (Autumn 1986): 11.

[66] Naomi Smith and Anne Boland, "Easter Ceremonies at Yaruman," *Nelen Yubu* 30 (Autumn 1987): 4.

Water. St. Mary's College students.
Copyright © 2023 Diocese of Broome

Ongoing Inculturation

Some four decades later, missionary Matthew Digges analyzed the Good Friday ceremonies in the Kutjungka (Balgo area), arguing that they "convey the same theological content and are the same basic ritual of the Christian mysteries to those who are attending them, but in a different context."[67] Many elements of the ceremony reflect those of his predecessors, but in his view, their involvement was "a pragmatic one, that has not been approached systematically or viewed through the lens of liturgical theology."[68] The missionaries at the time may not have had the tools for evaluation or known the formal theories of inculturation, but they did break new ground in bringing together the Roman Rite and First Nation traditional ceremony, where all felt able to contribute and be at home in the liturgical celebration. Church leaders, together with their Aboriginal counterparts who were lawmen skilled in the preparation and

---

[67] Matthew Digges was at the time a missionary priest in the Kimberley. See *Good Friday in the Kutjungka: Aboriginal and Catholic*, unpublished manuscript, University of Notre Dame Australia, December 2007, 6.

[68] Ibid., 16.

performance of ceremony, saw themselves as equal partners, actively inculturating the liturgy in the Kimberley in the years following the Vatican reform and Congress Mass.[69]

The Darwin Story of Liturgical Inculturation

Like their counterparts in the neighboring Diocese of Broome, the Darwin missionaries were keen to adapt the liturgy to make it more culturally appropriate for their communities.[70] In 1972, missionary Fr. Michael Sims, MSC, seemed to put into words their collective frustration:

> Has there been any *organised* attempt ever in the Territory to investigate the liturgical needs of our aboriginal people, to see whether or not any of their sacred rituals could be incorporated into our liturgy, greater use of aboriginal melodies and words in the sacrifice of the Mass, and a look at the sacraments to see whether they may be used more effectively in the aboriginal culture which it must eventually help?[71]

Sims proposed elements of the traditional ceremony that might be added to the liturgy and sacraments, that would, in his words, give the liturgy "an aboriginal flavor." However, while Sims did champion ritual elements from the traditional ceremony that he identified as sacred, he seemed to accept the status quo when in the same paper he asked, "With the dying out of the initiation rites on our missions (due to evil tendencies) the question is asked what have we done in our religion, besides preaching, to overcome the ritual exclusion?" Hearn was of the opinion that Michael Sims' paper helped to change

---

[69] See, for example, the story of Clare Ahern's first encounter with a group of Aboriginal women in "A Religious Contract with the Kundat Djaru Community," *Nelen Yubu* 24 (Spring 1985): 3–8.

[70] In 1969, the Northern Territory Catholic Missions Council (NTCMC) was established. Resolution 26 called for "a study ... of the use of the vernacular" in all areas, including liturgy. Resolution 26, Diocese of Darwin.

[71] Fr. M. Sims, MSC, "Liturgy among the Aborigines," *Forum NT* 1 (November 1972). Found in Catholic Diocese of Darwin Archives.

"the largely negative attitude of the first generations of missionaries toward Aboriginal religion." While this attitude, as we have shown, was probably widespread, Hearn believed that church leaders in the Darwin Diocese had continued to retain it.[72] Following his contribution to the discussion, Sims was tasked by Bishop O'Loughlin to "develop a liturgy for the Aboriginal people."[73]

Nothing of note seemed to change, though, in the Darwin Diocese, except that it was decided that the La Grange liturgy of Fr. Kevin McKelson became the preferred translation to be used in mission territories in the diocese, rather than the Congress Aboriginal Mass. This was possibly to counter a variety of approaches that individual pastors might introduce, because in fact, as we have shown, the Congress liturgy was based on the La Grange Mass. Despite the input of scholars, including the careful work of his missionary Fr. Martin Wilson, Bishop John O'Loughlin continued to be very cautious and tentative in his approach to the liturgy. At a special meeting of church leaders just two years after supporting the Aboriginal Mass in Melbourne, the bishop instructed his leaders, "There is not much scope for changing the Liturgy, devotions are another matter and it is quite in order to do all possible to make these more meaningful for the people."[74] In other words, culturally adapt the devotional needs of the people to their needs, but leave the official work of liturgy as a formal Roman Rite with no Aboriginal or Islander elements.

It was thus left to the Catholic missionaries to continue to adapt the liturgy to the local communities without guidance or support. However, Fr. Malcolm Fyfe, appointed director of missions in 1979, urged the leaders of Aboriginal and Islander Catholic communities to engage in liturgical inculturation, stating, "Translating the scriptures and the wording of liturgical actions into a local language does not constitute inculturation, nor do we automatically achieve inculturation

---

[72] Hearn, *A Theology of Mission*, 192.
[73] Ibid., 172.
[74] Found in the minutes of a special meeting of MSC leaders held in Daly River in 1975, quoted in ibid., 223.

of the Christian message by indigenizing the clergy."[75] While Fyfe makes clear what is not liturgical inculturation, in the letter he does not offer a clear definition but promises to send papers on the topic in the future. Whether this occurred is doubtful, because, as Hearn comments, attempts foundered, at least in any formalized way. He attributes this to the fact that no missionary of the Sacred Heart was formally trained in liturgy or linguistics, nor were people with formal expertise invited to visit the diocese.[76] According to Hearn, the approach to bringing local culture and liturgy together seemed to rely on a "top down" approach, rather than any genuine dialogue with Aboriginal and Islander peoples, in the way of McKelson or his colleagues.

Liturgical Texts—Tiwi and Murrinnpatha

This dismal conclusion of Hearn appears to have overlooked the significant contribution by the religious of Our Lady of the Sacred Heart and trained linguist Tess Ward. Over four decades, Ward served in the Darwin Diocese in the communities of Nguiu / Bathurst Island and Wadeye. In Nguiu, in dialogue with elders, Ward translated the texts of the Mass and sacraments of the Roman Rite into Tiwi, and likewise with the Wadeye community into the local Murrinnpatha language. In Wadeye, Ward enjoyed the valuable assistance of fellow religious and local Aboriginal woman Beatrice Demkadath Thardim, FDNSC. Ward and her companions worked painstakingly over many years on both projects. We are given an insight into Ward's methodology in her own words, recently recorded:

> We began our work on the liturgy with the traditional ritual element at the beginning of Mass where we sign ourselves with a cross while saying: "In the name of the Father and of

---

[75] Correspondence from Fr. Malcolm Fyfe to priests engaged in the Aboriginal Apostolate in the Darwin Diocese (February 1979). Diocese of Darwin Archives.

[76] Hearn, *A Theology of Mission*, 200.

the Son and of the Holy Spirit." I asked the elders: "What does 'in the name of' mean?" The elders responded, "That is easy, the Father, The Son and the Holy Spirit are with us and we want to honour them." So we will say, "Yile Neki, Wakal Nhinhi i Ngepan Kangkarlmawu thaninganmardardi kathu." This means, in English, "Our Father Your Son and the Spirit of the one who lives above, enter into us."

Ward worked in a systematic way to translate the liturgical texts, not literally word for word, but rather beginning with the meaning of the text. The translations were attentive to the particular thought patterns, idioms, and forms of expression of the local people. While Kevin McKelson was translating the Roman Rite in La Grange / Bidyadanga in the western Kimberley, Tess Ward across the continent was also leading a team of vernacular translators. At the time, Ward did not see a need to "back translate" the texts into English, so her work was confined to the two communities.

What can be said of McKelson can equally be said of Tess Ward, who, guided by the exacting principles of dynamic equivalence, provides a further example of liturgical interculturation, resulting in two Aboriginal Catholic communities continuing to intelligently participate in the church's liturgy.

An Aboriginal Catholic Priest in Darwin

In 1975, Patrick Dodson became the first Aboriginal to be ordained a Catholic priest.[77] In a report from the Port Keats Mission, leader Fr. John Leary wrote, "One final and important area which I could not adequately begin to evaluate is the work that Pat Dodson did at the level of the Aboriginal ceremonies. Maybe only the future will really show the value of his work with the leaders and men of

---

[77] In preparation for ministry, Dodson spent a year immersing himself in his tribal culture in Broome. No other Aboriginal man has become an ordained priest, although Boniface Perdjert, from the Kardu Diminin people at Port Keats, spent a year with Pat Dodson and was to serve many years as an ordained deacon and leader in the community.

Port Keats."[78] High praise indeed for Dodson, who spent only one year in the Port Keats community, yet it seems that Dodson felt restricted in his ministry. He wrote to McKelson, "I have attempted a few [liturgical] things but like yourself am wary about developing something that the People have their heart in but hasn't the official backing of the Authorities."[79] Dodson is alluding to difficulties he had already experienced with his bishop.[80] Nevertheless, the Aboriginal Dodson expressed clearly in his correspondence to McKelson what he believed his fellow sisters and brothers would find "a suitable style of liturgy."

Catholic liturgy for Aboriginal and Islander Catholics should include, according to Dodson, three essential elements: (1) singing in the vernacular, (2) dancing that expresses central teaching, and (3) attending to formation and the setting for where and how we celebrate. Unfortunately, Dodson does not explain these components. While the first and third points perhaps seem self-explanatory, it is hard to know what he means by dancing that expresses central teaching. Is he referring to newly created dancing that interprets Church teaching in a traditional Aboriginal way? Or suggesting that comparable traditional ceremonial dance be included in the liturgy, as was the practice in the Eastern Kimberley? We do not have any written record of examples of the inculturation that Dodson developed at Port Keats; however,

---

[78] Acts and Proceedings of the Northern Territory Catholic Mission's Conference, 1979, 61. Diocese of Darwin Archives.

[79] Correspondence from Patrick Dodson, at Casuarina, to Kevin McKelson, May 11, 1977. ATSIS, Canberra. This liturgy is important because it is the only available documentation concerning inculturation of the Catholic liturgy from an Aboriginal perspective.

[80] While at the Port Keats Mission, Fr. Patrick Dodson restored traditional culture that had been officially suppressed for Catholic Aboriginals by the church over decades. He also worked at inculturating the Roman Rite. However, he caught the ire of Bishop John O'Loughlin, who is known to have remarked that he had "tolerated (Fr Dodson), but not approved of the resurrection of pagan ways." The conflict between Dodson and O'Loughlin became very public and is recorded in Hearn, *A Theology of Mission*, 265–74. The honorary Patrick Dodson is currently a celebrated and revered elder, and federal senator in the federal Government.

cultural elements continue to enrich local liturgical celebrations. In a community where tribal unrest often sits just beneath the surface and violence can break out at any time, art that illustrates the local language missal text expresses hope for a peaceful future.

Painting. Wadeye landscape. The peaceful dove
is the totem of the Kardu Diminin Clan.
Copyright © 2022 Barbara Nimpangarl Narndu

Dodson affirmed McKelson's continuing development of the liturgy celebrated at La Grange. He makes clear that the celebration of the liturgy must remain fluid and not become fixed in a time or place. Dodson is completely against liturgy that becomes "the *total* or *only form* associated with that place and way of doing it." He then makes the point that the style of liturgy has to centre around the Catholic Eucharist but its story has to be linked with God's dealing and presence amongst Aboriginal People. An Aboriginal man has to worship God as an Aboriginal man and not as a quasi white man. Unfortunately the Eucharist is associated with being non-Aboriginal in character, but the theology is obviously something greater than the culture it finds expression and form in.[81]

There can be no doubt that Dodson, the then-Aboriginal priest, was inviting a much deeper conversation about liturgy celebrated with Aboriginal people than had yet been envisaged. He was not speaking of simply adding elements of Aboriginal culture to the liturgy. Neither did he wish to change the essential elements of the Roman Rite, that is, to center around the Catholic Eucharist. Rather, Dodson wanted Aboriginal spirituality/religion to find its own way into the church's liturgy. This seems a similar cry to his Indigenous sister Canadian Eva Solomon:

In our brokenness, are we still looking outside our culture for a saviour instead of the Christ who must rise out of our own tradition, just as salvation came from the Jews because Jesus himself came out of the Jewish culture? What if the Son of God had been born among the Anishinaabeg? Would the Gospel images then be sheep and shepherds, wine, and olive oil? What Christological images would we have?[82]

Dodson is asking that his sisters and brothers need to identify with Christ as an Australian Aboriginal or Torres Strait Islander, one who is truly their ancestor from the dreaming, whom they continue to remember in their own cultural way. In this he is affirmed by St. Pope John Paul II, who notably said to First Nation Australians in Alice Springs, "All over the world people worship God and read his

---

[81] Correspondence from Patrick Dodson, at Casuarina, to Kevin McKelson, May 11, 1977.

[82] Solomon, *Come Dance with Me*, 112.

word in their own language, and color the great signs and symbols of religion with touches of their own traditions. Why should you be different from them in this regard, why should you not be allowed the happiness of being with God and each other in Aboriginal fashion?"[83]

Conclusion

Australia's First Nation Christians continue to be immersed in their long traditional heritage where the creative and life-giving forces are still very much alive. In Dodson's words, "The spirits of the ancestors of all human, plant and animal life are represented in the life forms.... It is from these life forces that Aboriginal people get their identity."[84] And that identity is nurtured by ceremony celebrated continuously over sixty-five thousand years. Ancient traditional ceremony, like the Roman Rite, follows certain principles. We know that all in the community know their proper place, and all participate. Dancing and singing bring to life the foundational myths that are essential to the remembering that links the past to the present. Certain dances are reserved for men or women, and songs, expressed in different genres according to the performers, are simple and repetitive in nature. Special places are significant—for example, certain water holes are considered sacred and the water is used in ceremony. Importantly also, stories told in ceremony are adapted according to events that affect the community.

---

[83] This is eloquently expressed in what has become a watershed speech for Australian First Nations Catholics. See Address of John Paul II to the Aborigines and Torres Strait Islanders in Blatherskite Park, Alice Springs (Australia), (1986), 12.

[84] Patrick Dodson, "The Land Our Mother, the Church Our Mother," in *Discovering an Australian Theology*, ed. Peter Malone (Homebush: St. Pauls, 1988), 83. See also Anne Pattel-Gray, ed., *Aboriginal Spirituality: Past, Present, Future* (Blackburn, Victoria: HarperCollins Religious, 1996), and *Rainbow Spirit Theology: Towards an Australian Aboriginal Theology by the Rainbow Spirit Elders* (Blackburn, Victoria: HarperCollins Religious, 1997).

Dr. Miriam Rose Ungunmerr-Baumann tells it this way:

> We wait for the right time for our ceremonies and our meetings. The right people must be present. Everything must be done in the proper way. Careful preparations must be made. We don't mind waiting, because we want things to be done with care. Sometimes many hours will be spent on painting the body before an important ceremony.[85]

It goes without saying that aspects of the traditional ceremony need critique if they are to become part of the Roman Rite, in the same way that the Roman Rite itself continues to undergo reform. In 2010, a group of young Aboriginal Catholics met in Darwin as part of the preparation for the celebrations of the canonization of Australia's first saint, Mary of the Cross MacKillop, in Rome. After becoming acquainted with Mary MacKillop, the young ones decided that Mary is a brolga: a large, strong, and stately bird, yet one that treads delicately on water lilies. Next, the young First Nation Catholics composed a chant, accompanied with clapping sticks and didgeridoo. Finally, they prepared a dance to bring the gifts to the altar at the Mass following the canonization.

The young Indigenous Australians, unfamiliar with Mary MacKillop, needed to hear the story in its historical context. And the organizers needed to listen respectfully to another way—the way of remembering by young Indigenous people who were steeped in their ancient ceremonial heritage. The respectful engagement between equal partners recognized that we share a spirituality but express it differently, according to our cultural traditions.

While this is one successful example of liturgical interculturation, serious obstacles remain. For example, First Nation Australians continue to live with the pain and trauma of colonialism. At sporting events and in other public arenas where significant Indigenous peoples are targeted, racism is manifestly obvious. And in the ecclesial

---

[85] Miriam Rose Ungunmerr-Baumann, "*Dadirri:* Inner Deep Listening and Quiet Still Awareness," *EarthSong Journal: Perspectives in Ecology, Spirituality and Education* 3, no. 4 (Autumn 2017): 14–15.

Dance. Brolga dance accompanying gifts,
St. Paul's Outside the Walls, Rome.
Copyright © 2010 Sisters of St. Joseph of the Sacred Heart

space, the Roman Rite is considered superior, often reflected in a preoccupation with rubrics. There is also a lingering opinion by some that pre-Christian ceremony is pagan.[86] In the midst of these barriers, Pope Francis calls for change:

> We can take up into the liturgy many elements proper to the experience of indigenous peoples in their contact with nature, and respect native forms of expression in song, dance, rituals, gestures and symbols. The Second Vatican

---

[86] At the opening Mass of the Second Assembly of the Fifth Plenary Council of the Catholic Church in Australia on Sunday, July 3, 2022, which began with a smoking ceremony and welcome to the country, a number of delegates declared that they would not participate if the Mass began with a "pagan" ceremony.

Council called for this effort to inculturate the liturgy among indigenous peoples; over fifty years have passed and we still have far to go along these lines.[87]

But major shifts are needed that call for cultural conversion. We will require openness and deep listening to the Spirit if we are to recognize Dodson's claim that "ritual practice in Aboriginal culture [is] capable of the same salvific encounters as the performance of the sacramental rite in the Roman rite."[88] While not insurmountable, when barriers are broken down and genuine dialogue and goodwill occur, only then will we achieve Miriam Rose's desire that "deep Aboriginal ceremonial instincts can find genuine expression in our Christian celebrations."[89]

---

[87] Pope Francis, *Querida Amazonia*, post-synodal exhortation, February 2, 2020, section 82, www.vatican.va.

[88] Patrick L. Dodson, Jacinta K. Elston, and Brian F. McCoy, "Leaving Culture at the Door: Aboriginal Perspectives on Christian Belief and Practice," *Pacifica* 19 (October 2006): 257.

[89] Miriam-Rose Ungunmerr-Baumann, "Autobiographical Reflections," *Nelen Yubu* 28 (Spring 1986): 13.

5

Silent Inculturation

Japan's Hidden Christians and the Criterion of the Cross

Antonio D. Sison

The Martyrs of Nagasaki (1597), engraving by Wolfgang Kilian, Augsburg (1581–1663).
Public domain

The road traversing a dense residential area is narrow and steep, until the vista opens to a wide plaza with a single focal point at its far end. As I walk alone in its direction, I feel that I am being ushered into a space of great solemnity and stillness. It is a bronze and stone monument, severe in its rectangular lines, and striking for its large sculpture of several praying human figures lined up in a straight, horizontal row to form a cruciform configuration. Immediately, I noticed two things. First, each appears to be floating on air; belying the weight of the bronze, their feet do not touch the ground. Second, my eyes are drawn to three conspicuously smaller figures among them. It is disquieting to realize that they are minors. In fact, it is disquieting to know that on February 5, 1597, each of the persons represented in this sculptural tableau were crucified to their deaths on this very spot. Nishizaka Hill in Nagasaki is the Japanese Golgotha where the first twenty-six of an estimated six hundred Christians were publicly executed. Counted among these martyrs were three Japanese Jesuits; four Spaniards, one Mexican, one Portuguese from India, who were all Franciscan Missionaries; and seventeen Japanese members of the Third Order of St. Francis. So pitiless was this execution that it did not spare the young—João Gotó, seventeen; Antonio, thirteen; and Luis Ibaraki, twelve.

Less than a year earlier, on October 19, 1596, the Spanish ship *San Felipe* crashed into the rocks off the coast of Urado. The cargo vessel was plying the Manila-Acapulco galleon trade route laden with fine silk, brocade, and gold. When the local authorities, in accordance with Japanese law, sequestered the cargo and detained the crew, the incident escalated to Toyotomi Hideyoshi (1537–98), the ruling shogun of Japan.[1] Hideyoshi gave the Jesuit intermediaries hesitant assurances of

---

[1] Toyotomi Hideyoshi is the second of three "Great Unifiers" of Japan, the other two being Oda Nobunaga (1534–82) and Tokugawa Ieyasu (1543–1616). In "Christian Martyrdom in Asia: Bearing Testimony to the Love of God," Peter Phan summarizes Hideyoshi's contribution: "Hideyoshi furthered Nabunaga's project of unifying Japan by systematically confiscating weapons from peasants and soldier-monks, subjecting landowners and tenant farmers to the samurai class, opening free trade, encouraging economic growth through tax incentives, controlling the currency, and subjugating the domains of independent daimyos, including those in Kyūshū and Shikoku, where there were a large number of Christians." Paul Middleton, ed., *The Wiley Blackwell Companion to Christian Martyrdom* (Hoboken, NJ: John Wiley & Sons, 2020), 383.

returning the seized cargo in view of maintaining good trade relations with Spain. He changed his mind, however, when the ship's pilot, in an ill-conceived display of colonial arrogance, warned that it was Spain's modus operandi to send missionaries as the king's advanced guard to a military invasion as it previously did in the conquest of the neighboring Philippines and, earlier, the Americas.[2] Already wary of the politicized power play between the rivaling Franciscans and Jesuits, and goaded by his cronies, the infuriated Hideyoshi was convinced that the growing foreign influence was a threat to his rule, indeed, to the sovereignty of Japan.[3]

Nine years earlier, Hideyoshi demanded that the Portuguese Jesuit vice-provincial Gaspar Coelho respond to a set of queries regarding the missionaries' motives and actions. As detailed by the noted historian C. R. Boxer,[4] they read as follows:

---

[2] C. R. Boxer asserts that this very suspicion was already expressed by the bonzes as early as 1570. Richard H. Drummond, *A History of Christianity in Japan* (Grand Rapids: William B. Eerdmans, 1971), 166.

[3] Following his predecessor Oda Nobunaga, Hideyoshi previously maintained friendly relations with Christianity; his real hostility was directed toward militant Buddhism. He was even reported to have intimated that had it not been for the Christian prohibition on polygamy, he would have been a convert himself. Drummond, *A History of Christianity in Japan*, 76–77. Moreover, on July 21, 1590, he gave a cordial reception for an embassy of four young Japanese nobles returning from a goodwill mission to the pope and the Spanish king. The embassy was organized by the charismatic Italian Jesuit missionary Alessandro Valignano. See ibid., 70–71. The historical episode was fictionalized in the Japanese television miniseries *Magi: The Tenshō Boy's Embassy* (dir. Shunichi Nagasaki, 2019). Valignano made significant contributions to the Christian mission in Japan, such as advocating for native clergy and the establishment of seminaries. See Drummond, *A History of Christianity in Japan*, 66–73.

[4] C. R. Boxer, *The Christian Century in Japan, 1549–1650*, 3rd ed. (Berkeley: University of California Press, 1974), 146. Regarding the charge of desecrating shrines and temples, the Jesuit Coelho qualifies that zealous Japanese converts were likely to have been responsible for this since the missionaries did not wield political power. See ibid., 147. Neil S. Fujita argues, however, that Coelho was incorrect. "Many padres encouraged and praised the Japanese Christians' violent actions against the idols and buildings of 'the teachings of the devils.'" Fujita,

1. Why are the *padres* so desirous of making converts, and why do they even use force on occasion?
2. Why do they destroy Shinto and Buddhist temples, and persecute the bonzes, instead of compromising with them?
3. Why do they eat useful and valuable animals like horses and cows?
4. Why do the Portuguese buy many Japanese and export them from their native land as slaves?

On one hand, the questions point to the cracks and inconsistencies in the missionaries' engagement with Japanese culture, religion, and political authorities. On the other hand, they also bespeak Hideyoshi's suspicion that, ultimately, the goal of the Christian missions was the conquest of Japan.[5] This had been weighing heavily on the shrewd Hideyoshi, who, in the same year, issued an edict of expulsion against the Jesuit missionaries. Stipulated therein were eleven policies and charges against them and the Japanese Christian converts. The edict asserted, "Japan is a country of the Kami [Gods], and for the padres to come hither and preach a devilish law, is a most reprehensible and evil thing."[6] Be that as it may, Hideyoshi was lenient in enforcing his own injunction, at least, until the fateful *San Felipe* shipwreck.

On January 8, 1597, Hideyoshi, with the intention of creating a public spectacle, issued the death sentence for the twenty-four *San*

Japan's Encounter with Christianity: The Catholic Mission in Pre-Modern Japan (Mahwah, NJ: Paulist Press, 1991), 123.

[5] Hideyoshi's suspicion was also fueled by staunchly anti-Christian personalities in his inner circle. Apparently, one of his personal counselors, Seyakuin Zenso, brought forward slanderous accusations against the Christians to a drunken Hideyoshi, who lost no time issuing the edict of expulsion, notwithstanding a previous cordial meeting with Coelho. Fujita, *Japan's Encounter with Christianity*, 111–13.

[6] Boxer, *The Christian Century in Japan*, 148. Coelho's reaction to Hideyoshi's injunction was impulsive and belligerent, attempting to incite armed resistance among the Christian *daimyo*, and imploring Manila to send armed soldiers. Widely opposed by his confreres, including Alessandro Valignano and the Jesuit superior in Manila who rebuked him, Coelho's efforts were in vain. See ibid., 149.

Felipe missionaries. This was bannered on a wooden board through a tortuous, monthlong death march, mostly on foot, from Sakai in the south of Osaka to Nagasaki, where they were to be crucified.[7] The charge was based solely on religious grounds.[8] In August of the same year, Hideyoshi issued these words to an envoy sent by the Spanish governor-general of the Philippines, who requested a return of the confiscated cargo and the remains of the martyrs.

> If some Japanese preachers and laymen come from Japan to your country, preach the teaching of Shinto, and create disorders by leading your people astray, are you as the ruler pleased with it? You would not be. So, can you blame me for that?[9]

Without suggesting that the massacre of innocent people can be justified, the shogun's question is a valid critique of the Eurocentric colonial mindset and the scarlet thread of genocide and cultural liquidation that, in the name of religion, runs through its historical trail in Asia, Latin America, and Africa.

The Nagasaki crucifixions did not generate the impact that Hideyoshi had expected. Paradoxically, they shone a brighter light on Christianity as a religion worth dying for. They also inflamed the zeal

---

[7] The edict reads, "These men have come from the Philippines with the title of ambassadors and remained in Kyoto preaching the Christian religion, which I rigorously prohibited in past years. I thus command that they be executed along with the Japanese who have joined their religion. And so these twenty-four will be crucified in Nagasaki. Let all know that I again prohibit from now on said religion. If anyone dares to disobey this order, he will be punished together with his family." Diego Yuuki, SJ, *The Twenty-Six Martyrs of Nagasaki* (Tokyo: Ederle, 2006), 47. Hanging from his cross, the Japanese Jesuit Paul Miki, who was a gifted preacher, was reported to have made a correction to Hideyoshi's sentence, exclaiming, "I am not from the Philippines. I am a Japanese, and a Jesuit Brother. I have not committed any crime but die only for having preached the religion of our Lord Jesus Christ." See ibid., 77.

[8] Yuuki argues that "the gist of the degree was exclusively religious—Hideyoshi had condemned them for preaching the gospel." Ibid., 47.

[9] Fujita, *Japan's Encounter with Christianity*, 138.

of Christians who were present, several of whom rushed to secure relics from the martyrs' blood.

Tokugawa Ieyasu (1542–1616), the third great unifier of Japan, shared the same antipathy toward missionaries and Christian converts as his predecessor Hideyoshi. Credited for stabilizing the *bakufu*[10] feudal political system laid out by the succession of two shoguns who preceded him—Hideyoshi and Oda Nobunaga (1534–82)—Ieyasu's "pax Tokugawae" practically ensured the exclusion of the Christian missions. The reason for this lies in the fact that the rigid feudal structure he saw to completion was ideologically supported by the three traditional Japanese religions: Shintoism, Buddhism, and Confucianism.

In the years that followed Ieyasu's reign, two events are worth mentioning. First, Ieyasu's successors firmly established the extreme measure of shutting the doors of Japan to foreign influence; this meant a radical suppression of Christianity by expelling all missionaries and annihilating local Christian converts, accompanied by stringent restrictions on European trade. Second, a revolt in Shimabara and Amakusa involving thousands of oppressed Christian peasants erupted in the autumn of 1637 and lasted for two years; for the Tokugawa *bakufu*, this major civil uprising was a clear indication of Christian motives to take over the reins of power in the country. This precipitated a total ban of Portuguese vessels from entering Japan, and "the search and destroy mission against the Christians was intensified even more thoroughly than before."[11]

---

[10] The *bakufu* or central government vis-à-vis *han* or regional governments are also jointly referred to in the appellation *bakuhan*. As described by James W. White, "Its particular political perspective involves the defining aspect of the state, that is, the creation of a governmental monopoly of the legitimate use of physical force within a given territory—in this case, the entirety of Japan." White, "State Growth and Popular Protest in Tokugawa Japan," *Journal of Japanese Studies* 14, no. 1 (Winter 1988): 1.

[11] Fujita, *Japan's Encounter with Christianity*, 186. For fuller treatment of the Tokugawa *bakufu*'s anti-Christian campaign, see ibid., 147–247.

The *Fumi-e* Apocalypse

At first glance, there is nothing unusual about a *fumi-e*. It is a Christian icon, customarily in bronze relief, embedded on a piece of wooden board. The historical context of its use, however, makes the icon stand on its head. The *fumi-e* was created specifically as a tool to effectuate apostasy during the anti-Christian inquisition of the Tokugawa period. The method is simple. The suspected Christian is compelled to publicly declare that he or she has chosen to apostatize by trampling on the *fumi-e*; refusal or hesitation meant torture and death. This explains why the image has a worn away appearance; it is the result of the treading underfoot from untold apostasies. Also known as *ebumi*, the *fumi-e* was first introduced as a method of torture by Takenaka Umene, *bugyō* or magistrate of Nagasaki from 1626 to 1631.[12] The one I've seen is a replica created for Martin Scorsese's riveting historical epic *Silence* (2016), which is credited for generating global attention to the Hidden Christians.[13] However, an earlier film, Masahiro Shinoda's *Chinmoku* ("Silence," 1971), more effectually captures the tinderbox moment of the *fumi-e* inquisition. The poetics of the human face, through Shinoda's lens, becomes a threshold of an inner and outer Gethsemane experience, particularly when the woman character Kiku (Iwashita Shima) is pressured to step on the *fumi-e* while witnessing her husband's torture.

---

[12] Stephen Turnbull, *The Kakure Kirishitan of Japan: A Study of Their Development, Beliefs and Rituals to the Present Day* (London: Routledge, 2013), 41. For this historical information, Turnbull draws from an illustrated book by Gizaemon Kondō, a former mayor of the town of Ikitsuki. *Ikitsuki no Kakure Kirishitan* (Ikitsuki, Nagasaki Prefecture: Ikitsuki Town Office, 1973), 48.

[13] The other *fumi-e* I've seen exhibited at museums within Nagasaki Prefecture—Hirado, Sotome, Nagasaki City—are also reproductions. The few originals that remain extant in Japan are permanently emplaced and seasonally exhibited at the Tokyo National Museum. The collection includes nineteen brass *fumi-e* commissioned by the Nagasaki Magistrate's Office in 1669. *E-Museum: National Treasures and Important Cultural Properties of National Institutes for Cultural Heritage, Japan*, https://emuseum.nich.go.jp.

The scene mirrors a chilling account recorded in the *Kirishito-ki*, a 1658 official compilation of documents detailing the methods of the Japanese Inquisition under the grand inquisitor Inoue Chikugo no kami Masashige (1585–1661).[14] In another sequence when the *fumi-e* image is that of "Santa Maria," Shinoda appeals to the feminine impulse in Japanese culture that identifies with the figure of the Virgin Mary,[15] thus pushing the tensive moment even further to the edge.

Fumi-e inquisition in the Japanese film *Chinmoku*.
Copyright © 1971 Toho Company

---

[14] "Old wives and women when made to tread upon the image (*fumie*) of Deus get agitated and red in the face; they cast off their headdress; their breath comes in rough gasps; sweat pours from them. And, according to the individual, there are reportedly women who venerate the *fumie*, but in a way to remain unobserved." George Elison, *Deus Destroyed: The Image of Christianity in Early Modern Japan* (Cambridge, MA: Harvard University Press, 1973), 204. Innervated by the philosophy "apostates better than martyrs," the brilliant and ruthless Inoue Chikugo no kami Masashige was the supreme enforcer of the Bakufu Inquisition. "Inoue Chikugo was the ideal inquisitor, demonic because intellectual." Ibid., 187.

[15] In writing about Endō Shūsaku, author of the acclaimed novel *Chinmoku* ("Silence") and his special attachment to his mother, Japanese American artist Makoto Fujimura observes, "This feminine influence in Japanese culture affects deeply the orphaned psyche of culture, and beauty is tied to feminine sacrifice and the feminine fragrance. Such a relational reality points to the faith Endo embraced, the feminine God expressed through the Virgin Mother. For someone like Endo, it would have been even harder to step on the fumi-e of the Virgin Mary than to step on the image of Jesus." Fujimura, *Silence and Beauty* (Downer's Grove, IL: InterVarsity Press, 2016), 41.

From a modern, Western, non-Catholic mindset, the *fumi-e* test might seem insignificant, certainly not worth the sacrifice of one's life. From the perspective of a Japanese convert in the Tokugawa period, however, faith is not principally moored on abstract, doctrinal propositions; it is also nontextual, visual, material, and visceral.[16] Although he was not specifically theorizing Japanese religious culture, Charles Taylor, 2008 Kyoto Prize laureate for philosophy, offers relevant insights on the premodern understanding of material objects as they relate to belief. In a premodern, "enchanted" worldview, material objects were the very *loci* of causal power and influence. The human mind does not impute meaning on them; they are, in and of themselves, understood to be "charged" objects that can, exogenously and magically, wield power: "In the enchanted world, the meaning exists already outside of us, prior to contact; it can take us over, we can fall into its field of force. It comes on us from the outside."[17] This understanding from what Taylor terms as a self that is "porous" (as against one that is "buffered" by scientific, materialist thinking) would be most sensitive and receptive to a Catholic sacramental imagination where certain objects and relics are deemed sacred—the divine presence manifested in historical visibility. Thus, on a cultural (Japanese), perspectival (enchanted/porous worldview), and sacramental (Catholic) tri-level, the *Kakure Kirishitan* believed that trampling on a *fumi-e* was not simply a matter of stepping on an object; it meant trampling on the real presence of *Deus* or Santa Maria. Thus, the *fumi-e* was a precision-guided inquisition weapon. Coupled with a system of surveillance that tapped into the communal five-family

---

[16] For Fujimura, the power of the *fumi-e* is hinged on an either/or between Christian and Japanese identity: "But to a Christian who has internalized the image of Christ as their Savior, a fumi-e uniquely portrays their own experience of choosing between being a Christian and being a Japanese. Creation of this dichotomy, as false as it is, is the brilliance of fumi-e as a torture weapon." Ibid., 130–31.

[17] Charles Taylor, *A Secular Age* (Cambridge, MA: Harvard University Press, 2007), 34.

mutual support structure or *gonin-gumi*, the *fumi-e* proved to be a potent method to track, ferret out, and persecute Christians.[18]

The forms of torture employed by the *bakuhan* were marked by a barbarous excess of violence and cruelty that rivaled the Spanish Inquisition (1478–1834). The "disinterested" firsthand account of staunch Protestant François Caron, a seventeenth-century French-Dutch trader in Hirado, graphically and sympathetically describes some of the untold suffering of the martyrs under such methods:

> Firstly, they took a red-hot iron bar and branded all twelve persons in their foreheads, and thereafter demanded whether they would recant and renounce their faith? Whereupon they all resolutely answered "No; there is but one God through whom we can obtain salvation, and therefore we cannot deny him." Hereupon they were again branded twice, upon each cheek, and as they still refused to recant they were stripped stark naked, both men and women, and, with their arms and legs fully extended, were soundly flogged with heavy lashes until they were half dead.... It is indeed extraordinary that amongst them are so many who remain steadfast to the end, and endure so many insufferable torments, in despite of their scanty knowledge of the Holy Scripture.[19]

Within this cruel context, remnant communities of Christians in secluded mountain villages and offshore islands surrounding Nagasaki endured and survived, albeit surreptitiously, as *Kakure Kirishitan* or Hidden Christians.

Thus far, we've explored pivotal turns in early missionary history in Japan and the torrents of persecution under the Tokugawa *bakuhan*.

---

[18] "In the years from 1640 to 1658 well over two thousand Christians were detected in all but eight of the sixty-six provinces of Japan, and in the following decades many more were arrested often in substantial groups." Drummond, *A History of Christianity in Japan*, 110–11.

[19] François Caron and Joost Schouten, *A True Description of the Mighty Kingdoms of Japan & Siam*, ed. C. R. Boxer (1935; repr., Amsterdam: N. Israel; London: De Capo Press, 1971), 79–80. Citations refer to the N. Israel–De Capo edition.

The historical sketch, purposefully diachronic and relativizing, offers heuristic touchstones for an inductive exploration of inculturation as it may have occurred in the faith life of the *Kakure Kirishitan*.

Silent Inculturation

Consisting of released captives who survived the *fumi-e* inquisition, as well as believers who remained undetected, the *Kakure Kirishitan* continued to defy the anti-Christian zeitgeist of the Tokugawa period, finding incredible ways of preserving their Christian identity and persevering in their underground worship life bereft of support from missionary priests and institutional structures. From the crucible of persecution emerged religious symbols and articles, prayers and liturgies, even a normative text, all of which the *Kakure* re-created and developed from fragmentary recollections of sixteenth-century Portuguese missionary practice and oral tradition. These devotional expressions were often hidden behind the protective veil of Buddhist and Shinto forms and observances. Dorothea Filus notes that the degree of secrecy was directly proportional to the virulence of the *gonin-gumi* spy system; a higher number of suspected Christians caught and exposed meant a surge in persecutions—thus, the exigency of concealment. Not surprisingly, their way of worshiping varied according to region, which, Filus argues, is attributed to the duration of each area's exposure to the instruction of the missionaries.[20] In view of these distinctions, the following exploration of selected *Kakure* devotional expressions includes, as much as possible, some reference to the milieu or region within which they were discovered and presumed to have been practiced.

Maria Kannon

Maria Kannon is a feminine representation of a Buddhist deity, usually depicting a mother cradling an infant or a little child, that

---

[20] Dorothea Filus, "Secrecy and Kakure Kirishitan," *Bulletin of Portuguese-Japanese Studies*, no. 7 (2003): 94.

was adopted by the *Kakure Kirishitan* as a covert stand-in for the Virgin Mary. Since the *danka* system (temple system, also known as *terauke seido*)—enforced by the third Tokugawa shōgun Iemitsu (1604–51) in reaction to the Shimabara Rebellion—compelled every household to register with a Buddhist temple to keep Christianity in check, the practice of obscuring Christian devotions with a Buddhist smokescreen made strategic sense. I encountered various iterations of Maria Kannon—statuettes, scroll paintings, even miniature dolls—while doing on-site research at the Memorial Museum of the Twenty-Six Martyrs and the Ōura Cathedral in Nagasaki City, Museum of History and Folklore in Sotome, and Ikitsuki-cho Municipal Museum Shima no Yakata in Hirado. The diverse locales from which the images were sourced suggest that the veneration of Maria Kannon was widely practiced among the *Kakure* communities in the main island of Kyūshū. As the name denotes, the original image is that of Kannon or Kan'-on, the Buddhist deity of compassion. With an uncanny visual resemblance to traditional Catholic Marian icons, particularly the Madonna and child, it is not difficult to see how Maria Kannon could be a convincing Japanese / East Asian mirror of the Virgin Mary. Since the Kannon image did not need to be altered or camouflaged, the identity substitution was detectable only through the eyes of faith of the *Kakure Kirishitan*, allowing them to continue their Marian devotion below the radar of the shogunate and spying non-Christian neighbors.

In the period between the first and second centuries, Indian Mahāyāna Buddhism introduced the enlightened being of compassion known as the bodhisattva. Among numerous bodhisattvas is Avalokiteśvara, otherwise known in Japan as Kanzeon, or its simplified form Kannon (Kuan-shi-yin or Guanyin in China). As Maria Reis-Habito notes, an entire chapter on Kannon can be found in the *Lotus Sutra*, which describes the bodhisattva as a worker of miracles whose mission is to save every living being who, in the face of various natural calamities and human injustices, prays for help in the deity's name. Intangible spiritual gifts such as deliverance from materialism, hatred, and ignorance are also attributed to Kannon.[21] The bodhisattva is known to have multiform appearances, but it was the maternal feminine form that held special significance for the *Kakure Kirishitan* devotion to Maria Kannon.

Maria Kannon image from a
Kakure Kirishitan family.
*Copyright © Twenty-Six Martyrs Museum
and Monument, Nagasaki, Japan*

Notwithstanding fundamental differences between Kannon and Mary, they do share a similar maternal role in extending benevolence and care for a wounded humanity. In traditional Marian piety, the Virgin Mary holds an exalted status as an intercessor and mediator, drawing devotees to the redeeming grace of her Son Jesus Christ. The maternal face of divine compassion, Mary is in the frontline of devotion, receiving the supplications of devotees who seek her intercession for liberation from physical and spiritual maladies, social injustices, and needs of every kind. It is noteworthy that a maximalist

---

[21] Maria Reis-Habito, "Maria-Kannon: Mary, Mother of God, in Buddhist Guise," *Marian Studies* 47, no. 1 (1996): 52–53, https://ecommons.udayton.edu.

Mariology characterized post-Reformation Iberian Catholicism, and this is particularly significant among the Jesuits, whose founder, Ignacio de Loyola (1491–1556), had an impassioned devotion to *La Moreneta*, Our Lady of Montserrat, patron saint of Catalonia. His friend, confrere, and fellow Basque Francisco Xavier dedicated Japan to Mary when he landed in Kagoshima on August 15, 1549, the Feast Day of Our Lady of the Assumption. Conceivably, the *Kakure Kirishitan*'s devotion to Maria Kannon bears the legacy of Marian fervor espoused by the Jesuit missionaries.

To be sure, a special affinity with divine-maternal imagery was already ingrained in the Japanese religious imaginary long before the missionaries brought Marian devotion to Japan. Commenting on the works of writer Endō Shūsaku, particularly his 1992 nonfiction book *Kirishitan Jidai–Junkyō to kikyō no rekishi* ("The Christian Era: A History of Martyrdom and Apostasy"), Stephen Turnbull submits,

> Endō argues that the mother figure is at the heart of Japanese religion, so that this notion of the caring mother was already cherished by them when the example of the Virgin Mary was introduced. The images of her thus struck a chord of familiarity, which was reinforced by the European priests' own devotion.[22]

The local religious culture, already well disposed to the divine maternal, was to become the fertile humus upon which the imported Catholic Marian devotion would germinate and eventually flourish. The graciousness and compassion of a mother, Turnbull indicates, would play an important pastoral function to the *Kakure Kirishitan* who bore the guilt of apostasy in the aftermath of a *fumi-e* inquisition:

> To the underground believers, forced to deny their faith annually when they performed *fumi-e*, it was not to the stern judging God that they looked for comfort, but to his mother. This the missionaries had taught them, and it was accepted easily because it already fitted into the beliefs about the

---

[22] Turnbull, *The Kakure Kirishitan of Japan*, 104.

mother figure which the missionaries had not supplanted, but merely redirected.[23]

Another level of congruence can be found in the *Kakure Kirishitan* sacred text known as *Tenchi Hajimari no Koto*, "The Beginnings of Heaven and Earth."[24] The *Tenchi* is a collection of narratives drawn mainly from memories of oral catechetical teaching, interwoven with numerous elements from Japanese Indigenous folklore (fuller treatment appears in a succeeding section). Reis-Habito underscores the resonances between Kannon and the *Kakure Kirishitan*'s understanding of Mary or "Maruya," as she is referred to in the *Tenchi*. The young girl Maruya, who is mentioned forty-five times in the text, obeys a heavenly voice summoning her to live her life as a virgin. When a marriage proposal from the King of Luçon[25] threatens her virginal existence, she is taken up to heaven where she is named a "Santa," and comes back to earth with an intercessory role in the economy of salvation. Santa Maruya is then understood in Trinitarian terms and identified as the Holy Spirit: "Holy Mother, in heaven you take on the role of a helper; the Heavenly Father is Pater, the Son is Filio and the Holy Mother is Spirito Santo."[26] Fujiwara Ken argues for the Maruya-Kannon resonance on the basis of *ki*, which translates as "spirit" or "breath." Consistent with the Judeo-Christian conception, the *Tenchi* attributes Creation to the breath of God the Father, the same breath that filled Mary when she conceived Jesus by the power of the Holy Spirit (here, the immaculate conception occurs when the Holy Spirit, in the form of a butterfly, flies into the mouth of Maruya).

---

[23] Ibid., 105.

[24] Christal Whelan, *The Beginning of Heaven and Earth: The Sacred Book of Japan's Hidden Christians*, trans. Christal Whelan (Honolulu: University of Hawai'i Press, 1996), 19.

[25] Also "Luzon" or "Roson" denotes the Philippines. Currently, Luzon refers to the largest and most populous of the three major island groups (the other two being Visayas and Mindanao) of the Philippine archipelago.

[26] Fujiwara Ken, "Hendobutsu Maria Kannon no shinzō," *Kannon shinkō*, ed. Hayami Tasuku (Tokyo: Yusankaku Publishing, 1983), 290. As quoted in Reis-Habito, "Maria-Kannon: Mary, Mother of God, in Buddhist Guise," 62.

Elizabeth Johnson asserts that the Catholic piety in the period following the Council of Trent (1545–63) tended to ascribe traditionally pneumatological functions to Mary: "It is said that she is spiritually present to guide and inspire; that she forms Christ in believers and is the link between themselves and Christ; and that one goes to Christ through her. In the Scriptures, these are the actions of the Spirit. Furthermore, Mary is called intercessor, mediatrix, helper, advocate, defender, consoler, and counselor, functions that biblically belong to the Paraclete (Jn 14:16 and 26; 15:26; 16:7)."[27] Whether consciously or not, the *Tenchi* is a speculum of the pneumatological tendencies of Catholic Marian piety that burgeoned in the previous century.

On the Japanese side, the Shinto-Taoist concept of *ki* is akin to the biblical *ruach* or *pneuma*.

> The working of the spirit (*ki*) is described as transformation (*ge*) or miracle (*ki*). Kannon is the Bodhisattva mentioned most frequently in the *Nihon ryōiki*. This is probably because Kannon is described as transforming herself according to the needs of sentient beings. But there must be a human disposition for the working of Kannon, or, in Christian terms, an openness to the working of grace. This "disposition" is also pronounced as *ki*. The human disposition corresponds to the transformative working of the Holy Spirit....
>
> As Christians hold, according to the Tenchi, that everything is imbued with the Spirit or "breath" of God, so Buddhists believe that everything is sustained by *ki*. Both Mary and Kannon share in the transformative power of the Spirit, through Whom/which they are able to perform miracles.[28]

In Maria Kannon, the visual resemblance shared by Santa Maria and the Buddhist Kannon is validated by a deeper mutual assimilation, an inner relationship framed by a fair degree of dynamic equivalence.

---

[27] Elizabeth Johnson, *She Who Is: The Mystery of God in Feminist Theological Discourse* (New York: Crossroad, 1992), 129.

[28] Reis-Habito, "Maria-Kannon: Mary, Mother of God, in Buddhist Guise," 63.

Ohatsuhoage

Another devotional practice of the *Kakure Kirishitan* that merits discussion is the *Ohatsuhoage*, the celebration of a communal meal rooted in an ancient Shinto harvest ritual. The practice was conceived in the region of Kyūshū during the great persecution (1614–1873) of the Tokugawa period.[29] The Shinto ritual of *hatsuhō*, which literally means "the first ears of rice," is an autumn celebration at a local shrine or temple where devotees offer the new crop to the *kami* or deities. A staple of Japanese culinary culture, rice also holds a certain connection with the sacred.[30] Inasmuch as it is an essential component of Japanese cultural, political, and religious life, rice would find organic assimilation in the *Kakure Kirishitan*'s creative efforts to celebrate the Christian Eucharist in secret. Roger Vanzila Munsi describes how the elements of the Catholic sacrament of communion found analogically compatible substitutes drawn from *hatsuhō*:

> In point of fact, the early Japanese crypto-Christians took up, among other things, the specific Shinto tendencies of *hatsuhō* and intelligibly incorporated them, with very slight changes, into their basically Christian structures, rites and institutions, albeit in secret. More specifically, they axiomatically substituted the Eucharistic species of bread and wine (goodness of creation) by Japanese rice (the stuff and staple of everyday life) and *sake* as precious offerings to God. In so doing, they involved

---

[29] Roger Vanzila Munsi, "The Age-Old Ritual Practice of *Ohatsuhoage* among the Kakure Kirishitan Survivors: Intersection of Identities and Resources," *Annual Papers of the Anthropological Institute, Nanzan University* 9 (2019): 4, https://nanzan-u.repo.nii.ac.jp/records/3663.

[30] As Emiko Ohnuki-Tierney notes, "Because it embodied the sacred power of nigitama, rice was for a long time considered to provide sacred energy and power.... Traditionally, rice cakes are eaten when people need strength, such as the height of the agricultural season and the start of the New Year, a seasonal rite of passage. Even those Japanese who do not normally eat rice do so on New Year's ... when they were offered to the deities and shared among family members, relatives, and all other visitors." Ohnuki-Tierney, *Rice as Self: Japanese Identities through Time* (Princeton, NJ: Princeton University Press, 1994), 67–75.

themselves into a ritually prepared communal meal underlying a typically thanksgiving gathering. From that point on, they constructed seemingly integrated minority communities, and their secret corporate religious actions with patchy piecemeal adaptations consistently generated the so-called *Ohatsuhoage* religious ceremony as the alternative of the Eucharist.[31]

It has been noted as well that sashimi, a traditional delicacy consisting of delicately sliced pieces of raw fish, was also used in place of rice.[32] Evidently, the context of a shared meal connects the prescribed Eucharistic species of bread and wine[33] with the local fare used in *Ohatsuhoage*. Serving as relatively accessible substitute species when the extreme conditions made it difficult to source for bread and wine, rice or *sashimi* with *sake*, elements of a traditional Japanese meal, also offered a more immediate symbolic import, not to mention a deeper cultural equivalence for the *Kakure Kirishitan*.

Beyond the apparent equivalence of form and context of use is the *Ohatsuhoage*'s profound connection with the Catholic belief in *communio sanctorum* or the communion of saints, the spiritual union of all Christians, whether living or departed. In his study, Munsi refers to a firsthand narrative from a present-day *Kakure Kirishitan* community describing the institutionalization of *Ohatsuhoage* in 1630. The primary source discloses that the *Kakure* Eucharistic celebration "significantly made practitioners integrally become in communion and

---

[31] Munsi, "The Age-Old Ritual Practice of *Ohatsuhoage* among the Kakure Kirishitan Survivors," 10.

[32] I noted a similar rice/*sashimi* option at the re-created *Kakure Kirishitan* home on exhibit at the Memorial Museum of the Twenty-Six Martyrs in Nagasaki, which indicates both in text and diagram a liturgical meal consisting of rice or sashimi (also cooked fish) paired with sake; this practice was identified in a village in the Gotō Islands during the Christmas Eve celebration known as *Otaya* or *Natale*.

[33] The custom among the disciples of sharing an actual meal in Jesus' memory antedates the Eucharistic narratives of the Markan Gospel by forty years. Eugene LaVerdiere, *The Eucharist in the New Testament and the Early Church* (Collegeville, MN: Liturgical Press, 1996), 47.

or in communication with saints and their deceased predecessors."[34] The theological and ecclesiological significance of the communion of saints is vividly elucidated by Walter Kasper:

> For the communion which the church confers, and which it itself is, surpasses everything that purely human community can be. Death, at latest, is the inescapable frontier to human community. The loftiest utopian dreams about a kingdom of freedom and justice can never undo the injustice done to those who are already dead, the tortured and murdered of the past. So purely human utopias cannot provide a basis for a truly universal hope. But the communion of the church is communion even beyond death. This alone can satisfy the longing of the human heart. The communion of saints—the fellowship between the earthly and the heavenly church—is therefore the only final answer to the question about everlasting life and the unbreakable bond of love.[35]

For the Japanese cultural and religious imaginary, the unbroken relationship between the community of the living and the mystical community of the departed is not foreign by any means; ritualized ancestor veneration is a deeply rooted practice in Shinto-Buddhist traditions. In Tokugawa Japan where the peasantry constituted 80 percent of the population, the practice of Folk Shinto was customary and widespread. In agricultural rituals, adherents gather to offer prayer and thanksgiving to the *kami*, of whose ranks the ancestral spirits have joined.[36] During the summer festival of the dead known as *bon*,

---

[34] Munsi, "The Age-Old Ritual Practice of *Ohatsuhoage* among the Kakure Kirishitan Survivors," 11.

[35] Walter Kasper, *Theology and Church*, trans. Margaret Kohl (New York: Crossroad, 1992), 164.

[36] Inoue Nobutaka, "Perspectives toward Understanding the Concept of *Kami*," in *Kami: Contemporary Papers in Japanese Religion*, ed. Inoue Nobutaka (Tokyo: Institute for Japanese Culture and Classics, Kokugakuin University, 1998), 15–17.

the ancestors are believed to return to earth for a family reunion, "a celebration of the continuity of life."[37] With the introduction of Buddhism in 538 CE and its eventual harmonious fusion with Shinto, *kami* and Buddha identities came to be understood as somewhat merged, and the principles and practices of ancestor veneration took on a certain complexity.[38] In an enduring popular religious belief, family members who have passed are still considered to be part of the household, continuing to hold sway over the fortunes of their living kin and society in general: "The family as a social unit that includes not just the present but past and future generations is one of the most important institutions in Japan, playing a role in the continuing stability of Japanese society."[39]

It is fair to submit that the *Kakure Kirishitan*'s assimilation of the Catholic belief in the communion of saints was a near seamless one. Contextual considerations make this point even more compelling. For an underground Christian community barely surviving the constant threat of annihilation and bearing the dangerous memory of a great cloud of martyrs from among their own numbers, *Ohatsuhoage* and its affirmation of the communion of saints offered a liminal space where its members could still find a vital connection with transcendence. It allowed them to experience some semblance of a living, albeit invisible, community under the shadow of death.

---

[37] Ian Reader, Esben Andreasen, and Finn Steffánson, *Japanese Religions: Past and Present* (Honolulu: University of Hawai'i Press, 1993), 52–53.

[38] Nobutaka discusses some of the key changes in the ideology and practice resulting from the Shinto-Buddhist fusion. See "Perspectives in Understanding the Concepts of *Kami*," 4–6.

[39] Reader, Andreasen, and Steffánson, *Japanese Religions: Past and Present*, 56. For fuller treatment, see 54–58. For a contrasting perspective based on a study of the Japanese ancestral cult vis-à-vis Protestant missionary theology and practice, consult Mark R. Mullins, "Japanese Christians and the World of the Dead," *Mortality* 9, no. 7 (February 2004): 61–75.

Tenchi Hajimari no Koto

Translated as "The Beginnings of Heaven and Earth,"[40] the *Tenchi Hajimari no Koto* is considered a regional Bible of sorts for some *Kakure Kirishitan* communities. Excerpts from the diary of French missionary priest Bernard Thaddée Petitjean—in March 1865, some fifteen hidden Christians from Urakami revealed themselves to him, the first such disclosure for nearly three hundred years[41]—published in a nineteenth-century work indicates that the text was committed to writing sometime between 1822 and 1823 from an earlier transmitted oral tradition. Petitjean worked to transcribe and translate the text, noting the relative soundness of its content: "We found errors here and there, but so far nothing substantial."[42] Unfortunately, Petitjean's manuscript perished in the 1874 fire that gutted the *Société des Missions Étrangères de Paris* mission house in Yokohama. It was only in the 1930s when Tagita Kōya, pioneering scholar on the *Kakure Kirishitan*, discovered not just one but seven copies of the *Tenchi*. Four of the copies were sourced from Sotome, two came from the area of the Gotō Islands, and one from Nagasaki. Apparently, Tagita did not find any written text in either Hirado or Ikitsuki.[43]

As earlier mentioned, the *Tenchi* is not so much a translation or retelling of the entire Bible as an earnest recollection of biblical and catechetical fragments orally passed on by the missionaries, interwoven

---

[40] As in Whelan's translation *The Beginning of Heaven and Earth: The Sacred Book of Japan's Hidden Christians*. Stephen Turnbull's translation slightly differs: "Concerning the Creation of Heaven and Earth." See "Acculturation among the *Kakure Kirishitan*: Some Conclusions from the *Tenchi Hajimari no Koto*," in *Japan and Christianity: Impact and Responses*, ed. John Breen (London: Macmillan Press, 1996, and New York: St. Martin's Press, 1996), 63.

[41] Drummond, *A History of Christianity in Japan*, 303–4.

[42] Ann M. Harrington quotes Francisque Marnas, *La "Religion de Jésus" (Iaso ja-kyo) ressuscitée au Japon dans la seconde moitié du XIX siècle*, vol. 1 (Paris: Delhomme et Briquet, 1896), 507, in *Japan's Hidden Christians* (Chicago: Loyola University Press, 1993), 77.

[43] Turnbull, "Acculturation among the *Kakure Kirishitan*," 64.

with elements drawn from Buddhist concepts and Japanese folklore. Organized in a structure somewhat akin to a systematic theology, it is topically presented as follows:

1. Creation of the Heavens and the Earth
2. Creation of Adam and Eve
3. Temptation and Fall of Adam and Eve
4. The Great Flood
5. Annunciation and Immaculate Conception of Mary
6. Birth, Death, Resurrection, Ascension of Jesus
7. The End Times

Notably missing are all the books of the Old Testament following Genesis, abruptly jumping to a narrative of Mary's Annunciation. The role of the Virgin Mary in the economy of salvation acquires a distinct prominence here, validating, in all probability, the traditional Japanese attraction to the divine maternal as discussed earlier. So significant is the Marian influence here that unambiguous references to the mysteries of the rosary, both in its structure and meditations, characterize the *Tenchi*.[44]

The work of putting together the jigsaw pieces to codify the *Tenchi* from oral tradition into written form may be described as a conservative process. It involved a sustained, resolute effort to retrieve memories of missionary catechism, biblical and extrabiblical stories, ritual practices, and other sensory data that had been storehoused and transgenerationally imparted. Although the exact origin of the *Tenchi* remains unknown, scholars such as Christal Whelan who translated the entire text have identified its probable sources. Pointing to the numerous Latin and Portuguese words in the *Kakure* text, Whelan asserts that the 1592 Jesuit catechism known as the *Doctrina Christan* "had left an indelible impression in terms of its lexicon on the minds of those who created the *Tenchi*."[45]

---

[44] Ibid., 66.
[45] Whelan, *The Beginning of Heaven and Earth: The Sacred Book of Japan's Hidden Christians*, 20.

While textual analysis falls outside the scope of this study, I draw attention to a section of the *Tenchi* for its presumable resonance for the *Kakure Kirishitan*. Upon reading Whelan's translation of the text, I was taken by the final chapter and its allusion to the eschatological reversal found in the book of Revelation:

> Deusu the Almighty will descend from Heaven and blaze a trail for the myriad souls. Within three units of time Deusu will select some and mark them with his seal. All of them will be divided either on Deusu's left or Deusu's right. What a sad thing to see those on the left who, because they did not receive baptism, will fall together with the *tengu* to the hell called Benbo and get their stamp there. For all of eternity they will never float up to the light from the depths to where they have sunk.
>
> Those people on the right who received baptism will accompany Deusu to Paraiso where, once judged, their good works will be the basis of the ranks they will receive. It is guaranteed that they will all become buddhas and know unlimited fulfillment for all eternity. Ammei Zesusu.[46]

For comparison, it is instructive to refer to Revelation 22:12–14 (NRSV):

> See, I am coming soon; my reward is with me, to repay according to everyone's work. I am the Alpha and the Omega, the first and the last, the beginning and the end. Blessed are those who wash their robes, so that they will have the right to the tree of life and may enter the city by the gates. Outside are the fornicators and murderers and idolaters, and everyone who loves and practices falsehood....
>
> The one who testifies to these things says, "Surely I am coming soon." Amen. Come, Lord Jesus!

---

[46] Ibid., 66.

The prophetic admonition of an eschatological reversal in the *Tenchi* is strikingly similar to that of the latter chapter of Revelation, which does appear to be its likely basis. They share an analogous circumstantial background, reflecting the perilous historical milieu in which Christian communities were made to live—the former, the great persecution under the Tokugawa shogunate; the latter, the great persecution under the emperor Domitian (c. 95 CE).[47] Moreover, they both refuse to accord the last word to evil and their perpetrators; the Christian God is the sole and final arbiter of humanity's existence, and it is divine justice that will ultimately be served notwithstanding the temporal reign of terror and suffering. In the secret pages of the *Tenchi*, the *Kakure Kirishitan* hold a subversive prophetic-liberating message that militates against the oppressive status quo. While in the historical meantime, Christian identity is a death warrant, the opposite is true in *Deusu*'s eschatological future. The *fumi-e* apocalypse is reversed. Recalling the Matthean separation of the sheep from the goats (Matt. 25:31–33), the Christians will be saved while the unbaptized (those who do not wash their robes) will perish. It is not unreasonable to propose that this must have contributed to the uncanny fortitude and defiant faith of the *Kakure Kirishitan* as they faced torture and genocide.

While the development of the *Tenchi* can be described as conservative, it was, in like manner, "productive" because the process demanded filling in with narrative elements from Japanese religious culture the lacunae caused by the limits of memory and transmission under extreme conditions, not to mention the sheer passage of time. Threads from Buddhism, precisely because it was the religion prescribed by law, form part of the weave that make up the pages of the *Tenchi*. Among many other references as discussed in the works of Whelan, Turnbull, and others, the Buddhist influence is clearly seen in the penultimate line of the above eschatological section where the path to transcendence—becoming buddhas—is reserved for the baptized:

---

[47] M. Eugene Boring, "The Revelation to John," in *The New Interpreter's Study Bible: New Revised Standard Version with the Apocrypha* (Nashville: Abingdon Press, 2003), 2211.

"It is guaranteed that they will all become buddhas and know unlimited fulfillment for all eternity." The preceding line also alludes to the Buddhist concept of "ranks," the attainment of which is determined by one's virtuous actions.[48]

In sum, for the *Kakure Kirishitan* communities of Sotome, the Gotō Islands, and Nagasaki within which it had found devotional significance, the *Tenchi Hajimari no Koto* was a lifeline for their Christian faith. As Whelan's interview with Shigenori Murakami, a seventh-generation *Kakure Kirishitan* leader, reveals, "If it weren't for the Tenchi, Christianity would have completely died out in Japan."[49]

Two other inculturated *Kakure* devotions are worth noting. *Bastian no Higuri* or the "Calendar of Bastian" is a transposition of Catholic liturgical feasts from a Western solar calendar to a Japanese lunar calendar based purely on memory. The work of a Japanese catechist who was an apprentice of a revered Portuguese missionary martyr known as San Jiwan, Bastian or Sebastian, who would himself become a martyr, heroically took on priestly responsibilities and ensured the continuity of liturgical celebrations among *Kakure Kirishitan* by way of his calendar.[50] Notable as well is a set of recited prayers known as the *Orasho* (derived from the Latin "Oratio"), an unintelligible oral bricolage of prayers consisting of Portuguese, Latin, and Japanese words remembered from sixteenth-century texts. Munsi notes that the real value of the *Orasho* for the community is in its recitation, not its meaning.[51] It is reasonable, I believe, to describe *Orasho* as a return to a

---

[48] Deusu, Jesuheru, and Maruya, the main figures in the *Tenchi*, are described in terms of rank. Whelan, *The Beginning of Heaven and Earth: The Sacred Book of Japan's Hidden Christians*, 30.

[49] Ibid., 27.

[50] For a fuller discussion of *Bastian's Calendar*, see Turnbull, *The Kakure Kirishitan of Japan: A Study of Their Development, Beliefs and Rituals to the Present Day*, 55–57. Copies of the original are on exhibit at Sotome's Museum of History and Folklore.

[51] As an example, Munsi notes that the first words of the Hail Mary prayer in Latin "*Ave Maria gratia plena*" become an unintelligible "*Abe Mariya hashiyabena*." Refer to Munsi, "The Age-Old Ritual Practice of *Ohatsuhoage* among the Kakure Kirishitan Survivors," 8.

kind of primal spirituality, a phenomenon comparable to glossolalia—speaking in unknown tongues, as found in Acts 2:1–4. More than a recollection of conventional prayer, the *Orasho* meaningfully resonates with the pneumatic utterances of the early Christians who, in a milieu that threatened to crucify them to silence, found their spiritual voice.

The Criterion of the Cross

Persecution is the scarlet thread that runs through the historical timeline of the *Kakure Kirishitan* communities; they are, in the truest sense, an "ecumene of suffering."[52] What is clear, however, is that the *Kakure* had proven to be religious "extremophiles," preserving their Christian identity under murderous conditions, and persevering in their Catholic devotional practices against insurmountable odds. As a counterpoint, then, we can say that heroic faithfulness is the golden thread that runs through *Kakure Kirishitan* history. Be that as it may, the inductive journey leads us to the question: Is it reasonable to propose that *Kakure Kirishitan* faith birthed from a process of inculturation? To engage this question, it is necessary to clarify the term "inculturation" as it is applied in this study and distinguish it from "acculturation," the often-used theoretical term in anthropological studies.

As a theological notion, inculturation is described as "the creative and dynamic relationship between the Christian message and a culture or cultures."[53] It understands the introduction of the gospel into a culture as a transformative "incarnation"[54]—at its theological root is

---

[52] Edward Schillebeeckx, *Christ: The Experience of Jesus as Lord*, trans. John Bowden (New York: Crossroad Publishing, 1980), 725.

[53] Aylward Shorter, *Toward a Theology of Inculturation* (Maryknoll, NY: Orbis Books, 1988), 11.

[54] In a 1978 letter to all members, Pedro Arrupe, the twenty-eighth superior general of the Society of Jesus, defines inculturation as "the incarnation of Christian life and of the Christian message in a particular cultural context, in such a way that this experience not only finds expression through elements proper to the culture in question (this alone would be no more than a superficial adaptation), but becomes a principle that animates, directs and unifies the culture, transforming and remaking it so as to bring about 'a new creation.'"

the incarnation of the historical Jesus in a particular culture—vis-à-vis a corresponding recapitulation, connoting that the culture itself contributes to the enrichment of the gospel message by offering its own cultural wisdom to interpret it anew and to give it meaningful expression. St. Pope John Paul II's 1995 post-synodal exhortation *Ecclesia in Africa* truly captures the mutual interchange that characterizes inculturation; it is illuminating to reprise the description here:

> By respecting, preserving, and fostering the particular values and riches of your people's cultural heritage, you will be in a position to lead them to a better understanding of the mystery of Christ, which is also to be lived in the noble, concrete, and daily experiences of African life. There is no question of adulterating the word of God, or of emptying the Cross of its power (cf. *1 Cor* 1:17), but rather of bringing Christ into the very center of African life and of lifting up all African life to Christ. Thus, not only is Christianity relevant to Africa, but Christ, in the members of his Body, is himself African.[55]

In this sense, the linchpin for determining inculturation is the dynamic equivalence and mutual assimilation between Christian culture and local culture.[56] In anthropological studies, the definition of acculturation has been traditionally based on the 1936 "Memorandum for the Study of Acculturation":

> Acculturation comprehends those phenomena which result when groups of individuals having different cultures come into continuous first-hand contact, with subsequent changes in the original cultural patterns of either or both.[57]

"On Inculturation, to the Whole Society," *The Portal to Jesuit Studies*, https://jesuitportal.bc.edu.

[55] John Paul II, *Ecclesia in Africa*, post-synodal exhortation, September 14, 1995, section 127, www.vatican.va.

[56] In the Introduction of this book, I argue that the process of inculturation could also be understood as an "incarnation," not merely an "introduction" into Christian life.

[57] Robert Redfield, Ralph Linton, and Melville J. Herskovits, "Memo-

To be sure, the two terms overlap so that they have been, at times, used interchangeably.[58] The fine difference, however, can be identified. Aside from the express Christological perspective and grammar of the former, it also describes the character and dynamics of the encounter in more specific terms. Filipino liturgist-theologian Anscar Chupungco proposes a simple equation to illustrate a two-way mediation in inculturation: $A + B = C$. The Christian gospel and a particular culture find a deeper, mutually enriching connection, thereupon producing a tertium quid, a "new creation" (C). As I've proposed in another work, the image and cultural narrative of Mexico's *Nuestra Senora de Guadalupe* is a compelling example of a phenomenon of inculturation.[59] In comparison, Chupungco describes acculturation as $A + B = AB$ where a coming together also occurs but mainly in a frame of tolerance (AB).[60] Lacking an inner dialogical relationship or mutuality, it is, in a manner of speaking, a marriage of convenience. In theological studies, acculturation could be a prior moment to inculturation.

Having clarified the theological usage of inculturation, can it be argued that this was indeed the case for *Kakure Kirishitan* faith? If the approach to this question is based on a semiotic determination of "iconic" formal elements of their devotions—I mean this in the sense of a sign whose properties resemble its object or referent—it would be difficult to argue for the affirmative. As previously pointed out, especially in the case of the *Tenchi Hajimari no Koto*, the *Kakure* devotions are iconic of Buddhist, Shinto, and Japanese folkloric influences that render indistinct the Christian faith expression. Consequently, *Kakure* devotions are described in anthropological studies as having gone through a process of acculturation or syncretism.

---

randum for the Study of Acculturation," *American Anthropologist* 3, no. 1 (January–March 1936): 149–52, www.jstor.org.

[58] As an example, Shorter mentions the use of the term in Don Senior and Carroll Stuhmueller, *The Biblical Foundations for Mission* (Maryknoll, NY: Orbis Books, 1983), 37. See Shorter, *Toward a Theology of Inculturation*, 105.

[59] Refer to Sison, *The Art of Indigenous Inculturation*, 77–131.

[60] Anscar Chupungco, *Liturgical Inculturation: Sacramentals, Religiosity, and Catechesis* (Collegeville, MN: Liturgical Press, 1992), 27–30.

An alternative contextual approach, however, offers a compelling conclusion. I propose the "criterion of the cross," a regardful consideration of the extreme, cruel context the *Kakure* communities were forced to endure, as the reasonable and appropriate critical principle by which their faith must be examined. This is, in fact, the inductive pathway of this study. A protracted history of brutal persecution and forced *chinmoku* is very relativizing and cannot be left out of the account. In this case, a semiotic approach, not only of "iconic," but of "indexical" signification,[61] rends the veil of acculturation and goes deeper into *Kakure* faith beyond observable formal elements. As smoke signals a fire, *Kakure Kirishitan* faith points to a particular referent to which it has an existential connection: the Crucified Nazarene. In their profound suffering and forbearance, the *Kakure Kirishitan* bear in their bodies—indeed, in the hidden regions of their person—the wounds of Jesus Christ. Notwithstanding the many religious influences that had interwoven into the fabric of their practices, it is for the dangerous memory of Christ that the *Kakure Kirishitan* risked severe persecution and death in their continued underground existence. It would indeed be a great disservice to the *Kakure* to use the criterion of doctrinal and liturgical orthodoxy as the sole gauge by which their devotions are measured, arbitrarily disregarding the historical given that they had to find for themselves incredible ways to practice their Christian faith under extreme duress, at the risk of their own lives. With the exception of Bernard Petitjean who had a more creative and conciliatory approach, this was, in fact, the general attitude of the French missionaries when the *Kakure*

---

[61] The semiotic categories of "iconic" and "indexical" are drawn from the complex, extensive sign theory of nineteenth-century American philosopher Charles Sanders Peirce. For an accessible reference, see *Peirce on Signs: Writings on Semiotics by Charles Sanders Peirce*, ed. James Hoopes (Chapel Hill: University of North Carolina Press, 1991). For an elucidation of "index," see Thomas A. Goudge, "Peirce's Index," *Transactions of the Charles S. Peirce Society* 1, no. 2 (Fall 1965): 52–60. An earlier application to images can be found in Douglas N. Morgan, "Icon, Index and Symbol in the Visual Arts," *Philosophical Studies* 6, no. 4 (June 1955): 49–54.

reemerged from their underground existence in the Meiji period. For instruction—or, more accurately, reinstruction—they had wanted the returning *Kakure* to use a classic Catholic catechism propagated in China, a proposal Petitjean dissented as he believed that the *Tenchi* would be the best option precisely for its familiarity to the *Kakure*. A padre in Nagasaki by the name of "Salmon" was also reported to have dismissed the *Tenchi* as "worthless."[62] There have been doubts as well as to whether the *Kakure* themselves even understood their own brand of Christianity or whether this identity had supposedly been subsumed into the established Buddhist-Shinto belief system and had since lost its essence. If it is mainly acculturation that characterizes *Kakure* faith, this suggestion holds a measure of validity. However, if indeed inculturation had occurred on the level of the *Kakure*'s passion and crucifixion in the name of their Christian faith, who's to say that they had remained clueless about what it means to be a Japanese Christian? Yuri Isabelina Sugimoto of Uragami, the *Kakure* woman who, along with a remnant of fifteen, revealed their identities to Petitjean on March 17, 1865—they were searching for the icon of the Virgin Mary at the Ōura Church—proclaims: "The hearts of all of us here are the same as yours."[63]

With the simple and earnest devotional metaphor of "heart," Sugimoto's message connotes that she and her companions share Petitjean's Christian faith. Moreover, it's been noted that there are *Kakure Kirishitan* descendants who "still believe that they transmit the authentic Catholicism of Xavier."[64]

---

[62] Turnbull, "Acculturation among the *Kakure Kirishitan*: Some Conclusions from the *Tenchi Hajimari no Koto*," 65.

[63] Fujita, *Japan's Encounter with Christianity*, 244–45. In a message to Japanese bishops in commemoration of the reemergence, Pope Francis gave honor to the *Kakure* community: "This year you celebrate another facet of this rich heritage–the emergence of the 'hidden Christians.' Even when all lay missionaries and priests had been expelled from the country, the faith of the Christian community did not grow cold." Pope Francis, "Japan's 'Hidden Christians': A Model for the Church," *Vatican Radio*, March 20, 2015. www.archivioradiovaticana.va.

[64] Ichiro Hori, *Folk Religion in Japan: Continuity and Change*, ed. Joseph M. Kitagawa and Alan L. Miller (Tokyo: University of Tokyo Press, 1968), 15–16.

Bronze relief depicting the encounter between Sugimoto and companions, and Fr. Petitjohn. Ōura Church, Nagasaki, Japan.
Image courtesy Antonio D. Sison

The dismissal of these convictions as erroneous based on a decontextualized standard of doctrinal and liturgical conformity, I submit, is an expression of extraordinary arrogance. Certainly, the *Kakure Kirishitan* do not deserve to be silenced yet again, least of all by voices that do not have a stake in their faith. Across the scholarly landscape and media platforms, they have been insensitively characterized in terms that already seal their extinction. Yet, in a contextual light that recognizes and values a long view, we behold a heroic faith community that outlived more than two centuries of persecution, vilification, poverty, isolation, and exclusion.

By the grace of the Crucified-and-Risen One whose dangerous memory they embody, the *Kakure Kirishitan* are still here.

6

God, Canaan, Egypt, and the Stories of Migration in Intercultural Perspective

Ferdinand Ikenna Okorie

Since the rise of Egypt as a world power with an unmatched civilization in the narratives of the ancestors of Israel, and through the end of the Roman Empire in the third century AD, the nation's values, wealth, and resources supported the migration of peoples from around the ancient world, and world leaders jostled for control of the region (Isa. 45:14). It is a matter of fact that Egyptian civilization is the first in the African continent, but one that certainly integrated some cultural values in administration, social organization, and religious expressions from its East and Central African neighbors. Egypt's commerce was buoyed by the Nile Valley in the northeast corner of the continent. Therefore, the African fertile crescent, stretching from the eastern part of the Sahara into the Egyptian and Sudanese Nile Valleys supported agricultural activities, the population of Egypt, and the constant influx of migrants into Egypt from around the world.[1]

This essay is aimed at a careful and detailed interpretation of biblical texts and other relevant ancient sources on the historical

---

[1] Jean Vercoutter, "The Peopling of Ancient Egypt," in *The Peopling of Ancient Egypt and the Deciphering of the Meoroitic Script*, ed. Cheikh Anta Diop et al. (London: Karnak House, 1997), 24–25.

account of Egypt as a safe haven for migrants seeking a better life and safety away from a homeland ravaged by environmental disaster, political unrest, and war. Because of the extensive biblical narratives of the relationship between the children of Israel and the Egyptians, I shall only provide detailed exegetical interpretation of the migrations of the ancestors of Israel in the book of Genesis and of the remnant of Judah in the exilic period in the book of Jeremiah. A critical element of the hermeneutic of contextual expressions of religious value, as I discuss in this essay, involves the presence of the deity in the existential realities of a people who must leave their homeland in search of freedom and safety. I examine how, alongside the community or individual, the deity manifests the enduring presence of divinity to a people, or to an individual ripped apart by social and economic upheavals. Meaningful resonances in today's global migrant experience crystallize in an integrative section, "God, Homeland, Migration, and Inculturation." This essay contributes to the debate on the intersection of cultures and religious expressions through border crossing, the presence of the divine in the experience of migrants, who, then and now, emboldens the human spirit in the uncertain and treacherous journey.

God, the People of God, and Homeland

The relationship God establishes with the children of Israel has its origin in God's relationship with Abraham since his call and obedience to God's invitation to migrate to the land God has chosen for him. God initiates the terms of the relationship, and Abraham embraces them as he migrates away from home to the land of Canaan, the land that God has chosen for him (Gen. 12:1–2), a land that as a result becomes for Abraham and his descendants an everlasting possession by divine decree (see Gen. 17:8). During the exodus era, the land denotes the relationship God has established with the children of Israel as God reminds Moses of God's disposition to act on the status of the commitment God made to Abraham to bring back to the land the generation that is enslaved in Egypt (Exod. 6:5–8). Once more, the land is a critical element in God's relationship with the children of Israel. The terms of the relationship can be succinctly identified as the faithfulness of God to provide a divinely chosen habitation for the children of Israel, who are expected to faithfully acquiesce in obedience to the terms of their covenant with God. The children of Israel know that any infringement on the terms of this covenantal relationship with God merits banishment from the land (see Lev. 26:21, 32–33; Josh. 23:15). I will show later that the theological underpinning of the exilic period reveals the role Babylon plays as God's agent to drive the children of Israel away from the land because of disobedience (Jer. 21:2; 22:25; 25:8, 9; 27:6; 28:14; 29:21). Nevertheless, God promises to return repentant children of Israel back to the land on the terms of their covenantal relationship with God because the land is both a physical place for their habitation, and more so, a symbol of this relationship (Lev. 26:42). It is in the land that God lives on Mount Zion, in the temple in Jerusalem with the people of God (Zech. 2:7; Joel 3:17). In other words, the earthly habitation of God is in the land among the children of Israel.

It is clear to the children of Israel just as it is to the reader that the land belongs to God, and it is gratuitously given to them to be a place for their comfort, prosperity, progress, and identity formation as the children of God. It is a place for them to flourish in relationship with God and to develop their own identity. The book of Deuteronomy describes the land as fertile (Deut. 8:7–10; 11:10–12). The description of the land in Deuteronomy 8:7–10 as a good land, flowing with streams of water, valley and hill, barley, wheat, vines, figs, pomegranates, olive trees, honey, and minerals such as iron and copper, creates among the exodus community, who hunger for food and thirst for water in the uninhabitable and parched desert, the anticipation of God's gift of a land of their own. Walter Brueggemann provides a scholarly description of the significant place the land occupies in the relationship between God and the people of Israel. He agrees that the land is a gift that binds the receiver—in this case, the people of Israel—to the giver, God.[2]

---

[2] Walter Brueggemann, *The Land* (Philadelphia: Fortress, 1977), 47.

At the beginning of the formation of the children of Israel as a nation through the relationship between God and Abram, drought and famine threatened this relationship in the land, thereby sending Abram away from the place of relationship with God. The story of Abram's migration into Egypt to wait out the famine in the land is presented between the promises of divine blessings (Gen. 12:1–3, 7) and Abram's acquisition of riches (Gen. 13:2). Famine, drought, and the threat of malnutrition for the ancestral family introduces Egypt as a place of abundance and plenty. The same experience of famine in the land sends Isaac and his household away from the land (Gen. 26:1). But in his own case, Yahweh instructs him not to migrate into Egypt (26:2). Sparse rainfall, rudimentary irrigation, and low harvest make the land prone to food shortage and famine (2 Kings 6:25; 25:3). Egypt possesses what the land of Canaan lacks, promising survival and flourishing to the ancestral family that are unavailable to them in the land of Canaan. Egypt's agricultural abundance is supported by the Nile (see Deut. 11:10). Nahum M. Sarna suggests that Egypt serves as "a place of shelter and succor in time of distress" for the children of Israel.[3]

As immigrants, the ancestral family faces the challenges of life in a new country, seeking security amid the threats of harassment, displacement, and separation (Gen. 12:12–15). Gordon J. Wenham puts it bluntly as he describes Abram's experience: "as an immigrant there he would lack the support and protection afforded by the wider family network."[4] He will experience there the same exploitation that is often the experience of immigrant families today.[5] While some scholars suggest that the verb *gēr* indicates that Abram's migration into Egypt was for a long stay,[6] others suggest that it was a temporary

---

[3] Nahum M. Sarna, *Genesis: The JPS Torah Commentary* (Philadelphia: Jewish Publication Society, 1989), 93.
[4] Gordon J. Wenham, *Genesis 1–15*, vol. 1 (Waco, TX: Word Books, 1987), 287.
[5] Ibid., 287.
[6] Ibid. Peter C. Phan notes that a migrant could be a permanent resident and still remain a foreigner, being away from one's homeland. See "God, the Beginning and End of Migration: A Theology of God from the Experience and

migration (12:10).[7] Abram departs the land of the promise (see Deut. 10:11b) because the land has become for him and his household a place of impending starvation, malnutrition, and possible death. His family's experience of freedom will be determined by what Egypt is willing to offer them as migrants. Abram's trepidation concerning the journey to Egypt is betrayed by the request he made to Sarai that she give up her dignity for the sake of his safety by agreeing to lie about her marital status (12:11–13). Upon arrival at the border, they receive a traumatizing welcome, after their encounter with Pharaoh's security personnel, followed by arrest, detention, and separation (12:14–15). Sarai immediately becomes a victim of physical and emotional abuse, while silently acquiescing to her husband's request. We are lacking in enough evidence to suggest that Sarai protested against Abram's plan, which initiated the beginning of the denigration of her dignity and self-worth. We will never know whether she was coerced by her husband to agree to his plans or not. What we know, based on narrative evidence, is that she offered herself to the whims of Pharaoh for the sake of the survival of the ancestral family in a foreign land (12:15c). She sacrificed her identity, and she lied about her social and marital status; she presented a fake story and identity for the sake of the survival of her family. In terms of today's migration experience, Sarai handed over to the border control agent a fake passport and identity to give herself and her family a new lease of life in Egypt.

The affliction Pharaoh suffered on account of Sarai revealed that God was with the ancestral family in Egypt (Deut. 12:17–19). It is clear, therefore, that God traveled to Egypt with Abram's household,

---

Perspective of Migrants," in *Christian Theology in the Age of Migration: Implications for World Christianity*, ed. Peter C. Phan (Lanham, MD: Lexington Books, 2020), 106.

[7] James Chukwuma Okoye, CSSp, *Genesis 12–50: A Narrative-Theological Commentary* (Eugene, OR: Cascade Books, 2020), 46. Sarna is another scholar who agrees that the term connotes a temporary residence. As a key word in the book of Genesis, "it appears in one form or another fifteen times in relation to the wanderings and status of the patriarchs and their descendants, both in the promised land and in Egypt." See Sarna, *Genesis*, 93.

guiding, supporting, and defending them in a foreign land.[8] Abram's plan on how to survive as an immigrant in Egypt and Pharaoh's act of humiliating a migrant family met with God's disapproval. Disappointed, Pharaoh confronted Abram: "What is this you have done to me? Why did you not tell me that she was your wife? Why did you say, 'She is my sister'?" (12:18–19). Pharaoh was outraged, and he reprimanded Abram for his lies because Pharaoh paid a lavish dowry worthy of a nobleman to Abram as Sarai's "brother" (Gen. 12:16).[9] The divine plagues that afflicted Pharaoh and his household were indicative of the fact that God disapproved of Abram's plan and Pharaoh's behavior, and God restored Sarai's dignity and humanity. Notwithstanding Pharaoh's lavished gifts, Abram and his family were deported out of Egypt back to the land of Canaan, perhaps before the drought was over.

Another ancestral family was forced out of the land of Canaan as the global crisis of food shortage, drought, and famine "reached the land of Canaan" (Gen. 42:5). Just like the family of Abraham before them, the family of Jacob looked toward Egypt for survival. Once again, Egypt provided resources for the survival of the ancestral family. Jacob said to his sons, "There is grain in Egypt; go down and buy grain for us there, that we may live and not die" (Gen. 42:2). Twice the sons of Jacob traveled to Egypt to buy more food for the family because the famine was severe in the land of Canaan, and by extension in the whole world. The severity of the famine was revealed in Pharaoh's dream (Gen. 41:27, 30–31), which Joseph brilliantly interpreted, thus earning for himself the leadership of managing the food crisis during the time under review. Judah's words to his father, Jacob, who was deeply apprehensive about allowing his youngest son, Benjamin, to travel with his brothers to Egypt, reveal how vital Egypt was for their

---

[8] See similar view in Phan, "God, the Beginning and the End of Migration," 107.
[9] "It is quite likely that the bounty bestowed on Abram represented this sort of payment, though it may have been simply a mark of pharaonic goodwill toward Sarai's 'brother.'" See Wenham, *Genesis 1–15*, 289.

survival. He said, "Send the boy with me, and let us be on our way, so that we may live and not die—you and we and also our little ones" (Gen. 43:8). The threat of returning to Egypt loomed over them should they return to buy more grain without Benjamin. As the prospect of migrating to Egypt became imminent for Jacob and his family, they faced the challenges of life in a foreign land: the prospect of separation, displacement, and harassment at the hands of an Egyptian official, who, unbeknownst to them, is their brother Joseph, whose stable aristocratic life in Egypt paved the way for their own migration to Egypt. Today, several migrations are buoyed by a family and relative already living in the desired country of migration, who provide stability upon arrival for the new migrants. Jacob felt that the hope of surviving through the drought that Egypt presented to his family also brought pain and affliction to him. He said to his sons as he thought about the possibility of losing another child, "Why did you treat me so badly as to tell the man that you had another brother?" (Gen. 43:6).

When the time arrived for Jacob and his family to migrate to Egypt, Pharaoh gifted them with wagons for the journey to Egypt (Gen. 46:5), just as Pharaoh gifted Abraham with lavish gifts during his stay in Egypt. In the story of Abraham's migration into Egypt, God was present with him and his household. The act of carrying all their possessions into Egypt reveals that Jacob and his household understood their migration as long-term. It is important to point out the significance of Jacob's ritual act of sacrifice before migrating to Egypt seeking the protection of the God of his fathers. His reception of the divine encouragement not to fear the challenges of migrating to Egypt (Gen. 46:3) was followed by a twofold divine promise that Yahweh will accompany him to Egypt and will bring him back up again to the land of Canaan (Gen. 46:4).

It remains only to examine another major migration into Egypt by the children of Israel during a political uprising caused by a Babylonian colonial campaign in the land. Factions, violence, and killings of fellow countrymen undergird the relationship between Babylon and Judah. On one hand, Babylonian political presence in Judah was welcomed by one group of Jewish leaders, and on the other hand, an anti-Babylon faction used violence and intimidation against fellow Israelites to register their disdain for the Babylonian colonial enterprise in Judah (Jer. 41:1–3). Out of the bloodbath at Mizpah emerged a collective resolve of the remnant of Judah to migrate into Egypt rather than to live under Babylonian occupation. This determination was also motivated by warfare and famine (Jer. 42:14). The resolve of the remnant of Judah to migrate into Egypt did not diminish Yahweh's pledge to build them up and not destroy them (42:9–12). Nevertheless, the divine exhortation to the Judean remnant not to fear the Babylonians was not enough to deter them from their collective resolve to migrate into Egypt. By rejecting the prophecy of Jeremiah, they ipso facto rejected God, on whose behalf the prophet speaks. They said to Jeremiah, "As for the word that you have spoken to us in the name of the LORD, we are not going to listen to you" (44:16). Jeremiah was not losing the battle of trust to lead the community in his role as a prophet of God; rather God lost control of the children of Israel, Yahweh's chosen people.

God, the People of God, and the Other Nations

When Abraham migrated into Egypt, Yahweh approved of his decision and committed to be with him and to protect him and his family from the anxiety and trepidations of migrating to a foreign country. Two generations later, God encouraged Jacob to migrate into Egypt with the guarantee of divine protection in Egypt. Contrariwise, God forbade Isaac from moving into Egypt when famine struck the land of Canaan (Gen. 26:2). After the fall of Jerusalem to the Babylonians, when the exilic generation decided to migrate into Egypt, Yahweh intervened and persuaded them against their decision to move to Egypt, and rather to remain in the land under Babylonian rule. Yahweh played such a significant role in the relationship between the children of Israel and their more powerful neighbors, consistently deciding for them which alliances to forge and which warfare to wage. In this way, Yahweh continued to show divine leadership of the children of Israel.

Based on the scope of this research, I have established the limit of my discussions on the leadership of Yahweh in the relationship between Israel and its more powerful neighbors to only Babylon and Egypt, engaging extensively on the relationship between Egypt and the children of Israel. In 2 Chronicles 36:1–15, Babylon's political success in Judah is intrinsically linked to the disobedience of the children of Israel. The rise of the neo-Babylonian dynasty presented a significant sociopolitical challenge to Judah as the new leader of Babylon embarked on a campaign to expand his rule to the South. Judah's unwillingness to recognize Babylon's power triggered a political turmoil as one Judean king after another was violently removed from office, from Jehoiakim to Jehoiachin (see 2 Kings 24:10–12). Under Jehoiachin, Babylon raided Judah, looted the treasures of the temple of the Lord, and exiled the noble men and women of Judah (2 Kings 24:13–16). The forced deportation of Judean elites crippled the religious, administrative, and political leadership in the land. The Babylonian onslaught in Judah continued with the installation of Jehoiakim's uncle Zedekiah as ruler. But his political miscalculations that culminated with alliances with Egypt irked Babylon (Jer. 37:6–10). Consequently, between January 587 BCE and July 586 BCE, Babylon laid siege to the city of Jerusalem, destroyed what remained of the temple and homes, and established a forced deportation of Judeans of approximately seventy thousand men, women, and children. After quelling the rebellion of Zedekiah with disproportionate carnage in Judah, Babylon installed Gedaliah as governor, who championed an anti-Egyptian policy. He established the headquarters of his administration in Mizpah.

The remnant of Judah was challenged with dealing with the monumental and emotion-ridden reality of the unprecedented massacre and destruction in the city. Consolation and hope hung in their depressing lives, desiring a healing balm through the words of the prophet Jeremiah, who reminded them of the presence of Yahweh in their midst. An internal revolt and massacre of fellow Judeans ensued, leaving the remnant with the decision either to remain in Judah under

Babylonian colonial rule or migrate to somewhere else, perhaps Egypt for security, freedom, and a better life. The theological message consistently broached in the exilic period is the fact that the experience of Babylonian occupation was a consequence of Yahweh's wrath. In other words, it is a result of Israel's disobedience, plus the immediate obstinacy of Johanan and his followers against the prophecy of Jeremiah, warning them thus: "Do not go to Egypt" (Jer. 42:19), though they can choose to disobey at their own peril. Their request to Yahweh to intervene in their fate revealed the significant role Yahweh continued to play in their outlook toward life. They pledged to honor Yahweh's decision, professing that "whether it is good or bad, we will obey the voice of the LORD our God to whom we are sending you, in order that it may go well with us when we obey the voice of the LORD our God" (Jer. 42:6). Jeremiah returned to Johanan and the remnant of Judah with the words of Yahweh that showcase Yahweh's leadership and fidelity to the lived experiences of the children of Israel.

Yahweh wanted them to remain in the land notwithstanding the nightmare the Babylonian carnage inflicted on the collective psyche of the remnant of Judah and the bloodletting that happened when kinfolk turned against each other. Perhaps perturbed by the dangerous living conditions of the remnant of Judah, Yahweh offered a public apology to them, "for I am sorry for the disaster that I have brought upon you" (Jer. 42:10). Then, Yahweh further pledged to plant them and not pluck them up, which is one of the overarching theological messages of the book of Jeremiah and the prophetic ministry of Jeremiah as the servant of God (Jer. 42:10; see 1:10; 24:6; 31:28). Concerning the occupying Babylonian king, Yahweh exhorted the remnant of Judah not to be afraid of him because Yahweh pledged to be with them, to save them and rescue them from Babylon (Jer. 42:11). In addition to the divine promise of mercy, Yahweh pledged to restore them to their native land (Jer. 42:12–13). Once again, just as in the stories of the ancestors of Israel, likewise in the realities of the remnant of Judah: Yahweh's presence as the community navigated through the decision-making process of migrating into Egypt or to remain in the land of Judah under foreign occupation and the threat of death is apposite.

Migration into Egypt remained the preferred choice of the Judean remnant because, with the current state of affairs at home, Egypt was an attractive destination, promising life without war, bloodshed, and famine (Jer. 42:14). Migration into Egypt erased the fear of deportation to Babylon and the possible loss of lives at the hands of the Babylonians. Therefore, they were not assuaged by Yahweh's warning that they should stay in Judah (Jer. 43:3). What the land could no longer provide—namely, food and security—the remnant of Judah sought in Egypt. Johanan took everyone, including Jeremiah and Baruch, Jeremiah's secretary, and migrated to Egypt, settling in the city of Tahpanhes (Jer. 43:4–7). Because of their obstinacy and refusal to heed the words of Yahweh through the prophet, Yahweh reneged on the divine promise to the children of Israel about their future, which was rehearsed in Jeremiah 42:10: "If you will only remain in this land, then, I will build you up and not pull you down; I will plant you, and not pluck you up; for I am sorry for the disaster that I have brought upon you." Since they chose not to obey, Yahweh judged them and pledged "to break down what I have built and pluck up what I have planted—that is, the whole land" (Jer. 45:4). Their decision to take the prophet Jeremiah with them to Egypt is indicative of their hunger for prophecy and the need for the presence of Yahweh through the prophet. Johanan and the remnant of Judah knew that their history was undergirded by the uninterrupted presence of Yahweh among them. Notwithstanding their rejection of God's words to wait out Babylonian occupation of their land in preference for Egypt, they still expected God to go down to Egypt with them.

Before I go any further with the interpretation of the decision of Johanan and the remnant of Judah to migrate into Egypt, I wish to point out that between the famine that sent Jacob and his sons into Egypt and the choice of the Judean remnant to migrate into Egypt against God's wishes, other migrations into Egypt by the children of Israel are worthy of note. When King Solomon failed to unite the children of Israel under one monarch, then the ten northern tribes coalesced under Jeroboam, who eventually sought political asylum in Egypt on account of the threat to his life by King Solomon, who suspected a threat from Jeroboam to his imperial theocracy, and then plotted to kill him. This threat was revealed to Jeroboam by the prophet Ahijah, when he tore his garment into twelve pieces and offered ten pieces to Jeroboam to symbolize the prophecy of divine decision—to give Jeroboam ten tribes of the northern kingdom and leave only two tribes to King Solomon (1 Kings 11:30–31). Enraged, King Solomon took effrontery to this apparent divine decision with the result that Jeroboam sought political asylum in Egypt under the protection of Pharaoh Shishak until King Solomon died, when he returned home to Judah (1 Kings 11:40; 12:1–2). In the context of ritual offering to Yahweh, the children of Israel recited in ceremonial observance their ancestral history that paid tribute to Egypt as a land for migrants: "A wandering Aramean was my ancestor; he went down to Egypt and lived there as an alien" (Deut. 26:5).

In the book of Jeremiah, Uriah son of Shemaiah uttered prophetic words against Jerusalem and the land of Israel. Condemned for treason and sought by King Jehoiakim, he fled Jerusalem seeking political asylum in Egypt. Nevertheless, his escape to safety in Egypt was short-lived because King Jehoiakim's security network arrested him in Egypt, brought him back to Jerusalem, and executed him (Jer. 26:20–23). For the purposes of this essay, Uriah found Egypt to be a place of safety because of the threat to his life. The destruction of Jerusalem that Uriah son of Shemaiah predicted came to pass as Babylonian military action in Judah brought the nation under Babylonian colonial rule. The remnant of Judah (Jer. 42:2) had the choice of living under the colonial leadership of Babylon, visibly represented by Gedaliah, son of Ahikam son of Shaphan, a puppet appointee of the king of Babylon (Jer. 41:2–3), or seek political asylum in surrounding nations, such as Egypt.

Ancient accounts reveal that other rising powers found control over Egypt to be a symbol of the expansion of their powers and authority in world affairs. The ancient historian Herodotus recounted Persia's calculated attempts to take control of Egypt, and to govern the country through satraps and governors chosen from Persian aristocratic families who resided in Memphis, the capital.[10] They took control of the military and its defenses, enlisting both native Egyptians and foreigners into the Persian military forces. Herodotus notes that Egyptian servicemen were inherited by the Persian administration from the defunct pharaonic predecessors. Among the immigrants who called Egypt home during the Persian period and who were conscripted to serve in the military under the Persian leadership were the Jewish troops stationed in the garrison in Elephantine.[11] Drawing from the names of Jewish settlers in Elephantine, Michael H. Silverman finds correlation with the names of Jews during the Babylonian exile. Based on his findings, therefore, he suggests that the colony originated during the "last years of the kingdom of Judah" when Babylon administered the political structures of the nation.[12]

With Persian power waning in world affairs, Egyptians and immigrants living in Egypt saw Alexander the Great as a liberator after the battle of Gaza successfully upended Persian rule over Egypt. Alexander the Great's leadership over Egypt was a welcome development for the Egyptians and the migrant communities, including Jews in Egypt. One of his positive and diplomatic gestures to the native

---

[10] Herodotus, 3.1–29, 37.

[11] Herodotus, 7.25, 89, 97; 8.17; Alan B. Lloyd, "Egypt," in *The Anchor Yale Bible Dictionary*, vol. 2 (New Haven, CT: Yale University Press, 1992), 364–66. Through the examination of names, Michael H. Silverman attests to a Jewish settlement in Elephantine, who retained their ancestral religion and continued to worship the God of Israel. See Michael H. Silverman, "The Religion of the Elephantine Jews: A New Approach," *Proceedings of the World Congress of Jewish Studies* (1973): 377–88. Victor Tcherikover supports this point of view that identifies the destruction of Judea by Babylon as the beginning of the wave of migration of Judeans into Egypt. See Victor Tcherikover, *Hellenistic Civilization and the Jews* (Grand Rapids: Baker Academic, 1999), 269–70. Karl van der Toorn is specific with his observation that "by the fifth century B.C.E., there were various Jewish military colonies in Egypt. The famous among them lived on Elephantine Island at the northern Egyptian border." See Karl van der Toorn, "Egyptian Papyrus Sheds New Light on Jewish History," *Biblical Archaeology Review* 44 (2018): 34–35.

[12] Silverman, "The Religion of the Elephantine Jews," 381–82.

Egyptians was to appoint them into provincial roles and as tax officers. It is important to remember that before the conquest of Alexander the Great, Greek migrants lived in and called Egypt home. Greeks lived and worked in Memphis, the capital and administrative city of ancient Egypt. After Alexander the Great, Egypt came under the leadership of Ptolemy I Soter, who founded a Greek city in Egypt, Ptolemais, and turned Alexandria into the capital of Egypt.[13] Treating Egypt as an estate, he established the greatest library in the world in Alexandria, housing the largest collection of texts ever assembled in the ancient world. It was in this city that the Greek philosophical school of neo-Platonism flourished, and under which the great diasporic Jewish scholar Philo was educated. Under Ptolemy's leadership, Alexandria was the economic and cultural capital of the civilized world. Therefore, Jewish migrants found Alexandria attractive because of the opportunity for social and financial advancement that the city offered.[14] When Ptolemy II Philadelphus, the son of Ptolemy I Soter took over from his father, he expanded the empire into East Africa, setting out military outposts in the region, assigning lands to servicemen of both Jewish and Greek descent posted to the region. When Egypt came under Roman colonial rule (30 BC–AD 324), the nation and its peoples endured and lived under similar circumstances just as they did under previous colonizers. Rome benefited from Egypt's rich agricultural resources to meet the needs of an expanding population. For this reason, the stability of Egypt as the supplier of agricultural products was vital to the leadership of the emperors and the senate in Rome.[15]

During the Roman period, and based on the evidence of biblical narratives, a political tension and an impending suppression of

---

[13] S. Kent Brown, "Egypt," in *The Anchor Yale Bible Dictionary*, vol. 2 (New Haven, CT: Yale University Press, 1992), 367–73; John M. G. Barclay, *Jews in the Mediterranean Diaspora: From Alexander to Trajan (323 BCE–117 CE)* (Berkeley: University of California Press, 1996), 27.

[14] One example of assimilation into the local Egyptians' culture and the growing influence of Jewish migrants in Alexander was the political appointment of Philo's nephew, Tiberius Julius Alexander, as the governor of Egypt. See Barclay, *Jews in the Mediterranean Diaspora*, 105–6.

[15] Brown, "Egypt," 372–73.

nationalism sent Joseph and his family, from the tribe of Benjamin, out of Palestine, seeking security and asylum in Egypt on the advice of the angel of God, who forewarned the family to flee from King Herod (Matt. 2:13–15).

A Herodian archaeological site in Caesaria, Israel (c. first century BCE).
Image courtesy Ferdinand Ikenna Okorie

The anxiety of being dethroned by a newborn king of the Jews unnerved King Herod, setting him off on a campaign of murderous pursuit of the child, whose parents were forced into a hasty migration to Egypt. The angel of God instructed the family to remain in Egypt until the death of Herod. The hurried and clandestine departure meant that they had no time to prepare for the journey into Egypt. Probably, like most migrants today, they left Palestine with the hope of connecting with the Jewish community in Egypt. Based on Matthew's account of the infancy narratives, the early days of the newborn king of the Jews were spent as an asylum seeker, an exile, a refugee. His bar mitzvah and initial growth in God's presence took place in Egypt. Hence the divine affirmation that "out of Egypt I called my son" defined God's relationship with the children of Israel and the significant role Egypt plays in that relationship.

Based on our examination of biblical history from the time of Abraham through the Roman period, Egypt and East Africa were the economic bedrock of the ancient world. During the time under review, Egypt and East Africa also recorded the highest volume of migration in the ancient world.[16] During the time of the ancestor, Jacob, Egypt kept the world population alive during the seven years of famine as predicted by Joseph. The migration of Jacob and his family into Egypt revealed Egypt's open migration policy because of the nation's high moral principles. I have already examined how Egypt was important to the economy of the ancient world, supplying and satisfying the need for grain and abundant food production. Land was Egypt's most valuable resource, its arability enhanced by the flooding of the Nile in late summer.[17] Under the Ptolemies, Greeks and Macedonians were enticed to migrate into Egypt with the promise of land allocation.[18] Also, Egypt produced the papyrus that supported the dissemination of information, as well as the documentation and preservation of administrative and imperial transactions.

---

[16] The evidence proves that migrants settled in Egypt and East Africa along the banks of the Nile; these regions show gradual settlement and population growth. Migrants came from all parts of sub-Saharan Africa. The southern part of the Nile delta was inhabited by Africans. "Subsequently, various human groups came from different regions, increasing this population and altering its composition." See Anta Diop et al., eds., *The Peopling of Ancient Egypt*, 86–94.

[17] Brown, "Egypt," 367–68.

[18] Sylvie Honigman recounts, "Ptolemies built harbors on the Red Sea and set to exploit the mineral resources of the Eastern Desert, caravan routes connecting between Edfu and the Berenike harbor run through the Eastern Desert, branching out to the mining sites, whereas other routes led to the Kharga Oasis, 200km to the west of the Nile Valley, and to sandstone quarries to the south." See "Serving the Kings, Building Temples, and Paying the Jewish Tax: Aramaic-Speaking Judeans and Their Descendants in Upper Egypt from Persian to Early Imperial Times," in *Elephantine in Context: Studies on the History, Religion and Literature of the Judeans in Persian Period Egypt*, ed. Reinhard G. Kratz and Bernd U. Schipper (Tübingen: Mohr Siebeck, 2022), 79.

God, Homeland, Migration, and Inculturation

The experience of migration altered the relationship between Yahweh and the children of Israel as the symbolism of the land of Canaan and national identity assumed new meaning in a new context. In other words, their new lease on life as migrants in Egypt introduced another context to their relationship with Yahweh. In fact, Egypt became the contextual framework upon which the religious experience of the children of Israel found its latest expression. As a migrant community with all the trappings of homelessness, displacement, disorientation, and vulnerability, the dynamics of inculturation invited them to draw from their new context ways of engaging their histories, language, and religion in a foreign land. This is because the essence of inculturation was a dialectical interaction between their rich religious heritage and the Egyptian context. Egypt provided context for the children of Israel to navigate and express their religious experience and the role Yahweh played in their lives. The experience of inculturation invited them to embrace the benefits of a communal expression of their religious heritage in a foreign land. Inculturation opened their imagination to the fact that their relationship with Yahweh was not bound to the land of Canaan, but rather open to assuming new cultural affinity, and to some degree a different linguistic mode of expression in Egypt. Their experience in inculturation inexorably involved the ability to evolve into and embrace a hybridized lifestyle since their survival in a foreign land depended on it, and not in their effort to maintain the purity of their religious life that had been significantly changed by the experience of migration and departure from Judah.

We know that during the exilic period the Judean migrants settled in the Egyptian cities of Migdol, Tahpanhes, Memphis, and Pathros (Jer. 44:1).[19] Writing during the Roman period, Philo attested to diasporic Jewish habitation in "Alexandria and the country from the

---

[19] This is discounting the fact that some of the Judean migrants to Egypt moved to Elephantine, and Babylonian Jews collaborated in the founding of the colony. See Silverman, "The Religion of Elephantine Jews," 382.

slope into Libya to the boundaries of Ethiopia."[20] It is pertinent to mention here that as a migrating deity with the children of Israel, Yahweh was susceptible to the new modes of religious expressions of piety that Egypt offered the children of Israel. The traditional forms of Israel's worship of Yahweh underwent new forms of expression as the religious tradition of the children of Israel encountered the Egyptian context. For the migrant community in Egypt, inculturation became an experience in a radical altering of their expression of devotion to Yahweh through the use of Egypt's cultural categories. No doubt the worship of Yahweh in Egypt would undergo significant adjustments, so that through the process of inculturation the religious activities of the children of Israel assumed a profound meaning in a foreign land and culture. Because of the significant role played by context, namely, the existential arena of their activities as persons in community, the relationship between Yahweh and the children of Israel in Egypt took on the framework of inculturation, nudging them toward concretizing their religious experience within the local context of Egypt. The evidence of ethnic religious activities, the worship of Israel's deity in a foreign land, albeit with some vignette of syncretism with Egyptian deities, supports the view that the relationship between Yahweh and the children of Israel took on a contextual mode of expression in Egypt as they searched for a sense of belonging in a foreign land.

Archaeological evidence from ruins of synagogues and extant writings from Jews in Elephantine reveal to a greater degree an uninterrupted observance of religious activities and rituals honoring Yahweh, including pilgrimage to Jerusalem by diasporic Jews, especially from Alexandria in the Greco-Roman period.[21] Also, the religious activities of Jews in Elephantine revealed a degree of inculturation with their Egyptian context. The evidence of inculturation with

---

[20] Quoted in M. Stern, "Jewish Diaspora," in *The Jewish People in the First Century: Historical Geography, Political History, Social, Cultural and Religious Life and Institutions*, vol. 1, ed. S. Safrai and M. Stern (Philadelphia: Van Gorcum and Fortress, 1974), 122.

[21] See Stern, "The Jewish Diaspora," 123.

the Egyptian context is codified in a papyrus dated "to the first quarter of the 5th century BCE" on a benediction invoked in the name of Yahweh and the Egyptian deity Khnum (both the Egyptian deity, Khnum, and Yahweh had temples in Elephantine).[22] It is an important example of inculturation of the worship of Yahweh by diasporan Jews in Elephantine in the context of liturgy. In their liturgy, therefore, the Judeans adapted and permitted only "incense (and) meal offering, [which] traditionally belong to the Egyptian sacrificial cult, performed daily in front of the statue of god Khnum."[23] The Amherst papyrus 63 attests to the Elephantine Jews' consciousness of the religious traditions of their Egyptian context, and its influence on their own religious expression. Similarly, in the "Blessings of All the Gods" prayer in the same papyrus, one of the sections reads, "May the Throne of Yahō [Yahweh], and Asherah from the South bless you."[24] Holm suggests that "the Throne of Yahō might be an allusion to the well-known temple of Yahō at Elephantine, where Yahō was believed to reside."[25] Other evidence shows that "in their temple on Elephantine, the diasporan Jews of southern Egypt venerated the gods Eshem-Bethel and Anat-Bethel alongside their ancestral god Yahō. The same papyrus from Elephantine refers to Anat-Bethel—the traditional consort of Bethel, better known under the title Queen of Heaven—with the name Anat-Yahō."[26] In Elephantine, therefore,

---

[22] Bernd U. Schipper, "The Judeans/Aramaeans of Elephantine and Their Religion: An Egyptological Perspective," in *Elephantine in Context: Studies on the History, Religion and Literature of the Judeans in Persian Period Egypt*, ed. Reinhard G. Kratz and Bernd U. Schipper (Tübingen: Mohr Siebeck, 2022), 216–17.

[23] Ibid., 224.

[24] I depend on the translation provided by Tawny L. Holm, "Papyrus Amherst 63 and the Arameans of Egypt: A Landscape of Cultural Nostalgia," in *Elephantine in Context: Studies on the History, Religion and Literature of the Judeans in Persian Period Egypt*, ed. Reinhard G. Kratz and Bernd U. Schipper (Tübingen: Mohr Siebeck, 2022), 324.

[25] Ibid., 325.

[26] See Toorn, "Egyptian Papyrus," 37; idem, "The Background of the Elephantine Jews in Light of Papyrus Amherst 63," in Kratz and Schipper, eds., *Elephantine in Context*, 354; Holm, "Papyrus Amherst 63 and the Arameans of Egypt," 334–44. More evidence reveals that Judeans in Thebes in Egypt were

the Judean diasporan community was conscious and fully present to the cultural and religious realities of their context by adapting to the religious beliefs and traditions of their neighbors in their search of meaning in a foreign land.[27] The pairing of Yahweh and Asherah in cultic activities and the evidence of devotion to Asherah's divine majesty support the view that migrant Jews in Egypt were open to integrating new and foreign ways of religious expression in their search for meaning, belonging, and stability in Egypt.

Biblical evidence shows that their wives and daughters began to worship in the shrines and temples of Egyptian deities, making offerings to them for their divine attributes (Jer. 44:15). Adding the worship of Asherah, the queen of heaven, to their religious consciousness was not new to the Jewish community in Egypt, because devotion to her divine majesty was widespread in Judah and on the streets of Jerusalem (Jer. 44:17). Worshiping her in Egypt with libations and liturgical activities was for the purpose of seeking her divine benefaction to grant survival and prosperity to the migrant community of the children of God in a foreign land. This is based on the conviction that the calamities that have come upon them back home in Judah were a consequence of the neglect of their religious devotion to the queen of heaven (Jer. 44:18). What their conviction revealed is their belief that Yahweh alone could not save them in a foreign land. Famine, agricultural disaster, and the destruction of their nation had a divine consequence. It was, therefore, under this circumstance that in Egypt the communities embraced pious allegiance to the queen of heaven, Asherah, for the sake of their well-being and survival. Where Yahweh had failed, Asherah excelled as the people sought her divine providence as the goddess of fertility by pouring libations and votive offerings to her divine majesty (Jer. 44:15-19). Judean women confirmed their cultic allegiance to the queen of heaven by stating clearly that it was a family affair; every

---

also receptive to non-Judean gods as they became well integrated into Egyptian society. See Honigman, "Serving the Kings, Building Temples, and Paying the "Jewish Tax," 111.

[27] See Holm, "Papyrus Amherst 63 and the Arameans of Egypt," 331.

household and the entire diasporan community were involved in worshiping her (44:19).

In the *Metamorphosis*, Apuleius recounts that Lucius called Isis the "queen of heaven" (*regina caeli*),[28] as she was the queen of the heavenly beings;[29] she controlled the sun and the stars, and they obeyed her.[30] Also, in the aretalogy of Isis at Kyme, the goddess was associated with astral beings—sun and moon—and she was the only deity who charted the path of the stars, sun, and moon. She was the goddess who gave agriculture to humanity. Additionally, it is important to mention here that the Egyptians attributed the flooding of the Nile to the god Hapi, "who causes the water of the Nile to rise and brings the flood."[31] Similarly, the goddess Satet also is identified as the "pourer of the Nile flood."[32] In Greco-Roman times, the goddess Satet was linked with Isis. On this note, that Egyptian farmers honored these deities to help irrigate their farms revealed also a corresponding degree of devotional dependence of the migrant Judean farmers in Egypt on these deities.[33] Women called Isis their God, and Egypt was her earthly habitation from where she ruled humankind.[34] Jeremiah 44:15–19 confirms the ubiquitous presence of her cult in Egypt and the role women play in her cult and shrine.

---

[28] Apuleius, *Metam.* 11.2 (Hanson, LCL).

[29] Ibid., 11.5.

[30] Ibid., 11.25.

[31] Schipper, "The Judeans/Aramaeans of Elephantine and Their Religion," 210.

[32] Ibid.

[33] For the presence of the cult of Isis in Elephantine, see ibid., 210–14.

[34] See the translation of Frederick W. Danker, *Benefaction: Epigraphical Study of a Graeco-Roman and New Testament Semantic Field* (St. Louis: Clayton Publishing House, 1982), 197–99. Aristophanes calls the goddess Demeter, who is venerated in the Eleusian mystery the "Lady of Salvation, [who] promises to save our land in season." See Aristophanes, *The Frog*, 376–80, trans. Marvin W. Meyer, *The Ancient Mysteries: A SourceBook—Sacred Texts of the Mystery Religions of the Ancient Mediterranean World* (San Francisco: Harper & Row, 1987), 35. She is known as "the goddess who protects the growth of corn." See Hans-Josef Klauck, *The Religions of Context of Early Christianity: A Guide to Graeco-Roman Religion*, trans. Brian McNeil (Minneapolis: Fortress Press, 2003), 103.

Today, the migrants leaving behind their homeland in search of better living conditions elsewhere are convinced of a divine inducement for their decision to migrate. They carry on their persons religious items and objects as a symbolic act of invoking the deity's companionship just as the deity has done throughout human history, particularly in the relationship between the children of Israel and Yahweh. This is the reality of Abraham, his household, and Yahweh in the context of the harsh realities of living in Canaan together with the trepidation of moving to Egypt. On one hand, Yahweh shared with the household of Abraham the fear of death and the hostile living conditions in the land, hence the need to migrate. On the other hand, transcending human weakness and fear, Yahweh was a source of strength and courage as the companion of a migrating family who was weighed down by the uncertainty of life in a foreign land. This is the case because Yahweh rescued Sarah and restored the family unit from the actions of an ill-intentioned overlord to humiliate Sarah and embarrass Abraham. The same is true of the life of the ancestor Jacob and his household. Departing Canaan for Egypt, he performed a ritual honoring Yahweh, who assured him of divine companionship in Egypt. Therefore, Yahweh's presence in Egypt lends credence to the point of view that migrants, like Israel's ancestors, arrive in a foreign land with elements of their religious tradition, the providential presence of their deity, and openness to the opportunity for religious expression that their new context provides.

For migrants today, crucifixes, the different images of the Blessed Virgin Mary, rosaries, and religious cards are among the items carried in migrants' luggage or duffel bags. Certainly, the decision to carry among their belongings a symbolic reminder of the presence of the deity comes from a place of deeply ingrained belief that the migrant is accompanied by a deity or divine intercessor on whom the migrant's hopes and dreams of a better life depend.

For instance, the migrants fleeing poverty, violence, political unrest, and drug cartels from South and Central America, particularly from Mexico, carry in their luggage prayer cards and pictures of Our Lady of Guadalupe, because of the deeply held belief that divine

Migrants illegally enter the United States by crossing the Rio Grande in rubber boats near Los Ebanos, Texas, June 15, 2019.
Photo by Kris Grogan, CBP Office of Public Affairs, public domain

companionship provides assurances of success in a foreign land. Those who leave their homeland in Mexico for passage to the United States concretize the image and the cultural symbolism of Our Lady of Guadalupe as they retell her story of divine presence in their lives through their journey north; she is a sign of hope, liberation, and consolation in a foreign land that promises freedom and a better life.[35] For migrants from Mexico, inculturation is a profound experience of searching their religious tradition for a meaningful way to connect with Our Lady of Guadalupe in the present realities of their lives in the United States. Therefore, fleeing the experience of inhumanity caused by drug cartels and poverty, they embrace the nobility and dignity that the image of Our Lady of Guadalupe presents because she is the restorer of human dignity of the Indigenous people, the source of hope and strength to navigate an uncharted territory.[36] In fact, migrants

---

[35] Jeanette Rodríguez and Ted Fortier, *Cultural Memory. Resistance, Faith, and Identity* (Austin: University of Texas Press, 2007), 17.
[36] Ibid., 18–19.

crossing the southern border of the United States are consciously aware that Our Lady of Guadalupe enters into their lived experiences as a companion in their longing for dignity, self-worth, acceptance, and hospitality.[37] Indeed, their hope of human flourishing in the United States rests on the divine majesty of Our Lady of Guadalupe.

The walls of detention centers are designed with graffiti of the cross of Christ, left behind by migrants showcasing their convictions about divine companionship and connection with the cross of Christ, which represents both suffering and triumph, strengthening their hopes of surviving life in a foreign land, plus enduring the horror and the inhumanity of border crossing. Those who successfully arrive in Europe or North America—the most sought-after destinations for migrants from Africa, Asia, the Middle East, and Central and South America, following grueling journeys and horrifying stories in the hands of smugglers—are convinced that faith, belief, and divine providence brought them safely to their destinations.

African children arrive at a refugee camp, December 15, 2020.
Photo by Sam Mann/Unsplash, public domain

---

[37] See ibid., 31; also Antonio D. Sison, *The Art of Indigenous Inculturation: Grace on the Edge of Genius* (Maryknoll, NY: Orbis Books, 2021), 78–81.

Sub-Saharan African migrants who depart the city of Agadez in the Niger Republic en route to Tripoli in Libya through the desert are exposed to dehydration, harassment, extortion, and arbitrary detention, but their human spirit remains determined to cross the Mediterranean Sea into Europe through Italy. There have been numerous drownings at sea from fishing boats and rubber rafts crowded with migrants. On October 3, 2013, one of the most gut-wrenching and horrifying cases of fatality at sea was the drowning of more than three hundred migrants off the Italian island of Lampedusa. The victims, mostly from sub-Saharan Africa, panicked and tried to get out of the fishing boat at once when a rescue boat arrived. For every sea mishap, the bodies and belongings of migrants wash ashore, revealing, more often than not, articles of religious beliefs like crucifixes and rosaries, testaments to the migrants' determination and their faith in divine companionship. An Eritrean migrant who successfully arrived in Germany enthused, "Alhamdulillah," because of her firm belief in divine providence and companionship for her successful journey.[38]

Taken together, therefore, one can discern that when a migrant crosses a border, just as the children of Israel did, they take with them their culture and religious expressions as they search for meaningful life in a foreign land. As with the image of Our Lady of Guadalupe, so likewise the cross of Christ invokes Christ's triumph over death as a sign of their determination to seek a foreign land that offers life, dignity, and value.

---

[38] Reporting about Nasenet Alme Wildmikael, Alexis Okeowo writes, "She made her way through the Sahel desert, using a route where many migrants have died of hunger or thirst, and where sexual violence is so common that some women take contraceptives before embarking. In Libya, she was held in a detention center in Tripoli. The guards fed the prisoners once a day and frequently beat the male detainees. After a month, she was released, and paid almost two thousand dollars to board a boat to Italy. 'When I was on the boat, I thought I would never reach the ground again,' Wildmikael said. 'But, *alhamdulillah*, I arrived.'" See Alexis Okeowo, "The Missing. Many Migrants Disappear on Their Way to Europe. Most Are Never Identified," *New Yorker*, January 16, 2023, 17.

Syrians and Iraqi refugees arrive from Turkey at Skala Sykamias on the island of Lesbos, Greece, October 30, 2015.
Public domain

The Christian understanding of the kerygma, embodied in the ministry and life of Jesus Christ, encounters its most practical appropriation in the lived experiences of migrants. In fact, the passion of Christ in the Christian Scriptures stands out through time, history, and place in the kerygma, drawing believers into profound intimacy with Christ, who loves believers and has given himself up to death in order to bring to fulfillment God's plan for creation (see Gal. 2:19–20). Paul, as Michael J. Gorman observes, "claims that the reason for Christ's self-giving death was to rescue people from the hostile, apocalyptic powers of this evil age—sin, death, the 'elemental spirits,' and any other powers of [captivity and enslavement]."[39] These powers that stand in opposition to the cross of Christ manifest their enslaving dominance in the social, political, and economic realities of victimization, oppression, and death that drive many away from their

---

[39] Michael J. Gorman, *Cruciformity: Paul's Narrative Spirituality of the Cross* (Grand Rapids: Eerdmans, 2001), 276.

homeland in search of freedom elsewhere. It is for this reason that a relationship of divine belonging with Christ enlivens migrants' hope in the impermanence of suffering and the immutability of glory as proclaimed in the kerygma. The migrants "who live under the power of grace (Rom. 5:12–21; 6:15), the grace manifested in the cross," concretize their experience of divine companionship in Christ, who is their wellspring of their determination to succeed.[40]

To this effect, then, Christian migrants epitomize through a ritualized religious experience the central place the passion of Christ occupies in the tradition by carrying a crucifix on their person as they depart from their homeland to a foreign land. To this end, the self-gift of Christ on the cross represents for a migrant a totem of divine presence, whose life of suffering and glorification brings hope and reassurance in the migrant's context of suffering and uncertainty. Therefore, the invitation to believers in the letter to the Hebrews to look up to Christ who endured the cross and now is glorified by God is embraced by most Christian migrants as they navigate through the uncertainty of life in a foreign land (Heb. 12:2). Migrants have taught us that the cross is an adequate representation of their immediate contextual experience of suffering and struggle, along with a not-far-distant hope of triumph and joy.

Keeping in mind, therefore, that the cultural expressions of particular religious traditions find meaning in the life of a people and a community, migrants have deepened the affective meaning of the cross of Christ by embracing its complexities as a symbol of both dehumanization and divinization of personhood. Evidence reveals that for migrants today, the cross of Christ is relevant to their context, situation, and lived experiences. It is futile to engage the Christian tradition with a migrant community if such an interaction neglects to appreciate how their experience of migration has transformed and changed their Christian faith with the overarching centerpiece of the cross of Christ in their lives. If inculturation is the incarnation of the life, death, and resurrection of Jesus Christ in the context of the lives

---

[40] Ibid., 276–77.

of believers, then the experience of migrants, who contextualize the suffering and glorification of Christ, is apposite. Since the incarnation is an extraordinary outpouring of divine love in the humanity of Jesus Christ (John 3:16; Phil. 2:6–8), inculturation is essentially an experience in contextual expression of the presence of God in the world through the life, death, and resurrection of Christ. In other words, inculturation is a conscious act of uniting a community or an individual with Christ's life in a particular socio-cultural context. For many migrants today, the crucifix, as I have proposed here, stands out as a contextual expression of unity and belongingness in Christ. The context in which Christian migrants tell stories of their adventure is one of cross and glory, suffering and success, pain and joy, foregrounded in the human sphere in the life of Christ. Since the story of salvation is historically present in different cultures and in diverse human experiences, the experiences of Christian migrants are stories of an encounter with the Word of God, Jesus Christ, who enters into their experience of migration in order to bring about meaning and transformation.

Conclusion

The experiences of migration that I have examined in this essay speak to the human condition and the search for freedom and safety when a social context has become unhabitable. Because of the role that context plays in the formation of identity of a community's or an individual's outlook on life, a new context will present challenges that are not limited to linguistic and socio-cultural values, but also to the relationship with the divine. For migrants, the relationship with the divine is often forged and consolidated at the very moment they depart from their homeland in search of safety elsewhere. This was the same case with the Jewish ancestor, Jacob. The sacrifice he performed before leaving Canaan was a ritual act in divine companionship and reassurance that migration into Egypt was the best decision for him and his household (see Gen. 46:3–4). The anxiety of leaving behind their homeland is often mitigated by migrants' openness to new cultural contexts, as was the case with the Jewish migrants in Elephantine and other cities in Egypt. Egypt presented them with the opportunity to experience the process of cultural assimilation of their religious experiences for a meaningful life in a foreign land. I have examined the extant writings from Jewish settlements in Egypt, which reveal an activity of inculturation among diasporan Jews in Egypt. The same is true about migrants from places like Mexico, who identify with the socio-cultural and divine attributes of Our Lady of Guadalupe as they make their way to the United States for a better life. Just so, the cross of Christ, which they carry, serves as a symbol of pain and glory in the divine plan for the salvation of the world through Jesus Christ. By carrying this image, with its complex meanings of pain and suffering, joy and glory, they find a presentation of their own experience of crossing treacherous paths in the quest for human flourishing in Europe or North America.

7

Pedagogy of Hospitality

Transforming Missionary Onslaught into Mutual Transformation and Enrichment

Agbonkhianmeghe E. Orobator

Some missionary accounts of early evangelization portray it as a benevolent fulfillment of the gospel mandate to proclaim the good news to the ends of the earth, although local versions and perceptions show ample evidence of hubris founded on the presumed superiority and dominance of a foreign religion and laced with multiple forms of violence directed toward adherents of Indigenous religions. In the context of Africa, not only did African religion display an extraordinary resilience in the face of this missionary onslaught; it also responded with an approach that is best described as a "pedagogy of hospitality." Upon closer examination, this response entails a methodological path and offers a hermeneutical prism that reveals diverse ways in which African religion serves as the soil on which Christianity is rooted and, as such, engenders inculturation and exercises enduring transformative influence on Christian beliefs, practices, and rituals in the African church.

Africa of "All the Vices": Historical Backdrop

The early missionaries to Africa, as elsewhere, were motivated by the gospel mandate to "go and make disciples of all nations" (Matt. 28:19). Their strong, resolute, and enthusiastic response to this mandate led to a path of encounter between missionary Christianity and African religion that was propitious and turbulent at the same time. History shows that it was an encounter of two unequal religious self-consciousnesses and traditions, with the former claiming an unsurpassed superiority and the latter content to maintain its beliefs, rituals, and practices unfazed by the sophisticated theological resources of its interlocutor.

Africa's celebrated novelist Chinua Achebe captured the essence and complexity of this encounter in his award-winning novel *Things Fall Apart*. In the following excerpts, he recounts one of the first events of the encounter between missionary Christianity and African Indigenous religion.

> The arrival of the missionaries had caused a considerable stir in the village of Mbanta. There were six of them and one was a white man.
>
> When they had all gathered, the white man began to speak to them.... And he told them about this new God, the creator of all the world and all the men and women. He told them that they worshipped false gods, gods of wood and stone. A deep murmur went through the crowd when he said this. He told them that the true God lived on high and that all men when they died went before him for judgment. Evil men and all the heathen who in their blindness bowed to wood and stone were thrown into a fire that burned like palm-oil. But good men who worshipped the true God lived forever in His happy kingdom. "We have been sent by this great God to ask you to leave your wicked ways and false gods and turn to Him so that you may be saved when you die," he said....

> At this point an old man said he had a question. "Which is this god of yours," he asked, "the goddess of the earth, the god of the sky, Amadiora or the thunderbolt, or what?"
>
> The interpreter spoke to the white man and he immediately gave his answer. "All the gods you have named are not gods at all. They are gods of deceit who tell you to kill your fellows and destroy innocent children. There is only one true God and He has the earth, the sky, you and me and all of us."
>
> "If we leave our gods and follow your god," asked another man, "who will protect us from the anger of our neglected gods and ancestors?"
>
> "Your gods are not alive and cannot do you any harm," replied the white man. "They are pieces of wood and stone."
>
> When this was interpreted to the men of Mbanta they broke into derisive laughter. These men must be mad, they said to themselves. How else could they say that Ani and Amadiora were harmless? And Idemili and Ogwugwu too? And some of them began to go away.[1]

The hubris of these early missionaries was as comprehensive as their ignorance of the local context was profound—evidenced in the derisive laughter of their unimpressed and unbelieving audience.

A second factor is worth noting in the manner in which this evangelical hubris rapidly crystallized into a narrative of superiority and eventually morphed into a practice of domination and, in some cases, violence. Put simply, in the wider historical context of Africa and the world of the nineteenth century, missionary Christianity did not travel alone. In many parts of Africa, the advent of Christianity was almost always associated with the establishment of Western colonial political hegemony and its attendant project of massive economic exploitation. French, English, Portuguese, Spanish, Dutch, and Italian missionaries had the unique distinction of openly fronting

---

[1] Chinua Achebe, *Things Fall Apart* (New York: Anchor Books, 1994), 144–46.

the hegemonic agenda of their colonizing patrons to bolster their own evangelical ambition and extend their geographical sphere of influence. With only a few exceptions, such as Irish missionaries, they espoused overt political positions and economic interests that so often cast missionary endeavors in the shadow of an ambiguous adventure.

In reality, Africa was a daunting, unforgiving missionary terrain. Coming to Africa was considered a deadly or death-defying enterprise but one that was worthy of the gospel mandate to evangelize the world. The first cohorts of missionaries were guaranteed early and assured mortality. In his book *Sierra Leone: The Principal British Colony on the Western Coast of Africa*, the acting first writer to Her Majesty's Britannic Commissioners, William Whitaker Shreeve, offered a depressing account of Africa's religious identity and a frightful prognosis of Christianity's missionary adventure on the continent:

> Africa, like all countries where Christianity has not penetrated, or where it progresses but slowly, is doomed to the darkness of pagan superstition, or of idolatrous rites ... polygamy, lust, licentiousness, and all the vices.... For, until some great revolution in nature or some great and gradual human exertion takes place, it must ever prove the "white man's grave." ... And truly may it be said that "Africa's shores are paved with the white man's bones, and its grave-yards filled with monuments of lost exertions."[2]

Shreeve's assessment of the fate of an entire race pivoted on clichéd sociological and philosophical constructs. His account summarized the standard narrative of missionary Christianity: the object of the missionary mandate was a land of darkness, paganism, superstition, idolatry, and an assortment of unimaginable vices. Accordingly, missionary Christianity harbored no illusion about the undertaking and the fate that lay in wait.

---

[2] William Whitaker Shreeve, *Sierra Leone: The Principal British Colony on the Western Coast of Africa* (London: Simmonds and Co. "Colonial Magazine" Office, 1817), 2–3.

The ignoble project of a racially prejudicial taxonomy of Africa that Shreeve so eloquently articulated was a shared colonial construct across the disciplines of the day. Notably, his epistemological ancestor, Immanuel Kant, and philosophical heir, Georg W. F. Hegel, indulged in convoluted argumentation to prove the anthropological "stupidity" of Africans who are but pitiable specimens of "the natural man in his completely wild and untamed state"[3] and "the Unhistorical, Undeveloped Spirit, still involved in the conditions of mere nature."[4] For these colonial myth-makers, what was true of Africans was also true of their religion, though they would have been loath to consider any practice associated with Africans worthy of the label "religion."

Over several decades, the colonial enterprise of myth-making and racial stereotyping continued to yield a repertoire of nicknames and aliases gratuitously conferred upon Africa. Without exception, such nicknames denoted primitiveness and savagery—from Joseph Conrad's "heart of darkness" to Henry Morton Stanley's "dark continent" and *The Economist* magazine's "hopeless continent." This patronizing pastime of name-calling or nicknaming Africa reinforces a stereotypical thinking embedded deeply in mythical colonial portrayals of the continent's complex identity, history, and religion.

The historical and geographical context of Shreeve's morbid assessment would have justified his dark projections. As mentioned, nineteenth-century Africa was an intimidating terrain even for the most intrepid of missionaries, traders, and explorers, and the cast of colonial adventurers. High mortality rates, harsh tropical climate, rampant diseases, and poor sanitation guaranteed the certain demise of missionaries and colonialists and accentuated the urgency of their evangelical exertions and ambitions. For this reason, the African bishops at the first African Synod in 1994 paid a glowing tribute to the monumental evangelical exertions of Western missionaries:

---

[3] G. W. F. Hegel, *The Philosophy of History* (New York: Dover, 1956), 93; see also Immanuel Kant, *Observations on the Feeling of the Beautiful and the Sublime* (1764).

[4] Hegel, *The Philosophy of History*, 99.

The effort made by missionaries, men and women, who worked for generations on end on the African continent, deserves our praise and gratitude. They worked very hard, endured much pain, discomfort, hunger, thirst, illness, the certainty of a very short life span and death itself, in order to give us what was most dear to them: Jesus Christ. They paid a very high price to make us the children of God. Their faith and commitment, the dynamism and the ardour of their zeal have made it possible for us to exist today as Church-Family to the praise and glory of God. Very early they were joined in their witness by great numbers of the sons and daughters of the land of Africa as Catechists, interpreters and collaborators of all kinds.[5]

The habit of classifying or categorizing Africa and labeling its religious heritage has persisted into the twenty-first century, although it has evolved into a slightly more benign nomenclature. Accordingly, almost two centuries after Shreeve, Pope Benedict XVI created another pseudonym for the continent: "Africa," he declared, "constitutes an immense spiritual 'lung' for a humanity that appears to be in a crisis of faith and hope."[6] This manifestly complimentary description departs radically from the missionary vocabulary that branded all religious practices in Africa as paganism, superstition, and darkness. Implicit in Benedict's declaration is the confidence that the religious values of Africa could be spiritually refreshing for a humanity in dire need of renewal and rejuvenation. More importantly, the evolution of nomenclature from Shreeve's "white man's grave" to Benedict's "immense spiritual 'lung'" is symptomatic not only of the trajectory of the development of religion in Africa but also of the historical receptiveness of the continent to change and new opportunities. The main argument of this essay rests

---

[5] First Synod of African Bishops, "Message to the People of God," May 8, 1994, no. 10, Vatican Press Office, *Synodus Episcoporum*—Bulletin, English Edition (1995).

[6] Pope Benedict VI, Homily, Eucharistic Celebration for the Opening of the Second Special Assembly for Africa of the Synod of Bishops, October 4, 2009, www.vatican.va.

on the claim that this receptiveness is emblematic of and rooted in the heart of the spirit and practice of African religion. Such receptiveness is propitious for rethinking and re-rooting deep inculturation to the mutual benefit of diverse religious traditions.

It is perhaps not a surprise that Benedict would choose to flatter Africa with such an affirmative appellation. Africa is an indispensable part of the demographic fortunes of Christianity, particularly in the twentieth and the twenty-first centuries. The growth of Christianity on the continent is unprecedented. As the American commentator on religious history John Allen Jr. once remarked, "If I were asked to offer a history of Roman Catholicism in the twentieth century in one sentence, I would reply: 'The center of gravity shifted from North to South.'"[7] Such incontrovertible evidence of religious growth in Africa is interpreted by Benedict XVI as a sign of hope for the rest of the world. Africa holds a significant piece of the future of Christianity, or crucially, the future of Christianity passes through Africa. This fact is amply and strongly supported by statistics of the growth of Christianity in Africa.

For example, within the wider context of religious growth in Africa, Catholicism has recorded significant proportionate demographic expansion over the last one hundred years, climbing from 1,220,000, or less than 1 percent of the total global population of Catholics in 1910, to 171.48 million, or 16 percent of Catholics worldwide, in 2010.[8] These figures show the rapid growth of Catholicism on the continent in the span of a century, a fact that recently prompted an imaginative Spanish journalist to nickname Africa "a factory of Catholic souls."[9]

---

[7] John L. Allen Jr., *The Future Church: How Ten Trends Are Revolutionizing the Catholic Church* (New York: Doubleday, 2009), 17.

[8] World Christian Database, www.worldchristiandatabase.org; "Global Christianity: A Report on the Size and Distribution of the World's Christian Population," *Pew Forum on Religion & Public Life*, December 2011; corrected February 2013, www.pewforum.org.

[9] Joana Socías, "Una 'fábrica' de almas para la Iglesia," *El Mundo*, March 6, 2013.

A Resilient Religion or a Religion of Resilience

As mentioned, historically, African religion endured spates of vicious mischaracterizations, stereotypes, and denigrating labeling. Part of the missionary strategy to introduce, transplant, and ensure the survival of the "white man's religion" was to mount a frontal attack against Indigenous religions. The language of this attack was categorical: "Your gods are not alive and cannot do you any harm.... They are pieces of wood and stone." This ad hominem argumentation may have convinced many converts. Yet, quite clearly, the foreign religions—namely, Christianity and Islam—have failed largely to eradicate Indigenous religions from the vibrant religious landscape and deep consciousness of Africans. There are several examples that illustrate the persistence, tenacity, and resilience of African religion.

Consider, for example, the practice of voodoo. In the imagination of many people, this term evokes dangerous, diabolical, and malevolent beliefs, rituals, and practices, of the kind that Shreeve disparaged and maligned in his writing. Notwithstanding this patently negative perception, voodoo has a long-standing positive political profile, enduring social appeal, and widespread communal adherence in West Africa, particularly in the Benin Republic. For many people in this country, voodoo is an ancestral way of life that ritualizes and regulates relationships within the community of devotees and provides spiritual resources for individual and collective growth and flourishing. It is instructive that Benin honors the voodoo religion with an official national public holiday (January 10). The holiday is usually the occasion for colorful celebrations and unrestrained public display of pride in the tenets of voodoo among its adherents.

The second example of the resilience of African religion also comes from West Africa. Every year, in the month of August, an estimated one million pilgrims and devotees converge in Osogbo, an ancient town in Southwest Nigeria, to pay homage to Osun, the Yoruba goddess of the river. The deity is associated with water, fertility, purity, love, and sensuality. The nationalities of people who flock to this annual religious spectacle reflect the extent of Yoruba religious tradition, which encompasses not just its home in Nigeria but also people in the Caribbean, South America, North America, and Eastern Europe—Slovenia, Serbia, and parts of former Yugoslavia. As one Slovenian devotee was quoted as saying, "I am here to get blessing from Osun. We follow the culture of Ifa ... in search of primal energy." A Serb devotee added, "[I am] coming to Osun, to my mother and mother of all human beings to celebrate her and say thank you for my life ... and to ask support for the rest of my life." Over several decades, the Osun festival has grown in importance and reputation to merit listing Osogbo as a World Heritage Site by the United Nations Educational, Scientific, and Cultural Organization (UNESCO).

For the followers of these two Indigenous religions, the loathsome reputation and the attendant demonization of African religion that is often stoked by Christian preachers, pastors, and evangelists would be patently abhorrent. As the two examples demonstrate, this negative onslaught and willful mischaracterization have neither weakened nor eliminated its appeal to African religious consciousness. Besides, anecdotal evidence suggests that Christians and Muslims clandestinely revert to the practices of African religion in moments of crisis. My assessment of this phenomenon is markedly different from those of some African and Western theologians. Where they perceive syncretism, superficiality, and lack of depth of religious loyalty of Africa Christians, I tend to perceive something deeper and worthy of greater theological attention, particularly in regard to the project of framing a new and compelling discourse of deep inculturation:

> Whether driven by fear or circumstances, somewhere in the religious consciousness of Africans lies a counterpart to the "white man's religion." This counterpart functions neither as a foil or a foe, much less a competitor or rival. It is simply the ground on which the "white man's religion" was planted and on which it continues to grow. As one African

proverb says, a person who eats the fruit of a tree also eats the leaves, branches, trunk, and roots of the tree. So it is with Africans who have eaten the coveted fruit of the tree of Christianity; they continue to partake in its leaves, trunk, and especially, roots.[10]

In Africa, the root and the soil of the "white man's religion" is Indigenous religion, although, numerically speaking, Christianity would seem to have thrived at the expense of African religion. The significant growth of Christianity on the continent has no parallel in African religion. However, to think in such linear terms is to ignore the nature of African religion. In fact, religious practices and traditions in Africa are steeped in orality, embedded in cultural codes, and devoid of obsessive preoccupation with doctrinal rectitude, orthodoxy of belief, and proselytism. In reality, as I point out in my work *Religion and Faith in Africa: Confessions of an Animist*, quoting Benjamin C. Ray, what we call religion "is a late-comer to the scholarly discourse about Africa, and is still noticeably absent in most popular descriptions of African cultures."[11]

As I have argued across the broad spectrum of my theological scholarship, Indigenous religions resemble or form a cultural substratum on which a multiplicity of identities have been superimposed. John Barton has made a similar argument concerning the importance of Indigenous religions globally.[12] Thus, in Africa, Christianity or Islam cannot simply be understood as something planted in the wild and fallow forest of religious primitiveness. If my personal experience of conversion from Indigenous religion to Christianity serves as proof, African religious consciousness is anything but a tabula rasa. Like a dormant volcano, this religious substratum erupts repeatedly into the consciousness and beliefs of the imported religions. Thus the lava of African religion runs deep

---

[10] Agbonkhianmeghe E. Orobator, *Religion and Faith in Africa: Confessions of an Animist* (Maryknoll, NY: Orbis Books, 2018), 159.
[11] Benjamin C. Ray, *African Religions: Symbol, Ritual, and Community*, 2nd ed. (Upper Saddle River, NJ: Prentice Hall, 2000), xi.
[12] John D. Barton, *Better Religion: A Primer for Interreligious Peacebuilding* (Waco, TX: Baylor University Press, 2022).

in shaping the constantly rising profiles and identities of Christians and Muslims alike.

Missionary Christianity aimed to replace Indigenous religions in Africa by promoting its message as a substitute for something that it deemed false, obsolete, and uncivilized. For the missionaries, African religion had to cede ground to the Christian religion, considered modern, sophisticated, and superior. It was a zero-sum contest between the "true" religion and paganism, animism, or heathenism masquerading as a religion. Despite the sophisticated argumentation adduced to discredit Indigenous religion, the missionary understanding of African religion was patently flawed on several counts. This flawed understanding has persisted in contemporary times. What the early missionaries perceived—and modern-day evangelists continue to perceive—as African religion in all its nefarious manifestations resembles little of the organized religions of creeds, doctrines, and dogmas. It bears repeating that African religion is preeminently a way of life resourced by a deep universe of shared narratives, meaning, and wisdom. Were it just a repository of prescribed creeds, doctrines, dogmas, and Scripture, these could have been easily substituted and replaced, as the missionaries tried to do. But because it was a way of life, no amount of missionary exertion and theological argumentation would succeed in simply extirpating it from the religious consciousness and cultural landscape of its adherents. Here is how I have described the situation:

> Rather than replace the African way of life, Christianity built over it, which is another way of stating my position that Christianity is rooted in the soil of African Religion. This approach had the effect of unwittingly driving African Religion deeper into the hearts of its converts. Like a tropical tree the leaves and branches of Christianity flourished but the roots remained deeply anchored in the African way of life. It was this latter that nourished and shaped the growth of Christianity over centuries of evangelization in Africa. When today we reap the abundant fruits of missionary

Christianity, it is sweetened by the taste of its roots. To evangelical puritans, it is a bitter taste that they continue to attempt to wash away or dilute with the waters of baptism and the awesome force of the so-called "Holy Ghost fire."[13]

In a paradoxical sense, the fate and fortune of Christianity and African religion are intertwined in an intricate relationship of mutually assured survival. For the former to replace the latter "would amount to cutting off its own roots, which would mean a weakening of Christianity in Africa.... Christianity will continue to flourish, but influenced by the manner and form of its relationship with African Religion."[14]

In sum, the much-vaunted ascendancy of Christianity and Islam in sub-Saharan Africa over the last one hundred years may have weakened the practice of African religion, but—as the international Osun festival and voodoo national religious holiday demonstrate—it has not succeeded in eliminating the influence of Indigenous African religious beliefs, practices, and rituals.[15] These beliefs, practices, and rituals form the context wherein Christianity and Islam attempt to construct new and complex identities in Africa and where mutual transformation and enrichment happen for all three religious traditions. From a methodological perspective, it is also the site and soil of re-rooting inculturation, that is, of seeing and appreciating inculturation from the other side—from the perspective of Indigenous cultures and religions of the Global South and immigrant-heritage cultures in the interstices of dominant cultures.

By emphasizing the vital importance of Indigenous religion as the locus of deep inculturation, the aim is to focus attention on this dimension of depth. Oftentimes, the theological assessment of inculturation in Africa tends to concentrate largely though not exclusively on outward and observable manifestations of liturgical celebration. Among theologians, there is a wide consensus that credits

---

[13] Orobator, *Religion and Faith in Africa*, 164.
[14] Ibid.
[15] See "Tolerance and Tension: Islam and Christianity in Sub-Saharan Africa," *Pew Forum on Religion & Public Life,* April 15, 2010, 33–35, www.pewresearch.org.

the flourishing of liturgical inculturation to the reform and renewal engendered by Vatican II: "Led by the themes of Vatican II, sensitivity to popular religion and culture and a commitment to inculturation made it possible to refashion liturgy, celebrating rites to be relevant and familiar, intelligible, and also emotionally stimulating.... Now there was permission for Africans to be Africans."[16]

Celebrating "Culture Day."
Copyright © 2022 Hekima University College, Nairobi, Kenya

While this approach remains valid and has served useful purposes in the development and progress of liturgical adaptation, renewal, and creativity in Africa, it would be important not to ignore or overlook other promising sites for re-rooting deep inculturation. What makes Africans African goes beyond just the opportunity to participate in lively and emotionally stimulating liturgies, rites, and ceremonies.

The rest of this essay presents some elements of a hermeneutical prism for re-rooting inculturation that go beyond inherited ways of understanding and doing inculturation. The illustrative value of this

---

[16] Bede Jagoe, "Vatican II Comes to Africa," *Worship* 79 (2005): 544–54, 550.

description lies in the challenge it reveals to approach the task of a deeper inculturation through variegated facets that recognize and honor the genius, identity, and agency of Indigenous religious and cultural sensitivities and to fulfill the evangelical purpose of Christianity to make the gospel at home among peoples and places "wherever the Good News is preached in all the world" (Matthew 26:13). Each of the following sections identifies, develops, and situates a site among key areas and resources for deepening the theological understanding of inculturation where lived realities of culture, religion, and practice intersect, namely hospitality, relationality, and conversation.

A Religion of Hospitality

In several African cultures, a guest is considered to be a harbinger of blessings. A Swahili (Tanzania) proverb says, "A guest brings healing to the host." The arrival of a guest in a homestead is ritualized as an important event in the life of the host and the guest. In some cultures, the host offers a cup of water, symbolically, to quench the thirst of the guest who has come from afar and perhaps braved precarious situations along the way. In other cultures, the host may present a local beverage. Several West African cultures offer a kola nut. Each of these acts constitutes a social interaction and a religious ritual. For example, when a kola nut is presented, it is "broken," prayers are said, and its lobes are shared between the guest and the host-household. In the event that any of these items is withheld from a guest, it is generally assumed that he or she is not welcome. It should be said that African religion and cultures do not hold a monopoly over the practice of hospitality.

As in Africa, hospitality is a central feature of the Christian tradition. Many biblical stories recount the iconic experiences of wayfarers and their gracious and generous hosts. The list includes Abraham, Moses, Elijah, Mary, Martha, Zacchaeus, and Jesus of Nazareth. Every encounter of hospitality is an experience of mutual blessing. What is offered to the guest by way of nourishment and refreshment is returned to the host as multiple blessings.

The positive valuation of African ethics and a theology of hospitality has some downsides. This becomes evident when we consider, for example, the hospitality or the dearth thereof toward migrants and refugees. Unfortunately, the value of hospitality has come under close scrutiny and diminished in importance, especially in the particular situation of forcibly displaced people and migrants. More and more, countries are opting to close their borders, build walls, and push migratory people away from their shores. The message is clear: you are not welcome here. This approach is the antithesis of hospitality in a situation where the guests are for all intents and purposes vulnerable persons who face multiple exploitations and abuses, including hostilities of unwelcoming governments, confinement to dehumanizing conditions of living, and exploitation by organized criminal groups.

This situation has severely undermined the much-vaunted African spirit of solidarity, generosity, and hospitality. In the 1960s and 1970s, it was reasonable to rely on these virtues when the nascent problem of displacement seemed temporary and amenable to quick and easy solutions. But as the numbers have soared and the cost of hosting masses of displaced people proved unbearable for impoverished African countries, the compassionate disposition toward refugees and migrants has ceded ground to strategic economic calculations and stringent immigration and asylum policies, the cumulative effect of which has diluted hospitality as a cardinal virtue. As Jonathan Bascom has observed, "Today supportive evidence of 'African hospitality' for refugees has become harder to find."[17] The economic reason behind this decline of 'African hospitality' is not hard to fathom, given the fact that all the refugees in Africa are generated and hosted by the least developed countries. Thus, it is no longer considered a virtue that "the local community ... in the spirit of African solidarity, shares its poverty and becomes as poor as the refugees themselves."[18]

---

[17] Jonathan Bascom, *Losing Place: Refugee Populations and Rural Transformations in East Africa* (New York: Berghahn Books, 1998), 25.

[18] CIMADE, INODEP, MINK, *Africa's Refugee Crisis: What Is to Be Done?*, trans. Michael John (London: Zed Books, 1986), 131; UNHCR, *Statistical Yearbook 2001*, 65–70.

In this context, it is worth noting that Pope Francis has proposed pathways toward a solution for an ethical approach to the international management of migration based on the practice of hospitality. Francis' response is articulated by four verbs: welcome, protect, promote, and integrate. A generous approach of welcoming those who knock at our doors is the direct opposite of attitudes of rejection and indifference to the dignity of people on the move. In line with the core element of the practice of hospitality as exemplified in Africa, the most important component of the pope's approach is the recognition of the mutuality of hospitality. A guest does not always come as a burden; he or she comes with gifts and values to share with the host and to enhance the latter's life. As another Swahili proverb says, "A visitor is a guest for two days. On the third day, put him or her to work." In so doing, the guest begins to contribute to the social and economic well-being of the host household and community.

This excursus on the decline of hospitality may seem irrelevant to the subject of this essay. Quite the contrary, there is an important relationship. Of the many positive characterizations of African religion, none, to my knowledge, has applied the label of hospitality. As mentioned above, missionary Christianity and Islam did not encounter a tabula rasa; they encountered a flourishing religious experience complete with long-established beliefs, practices, and rituals that animated and gave meaning to and rooted the personal and communal lives of Africans in a spiritually charged universe. Despite the brutal force of imposition to which proponents of missionary Christianity resorted in several situations, African religion has remained a gracious host, albeit a long-suffering one. Therein lies a foundational element of African religion that ought to be given prominence in the discourse about re-rooting inculturation. In essence, it is a religion of hospitality. By nature, it does not proselytize. At heart, it is a religion of peace. This understanding of African religion as a repository of hospitality takes on an even deeper meaning in the present-day context.

In many parts of Africa, just like some other places in the world, religious tension points to the escalating animosity of religiosity and the emergence of sectarian cleavages that threaten the social fabric of the continent. With frightening intensity, these cleavages have unleashed deadly religious and tribal passions in different parts of Africa, turning them into zones of conflict, violence, and carnage. Strikingly, unlike Christianity and Islam, none of these events can be tied directly or indirectly to African Religion. Understandably, for this reason, the missionary religions, notably Christianity and Islam, have come under intense critical scrutiny. Critics like Nobel Peace laureate Wole Soyinka have repeatedly blamed Islam and Christianity of being "guilty not merely of physical atrocities on African soil, including enslavement of the indigenes, but of systematic assault on African spirituality in their contest for religious hegemony."[19]

As mentioned, Benedict XVI has correctly assessed the status of Africa as the lung of humanity, but religious zealotry and evangelical bigotry connive to choke this lung. In light of the purposes of this essay, this situation allows us to discover and consider seriously African religion as a viable and rich source of spiritual revivification and normative resources for re-rooting of inculturation, albeit one that has consistently been dismissed and combated by Islam and Christianity. I hold the strong conviction that the spirit of African religion is peaceable, hospitable, and inclusive. Without falling prey to the temptation of romanticizing the phenomenon, I believe that African religion serves a critical purpose as a bulwark against extremist attempts to dissolve the essence and value of religion in the pool of sectarian ideology and hypocrisy. Liberated from the zero-sum game of mutually assured destruction that characterizes Africa's two dominant religions in some instances, the spirit of African religion is a vital repository of humanity that can sustain belief in the future of the continent and school its people in the art of dignified existence and fraternal coexistence.

The inclusive and tolerant nature of Indigenous religion can be considered as a locus for generative inculturation, one that brings out the best of two religious traditions that encounter each other, while

---

[19] Wole Soyinka, *Of Africa* (New Haven, CT: Yale University Press, 2012), xi.

avoiding a tempestuous vilification and deliberate assaults, such as was the case with missionary Christianity.

What does inculturation re-rooted in African religion look like? Using three examples of elements of what I call the "pedagogy of hospitality," I attempt here to demonstrate how African religion and cultural practices serve as the soil on which Christianity is rooted and as such engenders inculturation and exercises an enduring transformative influence on Christian beliefs, practices, and rituals in the African church.

Inculturation as Relationality

A shorthand for the conceptualization of the core of African religion as the practice of hospitality is the notion of *Ubuntu*. In its imaginative sense, Ubuntu is a simple idea that prioritizes inclusivity over exclusivity, community over competition, hospitality over hostility, dialogue over confrontation, and respect over domination: "*Ubuntu* means we cannot turn our backs on anyone who genuinely wants to be part of our community.... *Ubuntu* in this sense places dialogue at the center of what it means to be fully human. It involves a future that seeks to rise above exclusion and alienation."[20]

One of my earliest puzzles in the study of philosophy was the Cartesian dictum, *Cogito ergo sum* ("I think, therefore I am"), which affirmed the priority of speculative reason as constitutive of human existence and knowledge. As an African, a different epistemological principle undergirds my worldview, namely, relationality as constitutive of human existence. Two expressions from southern Africa sum up this worldview: "*Umuntu ngumuntu ngabantu*" and "*Motho ke motho ka batho.*" Both translate loosely as "A person is a person because of/through other persons" and "I am, because we are."

Across Africa this approach is commonly known as Ubuntu. In its basic form, Ubuntu affirms the primacy of human relationship

---

[20] Gabriel Setiloane, quoted in Charles Villa-Vincencio, *Walk with Us and Listen: Political Reconciliation in Africa* (Washington, DC: Georgetown University Press, 2009), 113; see Cedric Mayson, *Why Africa Matters* (Maryknoll, NY: Orbis Books, 2010), 31–33.

in social, communal, and corporate activities. Humanity thrives on interdependence and relationality. Far from being isolated and self-sufficient, the human person depends vitally on other people to fulfill the deepest meaning of his or her existence. This approach recalls the values and principles of cooperation, solidarity, and shared purpose. To be human is to be open, that is, to reach out to others and to embrace them in their irreplaceable uniqueness and difference. Humanity is not a private, personal possession. Humanity is reflected through the mirror of the other's existence. Just as in God's light we see light (Psalm 36:9), the other's humanity illuminates my humanity, and vice versa.

Many African sayings emphasize Ubuntu as a normative resource that empowers people to situate themselves and their actions within a wider existential circle. Not only human existence, but also human capacity thrives on collaboration, cooperation, and communion. As one African proverb says, "If you want to go fast, walk alone; if you want to go far, walk with others." Another African proverb holds that "A single finger cannot catch a louse in the hair." Each proverb expounds the theme of interdependence and underscores the centrality of mutuality in human relationship. To say, "I am, because you are," is to embrace a horizon of relationships that is infinitely open and mutually enriching for a person, his or her community, and his or her environment. Although popularized in Africa, Ubuntu echoes key themes of the Christian tradition, notably the interdependence of the created universe and of all its constituents.

The narrative of creation in the Scripture affirms that the human person is created in the image and likeness of a loving God. Out of this inexhaustible font of love God confers dignity on the human person, making him or her "a little less than God" (Psalm 8:5). Yet the outcome of God's creative activity is anything but a monad: "male and female God created them" (Gen. 5:2). The narrative goes even further: God creates an environment designed to sustain human flourishing in return for care, solicitude, and stewardship toward all of creation. As Pope Francis teaches, biblical narratives of creation "suggest that human life is grounded in three fundamental and closely intertwined relationships: with God, with our neighbor and with the earth itself" (*Laudato Si'*, 66).[21] These relationships are "vital," because our life depends on them and we are because of them. Creation is eminently relational.

This Christian view of creation yields insights that align with the principle of the African worldview that we are fundamentally relational beings. Relationality is constitutive of our self-understanding. We cannot become fully who we are created to be while living in blissful isolation. To affirm the interiority, subjectivity, and humanity of my being, I must turn my gaze outward to see and recognize the other in his or her unique interiority, subjectivity, and humanity. This mutual recognition or intersubjectivity engenders a relationship of a spiritual "thou" who addresses himself or herself to another spiritual "thou," neither of whom is reducible to an expendable object of domination, exploitation, or violence (*LS*, 81).

In practical terms, the mutuality and relationality carry a normative value; they entail an ethical task to be realized. It is not enough to affirm the humanity of the other; it is morally imperative to defend and account for it. "Disregard for the duty to cultivate and maintain a proper relationship with my neighbor, for whose care and custody I am responsible, ruins my relationship with my own self, with others, with God and with the earth" (*LS*, 70). Thus, our shared humanity calls us to account for one another: "Where is your sister? Where is your brother?" (cf. Gen. 4:9). Yet as St. Francis of Assisi has taught, our sister and our brother include all of creation: "Brother Sun, Sister Moon, Brother Wind, Sister Water, Brother Fire...." ("Canticle of the Creatures"). The intersubjectivity of humanity encompasses the realm of nature. The earth, "our common home," is an integral part of a vital tripartite relationship (God, others, and nature). This triadic configuration "implies a relationship of mutual responsibility between human beings and nature" (*LS*, 67).

From the uniquely African perspective of Ubuntu, part of the vocation of the human person is to endeavor to overcome tensions

---

[21] Pope Francis, *Laudato Si'*, encyclical, May 24, 2015, www.vatican.va.

and divisions that hinder relationships—to sow seeds of peace, harmony, and hospitality. Again, St. Francis of Assisi provides the template for this creative task: "Where there is hatred, let me sow love; where there is injury, pardon; where there is doubt, faith; where there is despair, hope; where there is darkness, light; where there is sadness, joy …" ("Prayer for Peace").

The essence of Ubuntu is a pedagogy of love, precisely because it unveils the depth of love that anchors its message. Love flourishes in the mutuality of relationality—love that is neither self-serving nor exploitative. It is love for the other that seeks first to share and to give, rather than to hoard and plunder. Saint Ignatius of Loyola defines love in the following terms: "Love consists in a mutual communication between the two persons. That is, the one who loves gives and communicates to the beloved what he or she has, or a part of what one has or can have; and the beloved in return does the same to the lover. Thus, if the one has knowledge, one gives it to the other who does not; and similarly in regard to honors or riches. Each shares with the other" (*Spiritual Exercises*, no. 231).

Sharing the Eucharist.
Copyright © 2022 Hekima University College, Nairobi, Kenya

In the Christian narrative of salvation, the One who eminently exemplifies and embodies this selfless, generous, and gratuitous love is Jesus Christ: "You have no greater love than to lay down your life for your friends" (John 15:13). Jesus exhorts his followers to practice this rule of love: "Love one another as I have loved you" (John 13:34). The rich universe of meaning exemplified by and in Ubuntu reveals a captivating tableau of humanity that embodies a social premium epitomized by interconnectedness and mutuality. Our humanity grows in the measure in which we embrace, affirm, reverence, and celebrate the humanity of one another—for "A person is a person because of/through other persons," and "I am, because you are, and you are, because we are."

Viewed as a hermeneutical prism for anchoring or re-rooting deep inculturation, Ubuntu bears a striking resemblance to Pope Francis' pedagogy of fraternity. Interestingly, Pope Francis' encyclical *Fratelli tutti* contains an equivalent of the pedagogy of relationality modeled in Ubuntu: "Each of us is fully a person when we are part of a people; at the same time, there are no peoples without respect for the individuality of each person" (*FT*, 182).[22] In other words, we are "brothers and sisters all" (*FT*, 8). Francis credits South African Desmond Tutu, among others, as an inspiration for his encyclical (*FT*, 286). Tutu is the main proponent of Ubuntu as an African humanist philosophy based on a culture of sharing, openness, mutual dependence, dialogue, and interpersonal encounter. In Ubuntu, human existence reaches fulfillment as part of the whole, society thrives on a common humanity, and forgiveness and reconciliation are prerequisites for preserving social harmony.

Pope Francis' twin ideas of fraternity and social friendship underscore the urgency of Ubuntu in our present-day context, where the fabric of humanity is riven by atavistic conflicts, ideological division, isolationist paranoia, and political polarization that take a catastrophic toll on the weak and vulnerable (*FT*, 18–19). Devoid of a common uniting horizon, our ancestral fear of others drives us to

---

[22] Pope Francis, *Fratelli tutti*, encyclical, October 20, 2020, www.vatican.va.

build walls (*FT*, 26–27, 37, 41), thereby weakening our belonging to a common family and eviscerating our dream of a common purpose (*FT*, 30). Yet we are in this together (*FT*, 35)—hence the imperative of building a community of solidarity and belonging.

According to a Swahili proverb, "Mountains don't meet, but people do." As mentioned repeatedly, the foundational premise of Ubuntu recognizes the centrality of encounter with the other. For Francis, fraternity rests on a culture of authentic encounters whose precondition is creative openness to the other (*FT*, 50). Mutual openness, sadly, is assailed by a toxic digital communication saturated in social aggression, verbal violence, and ideological myopia. The result is a virtual closed circuit connected by shared fear and hatred for the other (*FT*, 42–46).

Francis proposes a new path toward a culture of fraternity founded on an "encounter of mercy" (*FT*, 83). Drawing on the parable of the Good Samaritan, he underscores the responsibility of love for others based on our shared Ubuntu. Such love builds a universal fraternity beyond considerations of its recipients' status, gender, origin, or location (*FT*, 107, 121). Universal fraternity entails suffering and requires time (*FT*, 48, 63) to forge a new social bond of solidarity that tends the vulnerability and fragility of others (*FT*, 66–69, 115). Francis likens this community to a polyhedral reality composed not of isolated monads (*FT*, 111, 143–45) but as "a family that is stronger than the sum of small individual members" (*FT*, 78). This reality exemplifies Ubuntu par excellence, because it is cemented by an inclusive social love that transcends narrow barriers, interests, and prejudices (*FT*, 83).

For Pope Francis, the radical mutuality of Ubuntu is achievable through love without borders that transforms humanity into a community of neighbors without borders. Like Ubuntu philosophy, Francis argues for a social premium on rights and duties on account of the relationality of humanity, whose deepest manifestation is the ability to transcend the self and create a solidarity of service of others (*FT*, 87, 88, 111).

Francis' social love goes beyond the immediacy of neighborliness; it is expansive and enriches the lives and existence of others. This kind of love manifests as hospitality, because it welcomes and values others for who they are (*FT*, 90–93), and recognizes every human person as an "existential foreigner" with an incontrovertible moral claim on our care (*FT*, 97). This expansive love forms the basis of an inclusive social friendship and borderless fraternity (*FT*, 94, 99). Far from being a leveling of difference or "false universalism" devoid of diversity (*FT*, 100)—or worse, a closed group of like-minded "associates"—fraternity, together with liberty and equality, offers a strong antidote to the virus of individualism (*FT*, 105). Thus, if "I am because we are," then true fraternity leaves no one behind (*FT*, 108), because we are saved together and are responsible for the life of all (*FT*, 137).

To quote another African proverb, "If my neighbor's house is on fire, I cannot sleep peacefully." In the spirit of Ubuntu, genuine fraternity eschews a "local narcissism" that constricts the mind and heart (*FT*, 146, 147). Authentic fraternity creates a family of nations, based on hospitality and gratuitousness (*FT*, 139, 141); it recognizes the rights of all peoples, communities, and groups both in private and social spheres (*FT*, 118, 124, 126). Unsurprisingly, in Francis' moral vision, the litmus test of the authenticity of fraternity is whether it welcomes, protects, promotes, and integrates migrants who come not as a nuisance or burden but as a gift and a blessing (*FT*, 129, 133).

As gospel-inspired virtues (*FT*, 277), fraternity and social friendship are the antitheses of pathologies of politics, like populism, nationalism, and neoliberalism, that negate the very meaning of "people," which is "open-ended" (*FT*, 160). Unlike these deleterious specimens of politics, the culture of encounter prioritizes multilateralism over bilateralism (*FT*, 174). Politics is healthy when it serves the common good and is animated by charity as its "spiritual heart" (*FT*, 180, 186). Political charity translates as "social love" founded on truth and the common pursuit of solutions to pressing problems (*FT*, 183). Universal fraternity and social friendship connect the local and the global in a mutually beneficial relationship (*FT*, 142). Cultural rootedness presumes openness to an encounter with the other, either as peoples, cultures, or countries. Cultural hospitality engenders communion and the mutual dependence of nations (*FT*, 146–49).

Besides encounter, another synonym for Ubuntu is dialogue. Dialogue promotes social friendship, because it respects the difference of opinions and points of view. Dialogue is open to others, recognizes our shared belonging, and is animated by the common pursuit of truth, the common good, and service of the poor (*FT*, 205, 230). On it rests the possibility of peace based on truth (*FT*, 228). This culture of dialogue and encounter transcends differences and divisions; yet it is inclusive of all and offers new possibilities and processes of lifestyle, social organization, and encounter (*FT*, 215–17, 231). As a form of kindness, social friendship makes a preference of love for the poor, vulnerable, and the least (*FT*, 224, 233, 235).

As mentioned, Ubuntu prioritizes forgiveness and reconciliation, especially when wrongdoing has sundered social harmony. Pope Francis agrees: social friendship values forgiveness and reconciliation, not as mechanisms for forgetting or condoning injustice and oppression, but as means of resolving conflict through dialogue (*FT*, 241, 244, 246, 251). As Tutu says, the pursuit of justice has "no future without forgiveness" (*FT*, 250, 252).

Inculturation as Conversation

In a certain sense, conversation may seem a banal and quotidian activity. This perception raises a question about how it can be considered a prism for re-rooting deep inculturation. "Conversation" ought not to be understood as a purely discursive activity of communication. Over the last ten years, in my theological research and scholarship, I have used "conversation" as a theological methodology to good effect both as a rationale and a method for convening diverse communities of scholars and practitioners for meaningful theological exchanges, collaboration, and mutual learning.

Not only is conversation a metaphor for theological methodology, but it also emerges as a dimension of theological inculturation at a deeper level. I consider this approach particularly apt for the purposes of re-rooting inculturation, mostly in regard to creating spaces of mutuality between and among cultures in the spirit of fraternity.

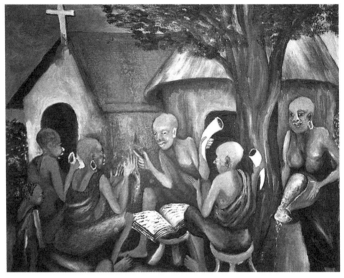

A Changing Generation by Shine Tani.
Image courtesy Agbonkhianmeghe E. Orobator

People who are conversant with African theology would be familiar with the practice referred to as palaver. As a model of conversational and communicative ethics in African cultures, palaver seems theologically fertile. Some derisive portrayals of this style also exist, including its depiction as pointless banter presided over by an African chief. As communicative ethics or ethics of communication, the African palaver embodies a model of dialogue and consensus in addressing consequential matters affecting the community and by extension—for the purposes of this essay—pertinent theological and ethical issues. A critical component of this approach is the readiness to listen and learn from one another, which entails intentionally avoiding the monopolization of the spoken and shared word.

This kind of conversation that is inclusive, mutual, and communal serves a form of theological methodology. Essentially, this approach combines dialogue and listening in conversation in an inclusive space where no voice is excluded and concerns of participants and interlocutors are accorded equal consideration. Listening is a condition for participation. Already it is easy to envisage how the practice is linked to hospitality and relationality, because palaver emphasizes open conversation in community and prioritizes consensus over confrontation. When applied to the enterprise of theology, the latter becomes the fruit of active dialogue, intensive listening, and mutual learning among theologians as members of a community of Ubuntu.

Journeying Together in the Service of Harmony by Okubasu Mukoya.
Copyright © 2021 African Synodality Initiatives (ASI)

For the keen observer of the path of synodality in the church, this conversational ethics of dialogue and listening is a fundamental characteristic of the synodal journey of walking and journeying together in view of discerning the will of God and achieving communion, participation, and mission in the church.

> Synodal listening is oriented towards discernment. It requires us to learn and exercise the art of personal and communal discernment. We listen to each other, to our faith tradition, and to the signs of the times in order to discern what God is saying to all of us. Pope Francis characterizes the two

interrelated goals of this process of listening: "to listen to God, so that with him we may hear the cry of his people; to listen to his people until we are in harmony with the will to which God calls us."[23]

In a particularly interesting manner, because palaver is an open, inclusive, and mutual practice of conversation, it renders possible and facilitates a global conversation among theologians engaged in the shared task of faith seeking understanding. This kind of global practice assumes a deeper significance at a time when local identity is gaining ascendancy and seeking increased recognition. Palaver is attentive to and actually promotes the complementarity or compatibility of purposes between global and local perspectives, thus allowing for and enabling mutuality in inculturation where Indigenous wisdom provides a critical leaven for the incarnation of the dynamic and transformative power of the gospel of Jesus for local cultures and religious traditions.

In the practice of palaver, no one person or participant can exhaust the conversations happening in the communal space, including issues they raise, the context they describe, the challenges they surface, and the strategies they propose as part of a wider process of sustaining the conversation. Another important dimension of palaver is that it is not a closed debate; it opens possibilities for conversation around issues that matter in order to create shared narratives, clarify assumptions, investigate issues, confront challenges, and propose new ways of walking and journeying together. Palaver creates the space where expanded conversation and inquiry can happen across ideological and doctrinal divides in view of achieving holistic, liberating, and life-affirming outcomes.

Given the foregoing, the basic methodological tools and attitudinal dispositions for re-rooting inculturation include the capacity to listen, discern, dialogue, engage, include, converse, collaborate, and immerse. The approach of palaver makes the theological enterprise an immensely collaborative effort or teamwork—all interlocutors

---

[23] Secretary General of the Synod of Bishops, *Vademecum for the Synod on Synodality*, September 2021, 2.2, www.synod.va.

are valued and respected participants, not spectators or bystanders. As a fundamental rule, in this communal enterprise, monopoly is a pathology of manipulation and monologue a symptom of deafness. Both contravene the ethics of palaver and Ubuntu.

Conclusion

People who know African religion credit it with essential values of inclusivity, hospitality, dialogue, and respect for other religious traditions.[24] When cultures and religions encounter one another, receptivity and mutuality of learning become important values. These values are informed and animated by attitudes of tolerance, inclusivity, and hospitality. Despite the challenge of religious intolerance and growing sectarian violence in some parts of Africa, there is tangible evidence of the practice of receptivity and mutuality in the ability of affiliates of divergent Christian denominations to coexist in extended interchurch familial, conjugal, communal, and social relationships.

Transposed to the realm of deep inculturation, African values, principles, and qualities—like hospitality, Ubuntu, and palaver—may serve a broader theological project by creating the context and modeling essential prerequisites for the mutuality that must enable and underlie inculturation rooted and re-rooted in lived faith where particular cultures are essential *loci theologici*, that is, sites of religious-theological discovery and insight. By not engaging in conflictual and antagonistic squabbles with arriving foreign religions, African religion models and offers a vision of deep inculturation, that is, openness to learn and to receive from the religious other, with mutuality and respect, but without surrendering its own Indigenous genius, cultural identity, and historical agency, for the benefit of realizing a wider religious synthesis.

As detailed above, in relation to deep inculturation, hospitality, Ubuntu, and palaver are vital pedagogical tools and characteristics of African spiritual and religious traditions for re-rooting inculturation.

---

[24] Soyinka adduces ample argumentation to elaborate this point in *Of Africa*.

In light of the foregoing, the gift of African religion lies not in the hubris of sectarianism and extremism but in its deep wells of humanizing values alive and active in the spirit of African religion. Devoid of hegemonic pretensions and proselytizing strategies, this 'spirit' "is peculiarly concerned with the aspiration to be human in a particular form and, therefore, with living satisfactory and responsible lives, both singular and in common, reflectively and actively."[25] Thus understood, Benedict stands vindicated, for the authentic spirituality of this continent is a profound repository of resources for the renewal of humanity. What I am arguing here is that the spirit of African religion entails a commitment to safeguard hospitality, tolerance, and inclusivity that characterizes African religion, as a global heritage in the face of the threat of sectarian terror. Consequently, as Soyinka argues, "If Africa falls to the will of the fanatic, then the insecurity of the world should be accepted as its future and permanent condition. There are no other options."[26]

There is a certain sense in which the elements presented above as African values are considered to be "traditional," that is, as static elements to be transposed across time and applied to current issues and questions. Yet of more analytical value would be studies that focus on and analyze African values—to the extent that they are actually identifiable as African—as dynamic entities and processes in a global context and the factors that influence or shape their dynamic evolution and development. African moral values, religious practices, and cultural norms undergo change, and they develop. Given this dimension of development, there is room for an authentic critique and fresh hermeneutics of the promises and limitations of African values to serve the goal of re-rooting inculturation on a firmer hermeneutical and theological ground.

---

[25] Timothy Jenkins, *Religion in English Everyday Life: An Ethnographic Approach* (New York: Berghahn Books, 1999), 14.
[26] Soyinka, *Of Africa*, 130.

Acknowledgments

The book editor extends his heartfelt thanks to the following:

• Robert Ellsberg, editor-in-chief and publisher of Orbis Books, for the continuing confidence and the gift of creative space. Managing editor Maria Angelini who is always a pleasure to work with.

• Catholic Theological Union for the Osiek-Sullivan sabbatical grant. Colleague and friend Richard E. McCarron for his intellectual generosity in a chapter review, not to mention the academic networking. The superb Bechtold Library staff for the invaluable research assistance.

• Nanzan Institute for Religion and Culture (NIRC) in Nagoya, Japan, for the enriching research environment that allowed the conceptual seed for an anthology to germinate. Special mention to Robert Kisala, President of Nanzan University, for the gracious welcome he extended to me as a visiting scholar, and faculty member Roger Vanzila Munsi for offering helpful information.

• The missionaries of the Society of the Divine Word (SVD), Japan Province, most especially Vu Khan Tuong and Jonathan Villacorta for the hospitality and thoughtful accompaniment in Nagoya and Nagasaki respectively.

• Shahar Caren Weaver, Chicago African-American artist and my former student, for the remarkable, inspirited cover image.

• Jeffrey Kirch, CPPS, Provincial Director, Society of the Precious Blood US Province, and Daryl Charron, CPPS Brother, for the earnest support.

- Joseph Quane, Executive Director of SPRED (Special Religious Development), Archdiocese of Chicago, for the brotherly presence and encouragement.

- Last but not least, our global voices, contributing authors Chris, Ángel, Marzanna, Carmel, Ikenna, and Bator, for the front row view of all their dedicated research, writing, and astonishing wisdom.

About the Cover Image

"Baptism" by professional Chicago artist Shahar Caren Weaver is a mixed media collage/painting that re-imagines a traditional scene of the biblical Jesus as he was baptized by his cousin John. The Holy Spirit dove image is a recurring motif in many of her African/Caribbean-inspired universal art pieces.

A priest in the Episcopal Church and a singer in the Chicago Community Chorus, Shahar studied at Catholic Theological Union, Lutheran School of Theology, and Seabury Western Theological Seminary. She also attended Howard University in Washington, DC, where she was trained in abstract art. Raised in Los Angeles, Shahar is currently a resident of Chicago.

INDEX

Aboriginal Mass, 107–9, 111, 116–17
Aboriginal peoples (Australia)
    and Catholicism, 101, 107, 112, 117, 119, 124
    genocide of, 98
    language, 95–96, 109–10
    and liturgy, 104, 107–9, 112–13, 116–17, 120*n79*, 122
    and missionaries, 99–101, 105, 115
    myths, 104–5
    and priesthood, 119*n77*
    traditions and beliefs, 89, 101–5, 107–10, 113–14, 116–17, 119–20, 122–23, 126
Abraham, 159, 163–65, 173, 179, 200
    as Abram, 161–63
acculturation, xi, xiii, 58, 93, 152–56
Achebe, Chinua, 188
Ad Gentes, xii
African Synod (1994), 191
Ahern, Clare, 113–14, 116*n69*
Aleluyah (1970 dance drama), 81
Alexander the Great, 170–71
Alexandria, 171, 174–75
Alice Springs, 122–23
American Academy of Religion, 24*n30*
Amherst papyrus, 176
Anat-Bethel, 176
Anatomy of Inculturation, xix–xx
Anat-Yahō, 176. *See also* Anat-Bethel
ancestors
    ancestral families, 161–63
    in Australian Aboriginal tradition, 92, 102, 113–14, 122–23
    in Buddhism, 145–46
    in Tarahumara legend, 37
anti-Semitism, 51*n32*

Apostles to the Slavs, The. See *Slavorum Apostoli*
appetitus, 34
Apuleius, 178
Arias, Miguel, 5–6
Arrupe, Pedro, xvii, 152*n51*
Art of Indigenous Inculturation, The, 18
Asherah, 176–77
assimilation, xi–xii, xvii
    Australian First Peoples, 90, 93, 97–100
    creative, 94–95, 108
    cultural, xi–xii, 6, 18, 186
    dynamic equivalence, 95–96, 108, 112, 119, 142, 153
    Egyptian Jews, 171*n14*
    Japan, 143, 146
    mutual, 27*n4*, 142, 153
    Tarahumares, 40
Augustine of Hippo, 34
Avalokiteśvara, 138

Babylon, 160, 164–70
    colonialism, 164–65, 167, 169
    and Jews, 170, 174*n19*
    occupation of Judah, 164–69
bakufu, 132. *See also* bakuhan
Bakufu Inquisition, 134*n14*
bakuhan, 132*n10*, 136. *See also* bakufu
balungan, 77–78
Barton, John, 196
Bascom, Jonathan, 201
Bastian no Higuri, 151
Batak Christian Protestant Church, 63, 84–85
Batak peoples, 57, 62, 69, 72, 78–80, 85
Batak Toba, 78–79
Baumgarten, Alexander, 8*n8*

Benedict XVI, 192–93, 203, 216
Benin Republic, 194
Benjamin, 163–64, 172
Berndt, Catherine and Ronald, 100*n27*, 102–3
Betancourt, Pedro José de, 5–6
Bethel, 176
Bevans, Stephen B., xx
Bhabha, Homi, 26, 54*n34*
Bhagavad Gita, 82
Bidyadanga, 109, 111*n57*, 119. *See also* La Grange
Bima, 82
Bishops' Conference of Indonesia, 84
Black Nazarene, xvii*n11*
Blomjous, Joseph, xxiii*n20*
bodhisattva, 138–39, 142
bodily theopoetics, 27, 53–56
Boxer, C.R., 129–30
brolga, 124–25
Broome, 90, 101, 111–12, 116, 119*n77*
Brueggemann, Walter, 160
Buddha, x, 146, 149–51
Buddhism, 129–30, 132, 137–38, 142, 146, 148, 150–51, 154
　Mahāyāna, 138
Bugnini, Annibale, 107

Calendar of Bastian. *See* Bastian no Higuri
Campos Morales, Javier, 32
Canaan, 159, 161, 163–65, 174, 179, 185
"Canticle of the Creatures", 206
Capps, Walter, 17*n16*
Carmelites, 57*n2*, 78
Caron, François, 136
Carrasco, Davíd, 3
cartels, 53, 179–80
Cartesianism, 204
Cerocahui, 32, 43, 48
Charles III, 31
Chihuahua, 27–28, 32, 41, 43–45, 52
Chikugo, Inoue, 134
China, 138, 156
Chinmoku, 133–34, 152, 155
Chopp, Rebecca, 21
Christal Whelan, 148
Christian Era, The. *See Kirishitan Jidai*
　"Christianisation as an Essential Part of Assimilation", 99
"Christian Martyrdom in Asia", 128*n1*
Chupungco, Anscar J., xi*n2*, xvii, 20, 27*n4*, 58, 90–91, 94–96, 108, 111, 114, 154
church music, 66, 68, 70–72, 74–75, 77
Coelho, Gaspar, 129–30
Comme le Prévoit, 95
Congress Mass. *See* Aboriginal Mass
Conrad, Joseph, 191
Constitution on the Sacred Liturgy, 96, 106*n39*
cosmovision. *See* Weltanschauung
Côte d'Ivoire, 62*n22*
Council of Trent, 142
creative assimilation, 94–95, 108
Creel, 32, 44, 53
Critique of Pure Reason, 8*n8*
Crollius, Arij Roest, vii, xi–xiv
cultural assimilation, xi–xii, 6, 18, 186
Cyril of Thessaloniki, xviii*n12*

daimyos, 128*n1*, 130*n6*
danka system, 138
Danzar o morir, 28*n7*, 32, 43, 53
Darwin (Australia), 89–90, 93, 99, 101, 104*n38*, 107–8, 116–19, 124
Deacon, Hilton, 107–8
Deus, 134–35
Deusu, 149–51
Deuteronomy, 160–62, 169
Dewey, John, 4, 14
Digges, Matthew, 115
Doctrina Christan, 148
Dodds, Tommy, 110
Dodson, Patrick, 119–23, 126
Dogmatic Constitution of the Church. *See Lumen Gentium*
Donovan, Dan, 105
drug cartels, 53, 179–80
dynamic equivalence, 95–96, 108, 112, 119, 142, 153

ebumi. *See* fumi-e
Ecclesia in Africa, xviii–xix, 153
Elephantine, 170, 174–76, 186
Elizondo, Virgilio, 16–17, 19
Elkin, P.E., 100*n27*, 105

Index

enculturation, 93
Engelhardt, Jeffers, 59–60
eschatology, 149–50
Eshem-Bethel, 176
Eurocentrism, xv, xx, 27, 131
Evangelii Gaudium, x, xxvi
Evangelii Nuntiandi, xii, 106*n39*
evangelization, xii, xxvi, 30, 90, 97, 187, 190, 197. *See also* missionaries
Evdokimov, Paul, viii

Feast of the Pharisees, 36
Federation of the Asian Bishops' Conferences, x
Filus, Dorothea, 137
First Nations (Australia)
  cultural traditions, 91–93, 103–5, 122
  and liturgy, 90, 93, 106–8, 114, 118, 120, 124
  and missionaries, 97, 99–100, 115
Flores, 57, 62, 64, 66–71, 73–74, 77, 83
foi, 73–74
Folk Shinto, 145
Font, Juan de, 30
Francis (Pope), x, xxvi, 13*n11*, 125, 156*n63*, 202, 205, 208–11, 213
Franciscans, 31, 128–29
Francis of Assisi, 206–7
Francis Xavier, 82, 140, 156
Fratelli tutti, x, 208
Fujimura, Makoto, 134*n15*, 135*n16*
Fujita, Neil S., 129*n4*
Fujiwara, Ken, 141
fumi-e, 133–34
Fyfe, Malcolm, 117–18

gamelan, 58, 62–63, 67–71, 75, 77, 82
ganokos, 40
Gaudium et Spes, xii, 106*n39*
gawi, 83
Gedaliah, 166, 169
"Gendhing Ratri Suci", 82
Genesis, 148, 159, 161–65, 205–6
Gereja Kristen Indonesia (Indonesian Christian Church), 63
gerong, 78
Ghono, John, 74
glossolalia, 152

goddess figures, x, 177–78, 189
gondang, 75, 78–80
gong gendang, 73–74
gonin-gumi, 136–37
Gordon, Sambo, 113
Gorman, Michael J., 183
gospel
  contextualizing, 63*n24*
  dependent on culture, ix, xxiii*n20*, 27*n4*, 56
  and evangelization, 99, 187–88, 190
  and inculturation, xxvi, 27*n4*, 152, 214
  and interculturation, 97
Gotō Islands, 144*n32*, 147, 151
Great Tradition, x
Groome, Thomas, 21
Guachochi, 27–28
Guadalupe. *See* Our Lady of Guadalupe
Guanyin, 138
Guatemala, 5–6
Gutiérrez, Gustavo, 21

hatsuhō, 143
Hearn, Peter, 99*n25*, 116–18, 120*n80*
Hegel, Georg W.F., 8*n8*, 191
hermeneutics
  of appreciation, xx, 18–19
  pragmatic, 14*n12*
  of serendipity, 18–20
  of suspicion, 18–19
Herod, 82, 172
Herodotus, 169–70
Hideyoshi, Toyotomi, 128–32
HKBP. *See* Batak Christian Protestant Church
Hogue, Michael S., 18*n17*
Holm, Tawny, 176
Horizontverschmelzung, ix
Huria Kristen Batak Protestan. *See* Batak Christian Protestant Church

Ibaraki, Luis, 128
Ieyasu, Tokugawa, 132
Ignatius of Loyola, 140, 207
Illman, Ruth, 20–22
inculturation
  assets-based approach, 20
  Chupungco on, 20*n20*, 27*n4*, 154

inculturation *(continued)*
　creative, xvii
　Crollius on, xi–xiv
　dialogical, xvii
　Engelhardt on, 60
　essence of, 174
　and Eurocentrism, xv
　Eva Solomon on, 96–97
　as evolving concept, xv–xvi
　generative, 203
　gospel origins, ix
　and hospitality, 187, 204
　vs. interculturation, vii, xvii, xxiii*n*20
　and interreligious dialogue, x
　John Paul II on, xviii–xx, 153
　and liberation, ix, 18–19
　Magesa on, xx
　and migration, 174–76, 180, 184–86
　mutuality, xvii, 27*n*4, 33, 43, 214–15
　Pope Francis on, xxvi
　and Protestant churches, 63
　and reconciliation, xiv
　as relationality, 200, 204–9, 213
　re-rooting, vii–viii, xvi, xx, 193, 198–99, 202–3, 208, 211, 214–16
　Shorter on, 58–59
　and syncretism, 26*n*3
　tactical approach, xii
　terminology, xi*n*2, 59, 152
　and Third Space, 27
　and Vatican II, 199
"Inculturation and the Specificity of Christian Faith", xiii
Inculturation: Working Papers on Living Faith and Cultures, xi, xiii–xiv
indexical signification, 155
Inoue Chikugo no kami Masashige. *See* Chikugo, Inoue
inquisition, 133–34, 137, 140. *See also* fumi-e
insertion model, xiii, xxiii*n*20, 58, 97
interculturation, ix–x, xxiii*n*20, 91, 97
　vs. inculturation, vii, xvii, xxiii*n*20
Introductory Lectures on Aesthetics, 8*n*8
Isaac, 161, 165
Isis, 178
Islam, 62, 67, 194, 196, 198, 202–3

Israel, 22, 158–61, 164–70, 172–75, 179, 182

Jacob, 163–64, 168, 173, 179, 185
Jadai, Madeleine, 111*n*57
Jehoiakim, 166, 169
Jeremiah, 159–60, 165–69, 174, 177–78
Jeroboam, 169
Jerusalem, 16, 160, 165–66, 169, 175, 177
Jesuheru, 151*n*48
Jesuits
　Japan, 128–30, 140, 148
　and Mariology, 140
　Mexico, 30–32, 34, 41–44, 48, 53, 55
Jews
　diasporan, 175–76, 186
　in Egypt, 170, 172, 177, 186
　in Elephantine, 170, 175
　migration, 171, 185–86
Jobst, John, 101, 106–7, 109
Johanan, 167–68
John Paul II, xvii–xx, 81, 122–23, 153
Johnson, Elizabeth, 142
Joseph, 83, 163–64, 172–73
Joy of the Gospel, The. *See Evangelii Gaudium*
Judah, 159, 165–70, 174, 177
Judas, 49, 51, 55, 82
Judea, 165–66, 168, 170*n*11, 174, 176–77

kami, 130, 143, 145–46
Kannon, 138–39, 141–42. *See also* Maria Kannon
Kant, Immanuel, 8*n*8, 191
Kanzeon. *See* Kannon
Karo peoples, 67, 75, 78
Kasper, Walter, 145
Keane, Webb, 63–64
Kelahiran Kristus, 81–82
Kenya, 18, 199, 207
keroncong, 66, 68
kerygma, 183–84
kethoprak, 81, 83
Kharga Oasis, 173*n*18
Khnum, 176
ki, 141–42

Kimberley (Australia), 97, 101, 108–9, 112–13, 115–16, 120
Kirishitan Jidai, 140
Kirishito-ki, 134
Kiti, Daniel, 68, 74
Kleinschaffer, Colleen, 114
Knox, James, 111*n58*
kórima, 36
Kriener, Werner, 112
Krishna, 82*n60*
Kuan-shi-yin, 138. *See also* Kannon
kulcapi, 75, 84
Kussudiarjo, Bagong, 81
Kyūshū, 128*n1*, 138, 143

La Grange, 109, 111, 117, 119, 121. *See also* Bidyadanga
La Moreneta. *See* Our Lady of Montserrat
Langen Sekar, 76–78
Leary, John, 93, 119
liberation theology, 3–4, 17, 21
liminality, 15–17, 25
Little Tradition, x
Loh, I-to, 66
Long, Charles H., 18
Lotus Sutra, 138
LS. *See* Langen Sekar
Lumen Gentium, xvii*n10*, 106*n39*

MacKillop, Mary, 124
Madah Bakti, 66
Magesa, Laurenti, xix–xx, 27*n4*
Magi: The Tenshō Boy's Embassy, 129*n3*
Mahabharata, 82*n60*
Mahāyāna Buddhism, 138
Maria Kannon, 137–40, 142. *See also* Kannon
Marianism, 13*n11*, 138, 140, 148
martyrs
  Cerocahui, 48
  Nagasaki, 127–32, 136, 138, 144*n32*, 146
Maruya, 141, 151*n48*
Mass for Aborigines. *See* Aboriginal Mass
Mass of the Land of the Holy Spirit. See *Missa Terra Spiritus Sancti*

Matovina, Timothy, 13*n11*
McKelson, Kevin, 96, 109–12, 117–21
Melbourne, 106–7, 117
"Memorandum for the Study of Acculturation", 153
Memorial Museum of the Twenty-Six Martyrs (Nagasaki), 138, 144*n32*
Memphis (Egypt), 170–71, 174
Mesa, José M. de, xx*n16*, xx*n18*
mestizo peoples, 31, 39, 53, 55
Metamorphosis, 178
Methodius of Thessaloniki, xviii*n12*
migrants and migration
  Abraham, 159, 161–62, 164–65, 179
  and Egypt, 158–59, 161, 168, 172–74
  and inculturation, 182, 184–86
  Isaac, 161
  Jacob, 164–65, 173
  Jeremiah, 165, 167
  Jeroboam, 169
  Jewish, 159, 162, 164–65, 172, 174, 177
  Johanan, 168
  Judean, 170*n11*, 174
  and kerygma, 183–85
  modern global, 159, 179–82
  and theology of hospitality, 201–2, 210
Mireles, Enrique, 44–45, 49, 51, 53
Missa Terra Spiritus Sancti, 112*n60*
missionaries and missions
  Africa, xix, xxvi, 187–92, 194, 197, 202, 204
  and assimilation, xi
  Australia, 90, 96, 98–101, 104, 106, 108, 110, 115–18
  and inculturation, xi–xiii, xvi, 108
  and interculturation, ix, xxiii*n20*
  Japan, 129–32, 136–37, 140–41, 147–48, 156*n63*
  O'Loughlin, 99–101, 120*n80*
  and Rarámuri communities, 30–32, 34–35, 41–44, 48
Mizpah, 165–66
moral imagination, 4, 6, 8–10, 14–15, 24
Mora Salazar, Joaquín César, 32

Munsi, Roger Vanzila, 143–44, 151
Murakami, Shigenori, 151
Murrinnpatha, 118
mutual assimilation, 27*n4*, 142, 153
mutual inculturation, xvii, 27*n4*, 33, 43, 214
Mveng, Engelbert, xix

Nabunaga, Oda, 128*n1*
Nagasaki, martyrs of, 127–32, 136, 138, 144*n32*, 146
National Liturgy Commission (Australia), 107
New Order government (Indonesia), 64–66
Ngada peoples, 70, 72, 74. *See also* Flores
Nicholls, Bruce J., 63*n24*
Nihon ryōiki, 142
Nishizaka Hill (Nagasaki), 128
Nkeramihigo, Théoneste, xiii–xiv
Nobunaga, Oda, 128*n1*, 129*n3*, 132
Northern Territory (Australia), 89, 99*n24*, 101
Northern Territory Catholic Missions Council (NTCMC), 116*n70*

Oderman, Gisela Petri, 111*n58*
Ohatsuhoage, 143–44, 146
Ohnuki-Tierney, Emiko, 143*n30*
Okeowo, Alexis, 182*n38*
O'Loughlin, John, 99–101, 107, 117, 120*n80*
Orasho, 151–52
organs (musical instrument), 69, 74–75, 78, 82
orthopraxis, 21*n25*
Osogbo, 194–95
Osun, 194–95, 198
Our Lady of Guadalupe, 13*n11*, 36, 49–50, 154, 179–82, 186
Our Lady of Montserrat, 140

paganism, 99–101, 104, 125, 190, 192, 197
palaver, 212–15
Palestine, 172
Pallottines, 96, 109
Pandawa brothers, 82*n58*

Paraclete, 142
Parkin, Evelyn, 90*n2*
Paul VI, 106–7
Peile, Anthony, 106*n40*
Peirce, Charles Sanders, 18*n17*, 155*n61*
pelog, 71, 77, 82
Perdjert, Boniface, 119*n77*
Persia, 169–70
Pésame ritual, 5–6, 9–12, 14–17, 20, 23–24
Petitjean, Bernard Thaddée, 147, 155–56
Petri, Helmut, 101–2, 111*n58*
Phan, Peter C., xxiii*n20*, 161*n6*
Pharisees
    dances of the, 38, 45, 49–51, 55
    Feast of the, 36
Philadelphia Mural Arts Program, 22
Philippines, xx*n16*, 18, 129, 131, 141*n25*
Philo of Alexandria, 171, 174
pneumatology, 142, 152
polygamy, 129*n3*, 190
Popular Catholicism in a World Church, xiv–xv
Port Keats, 103–4, 108, 119–20. *See also* Wadeye
Prabu Baladewa, 82
practical theology, 20–23
praxis, xxvi, 20–23
Protestant churches, xxv, 57–58, 63, 75–76
Psalms, 72, 77, 205
Ptolemies, 171, 173
Puji Syukur, 66–67

Querida Amazonia, x
Quetzalcoatl, 6

Rahwana, 82
Rama, 82*n58*
Ramayana, 82*n58*
Rappoport, Dana, 63–64
Rarámuri
    and conflict, 31–32, 53
    and dance, 37, 39–40, 42, 45, 55
    demographics, 28
    and feasts, 34, 40–42, 55–56
    and first missionaries, 30
    korima, 36

INDEX 227

living conditions, 29
resilience, 33
and Third Space, 26, 35
Ray, Benjamin C., 196
Redemptoris Missio, xii, 106*n39*
Reed, Daniel, 62*n22*
Reis-Habito, Maria, 138, 141
relationality, 200, 204–9, 213
Religion and Faith in Africa, 196
Religionswissenschaft, 3
re-rooting, xx, 193, 199, 203, 208, 211
revelation, xix–xx, 105
Revelation, 149–50
Rhodes, Alexandre de, viii
Roman Empire, 158, 171, 173–74
Roman Rite, 91, 94–97, 110, 114–15, 117–20, 122–26
Romero, Oscar, 3
Rome's pontifical universities, viii
Rose, Miriam, 126
ruach, 142
Rulfo, Juan Carlos, 28*n8*

salawatan, 67
Samachique, 27, 32, 43–45, 50, 52–53
San Antonio (Texas), 4–6, 10–13, 19, 23
San Felipe (ship), 128, 130–31
San Fernando Cathedral (Texas), 4–5, 7, 9, 14–16, 18–20, 23
San Jiwan, 151
San José del Parral (mine), 30
Santa Maruya. *See* Maruya
Sarah, 179
as Sarai, 162–63
Sarna, Nahum M., 161–62
sarunai, 75
Satet, 178
Schreiter, Robert J., xvii*n10*, 6*n4*, 21, 26*n3*
Scorsese, Martin, 133
Second Assembly of the Fifth Plenary Council (Australia), 125*n86*
Second Vatican Council. *See* Vatican II
Shikoku, 128*n1*
Shima, Iwashita, 133
Shimabara Rebellion, 132, 138
Shinoda, Masahiro, 133–34
Shintoism, 130–32, 137, 142–43, 145–46, 154

Shorter, Aylward, xi*n2*, xxiii*n20*, 27*n4*, 58, 91, 97, 106*n39*
Shreeve, William Whitaker, 190–92, 194
Shūsaku, Endō, 134*n15*, 140
Sierra Leone: The Principal British Colony, 190
Sierra Madre Occidental, 28, 32
Siete Palabras service, 9
Sijabat, Monang, 59, 78–80, 85
Silence (1971 film). *See Chinmoku*
Silence (2016 film), 133
Silverman, Michael H., 170
Sims, Michael, 116–17
sindhen, 71, 78
Sinta. *See* Sumbadra
Slavorum Apostoli, xviii
slendro, 71, 77
Smith, Alan, 20–22
social friendship, x, 208, 210–11
Soegijapranata, Albertus, 61
Solomon, 168–69
Solomon, Eva, xxiii*n20*, 96–97, 122
Sotome, 133*n13*, 138, 147, 151
South Sulawesi, 63
Soyinka, Wole, 203, 216
Spain, 19, 29–31, 45, 129, 136
Stanley, Henry Morton, 191
Stanner, W.E.H., 100*n27*, 103–5
Strehlow, T.G.H., 100*n27*, 105
Stuart, George, 113*n63*
Sturt, Junee, 113
Sugimoto, Yuri Isabelina, 156–57
Sumarsam, 62
Sumba, 63–64
Sumbadra, 82
Supriyanto, 81
syncretism, 26, 54, 60, 154, 175, 195
synodality, xxvi, 213

Tagita, Kōya, 147
Takenaka, Umene, 133
Tarahumara. *See* Rarámuri
Tarahumara Mountain Range, 28, 30, 32, 39–40, 42–44
Tarigan, Jasa, 75
Taylor, Charles, 135
Tcherikover, Victor, 170*n11*
Tenchi Hajimari no Koto, 141–42, 147–51, 154, 156

tesgüino, 35, 37, 41, 47, 51
Thardim, Beatrice Demkadath, 118
Theologies of Guadalupe, 13n11
theology, viii, xviin10, xxn16, xxn18, xxiiin20, 3, 7, 17–18, 20, 22, 24
  neo-Thomistic, viii
  practical, 20–23
Theology of Mission, A, 99n25, 120n80
Things Fall Apart, 188
Third Space, 25–27, 35, 42, 53–54, 56
Tiberius Julius Alexander, 171n14
Tillich, Paul, viii, 18n17
Tiwi, 118
Tokugawa
  Iemitsu, 138
  Ieyasu, 128n1, 132
Tokugawa shogunate, 132–33, 135–37, 143, 145, 150
Toorn, Karl van der, 170n11
Toraja, 63–64
Torres Strait Islander peoples, 90, 92–93, 95–97, 99–100, 103, 105–6, 108, 117–18, 120, 122–23. *See also* First Nations (Australia)
transculturation, 29
translation, x, 84, 95, 117, 119. *See also* vernacular
Turnbull, Stephen, 140, 150
Turner, Victor, 15–17
Tutu, Desmond, 208, 211
Twenty-Six Martyrs of Nagasaki, 127–32, 136, 138, 144n32, 146

Ubuntu, 204–11, 213, 215
Ungunmerr-Baumann, Miriam Rose, 89, 124
Uriah, 169

Valignano, Alessandro, 129n3, 130n6
Vatican Council, 95
Vatican II, viii, 90, 95–96, 106, 109, 116, 126, 199
Velasco Rivero, Pedro J. de, 26, 28n7, 32–33, 40–44, 46, 49–50, 53–54
vernacular
  use of, x, 90, 95–96, 111, 116n70, 120. *See also* translation
Via Crucis, 5, 8–9, 49–50, 55
voodoo, 194, 198

Wadeye, 104, 118, 121. *See also* Port Keats
Wallach, Jeremy Wayne, 66
Ward, Graham, 34, 118–19
Ward, Tess, 118–19
Warden, Nolan, 67n35
Wasitodipuro, Ki, 81–82
wayang wong, 81–82
Weltanschauung, 14, 32
West, Cornel, 3
Whelan, Christal, 148–51
White, James W., 132n10
Wignyosaputro, Darsono, 68, 76–78
Wildmikael, Nasenet Alme, 182n38
Wilson, Martin, 103–5, 117
World of the First Australians, The, 102–3
Worms, Ernst A., 101, 111n58

Yahweh, 161, 164–69, 174–77, 179
Yanawana, Maureen, 111n57
Yoruba, 194–95
yúmari, 37
Yuuki, Diego, 131n7, 131n8

Zenso, Seyakuin, 130n5